Phillip Adams

Insights & Reflections

Published by:
Wilkinson Publishing Pty Ltd
ACN 006 042 173
Level 4, 2 Collins St Melbourne, Victoria, Australia 3000
Ph: +61 3 9654 5446
www.wilkinsonpublishing.com.au

National Library of Australia Cataloguing-in-Publication entry
Creator: Adams, Phillip, 1939- author.
Title: Phillip Adams : insights & reflections / Phillip Adams.
ISBN: 9781925642025 (paperback)
Subjects: Adams, Phillip, 1939---Anecdotes.
Broadcasters--Australia--Anecdotes.
Mass media--Social aspects--Anecdotes.

Cover design: Matt Irwin
Internal design: Alicia Freile, Tango Media Pty Ltd.

Contents

Foreword

I GREW UP with the great Adams. I remember my older brothers would bring home copies of the *Nation Review* and we would lie in our bunk beds, four of us in the room, and listen, laugh and marvel, as one brother read aloud a new Adams column or reread an old one, copies of which we kept. Through the louvre windows would come the sound of the surf crashing in on the beach across the road, as if to emphasise the wild freedom of it all.

The first column I have a memory of concerned a perennial Adams favourite, the classical Greek philosopher Diogenes who lived in a barrel, and was celebrated for mocking power. When Alexander the Great came to visit the revered seer, and asked what he could do for him, Diogenes asked him to get out of his sunlight.

Adams has had a lifetime of sport reminding us of what obscures our sunshine, beginning with, in my memory at least, his mockery of Billy McMahon — an early, but more charismatic version of Malcolm Turnbull — and onwards to Billy Sneddon, and so on, and so forth. Of politics, of history, of classical Greek philosophers, I, of course, knew nothing. But what really connected his writings to a world I understood was a determined irreverence, a cheek, a dash, a daring, a determination to look beyond the shadows to the light.

I don't say Adams is without fault or sin. His refusal to die, for example, an odd affectation in a man so splendidly obsessed with death, may mean one of his greatest legacies is to turn Radio National into an antipodean equivalent of Breitbart as they load it up with yet one more dreary ideologue in the forlorn hope of rivalling Adams.

Adams! A word given incantory power by those who chant it ceaselessly as a synonym for everything decadent, cosmopolitan, suspicious, dubious, privileged, elite, urban, socialist. And, of course, *irrelevant*. Adams! A man whose views are *so* irrelevant a far right chunterer can't go a hundred words or five minutes on air without needing to spit his name out. Adams! Adams! Adams!

In the war without end that is the far-right wing's determination to destroy any semblance of alternative voices, it is frequently lamented by the George Grosz caricatures who appear before us as journalists and thinkers and leaders that there needs to be a balance to Philip Adams on the ABC, a right-wing Philip Adams.

This seems to me to miss the point entirely, which is that Phillip Adams isn't really of a faction or party or position, but rather of a different, if imperilled Australia.

I must confess I don't buy *The Australian* and so only get to marvel at its strange death rattles in places where it continues to exist as a quaint decorative detail, such as airports and hotel foyers. So it is always a pleasure to be able to read Philip Adams in a collection such as this, without the encrustations of lunacy that package him each week, like a great shark who most only know as battered flake.

Some people, of course, loathe Adams. Some have reservations. I don't. When he's gone, we will understand how important he was, speaking truth to power with a sly, wry irreverence that never bowed nor faltered no matter what pressures were brought to bear. He took what was best in us — our humour and our suspicion of power — to bravely upbraid us about what was worst — our conformity and our servility. And he's done it for a life time.

Most others break, go mad, write about their dog, or acquire dubious friends at the IPA. How he's evaded the sad progression, how he's done it, I can't say.

But I think I have discovered his secret. There is no gap between the broadcaster, the columnist, and the man. To sit and chat with him is no different than to switch on the radio at 10 in the evening or to find his column on a Saturday afternoon beneath an abandoned burger at Tullamarine. Low gossip, high politics, and endearing anecdotes of politics and other failures, love, art and his beloved farm, come together in a vision of life that is above all human, a world of frailties, vanities, and acceptance of, and wonder in, what we human beings are.

Here he is writing about his one-time mentor and dear friend, the legendary and visionary Nugget Coombs, who near the end of his life ended up in the sadness of a secure wing of an old age home.

> "Every few weeks I'd break him out and take him for a drive. We'd talk. Or rather, I'd talk and he would repeat every sentence. Dementia? Perhaps, but I felt Nugget understood everything.
>
> "The last time I saw him? After a drive around North Sydney — passing Kirribilli House where he'd spent a lot of time — I was easing my frail, feather-light friend into a wheelchair on the 20th floor of this geriatric gulag when, suddenly, wordlessly, he pulled my face down to his and kissed me on the mouth.

"Almost twenty years on I can still remember the dry lips of the old man — and his desperate need. It was, and remains, one of my greatest honours.

Diogenes famously carried a lamp around Athens in day time, saying he was searching for an honest man. In Philip Adams, Australia has been fortunate in having one for so long.

Style is the man, Chekhov said. And the man is a marvel, and every column a joy, and his work a reminder that the voices that matter are not of the right or the left, but of themselves, human, caring, comic, joyful, and unafraid. In our heavy age of terror, we need such lightly born courage more than ever.

Richard Flanagan

2003

Circus Royale

November 24, 2003

AN OLD CIRCUS act has clowns throwing buckets of water over each other. They work closer and closer to the audience who, expecting a bucketing, shrink back in their seats, only to be drenched in ... confetti!

At the Circus Royale last night, the rain came down in buckets — and the clowns, performers and rouseabouts used buckets to try and bale out the tent. But the deluge was too much for them and the show had to be cancelled.

So we went to this arvo's matinee, squelching on rubber mats laid over tonnes of sawdust. And I watched kids, used to digital effects in whiz-bang movies, marvelling at the simplest, silliest things. Like clowns throwing buckets of confetti and geese whooshing down playground slides.

The geese didn't mind the arena being a bit mushy but the circus owner, Frank Gasser, told me his camels were always a bit iffy after rain. Nonetheless, they went through their paces with patrician disdain, looking down their noses as only camels can. And the next performers were equally prima donna-ish. Pigeons, fanning their tails, puffing out their chests and strutting about, naturally theatrical.

I asked what had happened to the big cats. "I've retired them," he explained. "They were getting a bit long in the tooth." As is Frank, aged 68. Head of a circus family claiming 500 years of tradition. "Tigers only live around 10 or 12 years in the wild and mine were already 14 or 15. I reckon they'll live to be 20, but instead of training some youngsters, I thought up something else."

Before revealing what the "something else" was, he told me how tough it's been. "The circus is very close to the farm and when farms aren't doing well, the circus struggles. So I didn't mind cancelling last night's show. When farmers get some rain they get some hope. And if they make a bit of money they come to the circus."

He talked of the last few years on the dusty roads, zig-zagging their way across Australia, trying to find towns that weren't in total despair. Telling his competition that he'd be heading north, thus encouraging them to go south. Or west.

Not that there's as much competition as there used to be. After the best part of 200 years, Ashton's had closed down. Frank told me that Mrs A, the matriarch who'd held the show together, had finally died. Shortly after, they'd folded the big top for the last time. "As a matter of fact, it's Dougie Ashton's birthday today," he said, showing me the invitation to the party. Dougie, whom I remember as a powerful 50-year-old, is now 85.

"Trapeze? No, this tent's too small. But the Argentinians do a great high-wire act; tightrope walking right at the top of the tent." They ride bikes, have sword fights and tap dance on a silver filament at neck-craning height. Minus safety net.

Even if the drought has broken, Frank is sober about the future. Not just because he's 68, but because of the price of diesel and the fiasco of his new big top. It's taken a dozen skilled tent-makers months to stitch it together. "It was magnificent, but started to go wrong. The material was no bloody good. Couldn't handle the sun. Got sticky after a couple of weeks. We couldn't unroll it properly."

I sympathise about the sticky tent but, even worse, there's the GS bloody T. "I try and work it out, night after night, after the show, and it drives me crazy. As do the visas for international artists. We used to get visas that lasted a year. Now it's every three months, and each one costs hundreds and hundreds of dollars. So if you've got a lot of artists from Russia or, yes, Argentina, it's impossible. But not as bad as the insurance.

"It used to cost me $4,000 a year. Now it's $60,000. So I can't put money aside to help us over the bad times, over the droughts." When he introduces me to some of his children and grandchildren he says, "We're a circus family," with a mixture of pride and fatalism.

Inside the not-so-big-top, the miners' kids are literally screaming with laughter as clowns kick each other in the bum and drench each other with buckets. And then, Robin W Howell, the animal trainer, brings in the new act. Four Friesian cows. Looking like escapees from a dairy. Which is, in a sense, what they are.

Hey diddle diddle. Robin's cows don't jump over the moon but do manage some stately pirouettes and obligingly put their front hooves on little platforms so that the minuscule Welsh pony, Lobo, can run under them. Like Puffing Billy going through a rapid succession of tunnels. "We've had ten times more interest in the cows than we had in the big cats," Robin tells me. "Farmers, in particular, are enthralled." As Frank said, farms and circuses go together.

Like all of Robin's animals, the cows are trained by carrot rather than stick. Quite literally, as their rewards are pieces of carrot nuzzled from his palm. The only thing that affects the act is that, from time to time, one of the girls will notice a few blades of grass growing through the sawdust and stop for a nibble. This causes minor traffic jams. The cows are lucky to be in show business as it's far preferable to being rounded up at 5am for milking.

2004

Intelligence and war in Iraq

January 29, 2004

IN FEBRUARY 2001 Colin Powell told the world that Saddam Hussein "has not developed any significant capability in respect of weapons of mass destruction. He is unable to project conventional power against his neighbours."

The weapons inspectors agreed. As did Powell's colleague, Condoleeza Rice. "We are able to keep arms from him," she said. "His military forces have not been rebuilt."

Then the Bush regime changed its mind. Here's what Bush had to say in Cincinnati in October 2003: "The Iraqi regime ... possesses and produces chemical and biological weapons. It is seeking nuclear weapons. It has given shelter and support to terrorism. The danger is already significant, and it grows worse with time. If we know Saddam Hussein has dangerous weapons today — and we do — it doesn't make any sense for the world to wait ... for the final proof, the smoking gun that could come in the form of a mushroom cloud."

Obediently the CIA Reports ran hot: "The Iraqis possess chemical warfare, bulk fills for missiles, biological warfare programs are active and are larger and more advanced than they were before the Gulf War. Iraq has begun renewed production of mustard, Saran and other chemical weapons."

The claims from the White House got more detailed and specific. Nothing is merely suspected. Everything is known. Here's an extract from Bush's State of the Union message, January 2003: "Iraq has 500 tonnes of chemical weapons, 25,000 litres of anthrax, 38,000 litres of botulinum toxin, 30,000 prohibited bombs and warheads ... the British Government has learnt that Saddam Hussein recently sought significant quantities of uranium from Africa."

Colin Powell talked to the UN Security Council a few weeks later. "My colleagues, every statement I make today is backed up by sources, solid sources. These are not assertions. We are giving you facts and conclusions based on solid evidence ... I cannot tell you everything that we know, but what I can share with you ... is deeply troubling ... Iraq today has a stockpile of between 100 and 500 tonnes of chemical weapons agents ... Iraq retains a covert force of up to a few dozen scud-variant ballistic missiles ... Iraq has illegally imported 380 SA2 rocket engines ... Iraqi intelligence agents are driving around the countryside in cars full of key files from military and scientific establishments ... Baghdad has dispersed rocket launches and warheads containing biological warfare agent ... to various locations in Western Iraq ... hidden in large groves of palm trees ... Should we take the risk that he will not some day use these weapons at a time of his choosing? The United States cannot run that risk to the American people."

Paul Wolfowitz, the Principal Deputy to Secretary of Defence, Donald Rumsfeld, added undisputable facts of his own: "The CIA has collected solid facts about a decade of senior level contacts between Iraq and Al Qaida, facts about training of Al Qaida people, including in chemical and biological weapons, and facts about providing sanctuary for Al Qaida people, including senior Al Qaida people, including in Baghdad ... I believe those facts more than justify the concern the President has expressed that this regime is too dangerous to be left with the world's most dangerous weapons in its hands."

The CIA National Intelligence Estimate was less emphatic, admitting they didn't know everything. But this didn't matter because what they didn't know only intensified the problem: "Iraq is continuing and in some areas expanding its programs for WMDs; that we are not detecting portions of these weapons programs means it could be worse than we think; Iraq could make a nuclear weapon in a year if it had fissionable material."

Misinformation, disinformation, exaggerations, fantasies, fictions, propaganda and lies. Used to justify the war in Iraq. Thomas Powers, author of *Intelligence Wars: America's Secret History from Hitler to Al Qaida*, documents it thoroughly, quietly pointing out that none of the foregoing was true.

I was one of the many who believed that the threat from Iraq was being overstated by orders of magnitude. Though convinced that most of the weapons — and weapons programs — had been destroyed in Gulf War I or, as weapons inspections had demonstrated, subsequently dismantled, I accepted there'd be some nasty weapons deployed by Saddam. Or at very least found. The fact that a year of desperate searching yielded nothing is a devastating indictment of both the nonsense we were fed and the willingness, the enthusiasm, of the Howard government to believe it. And to act on it. Taking us into a war that put our troops in harm's way while exposing Australia to escalating danger in the aftermath.

"A source said that 1,600 death row prisoners were transferred in 1995 to a special unit for (chemical and biological) experiments ... an eye-witness saw prisoners tied down to beds, experiments conducted on them, blood oozing around the victims' mouths and autopsies performed to confirm the effects." — Colin Powell at the UN, February 2003.

Note the specific details. Not only do we have warheads hidden in large groves of palm trees, but a specific number of death row prisoners. Yet on the closest inspection, everything evaporates. Both the palm trees and the prisoners tied to the beds. All those specific details, known facts, things beyond doubt and dispute turned out to be tosh. We have lived through, been part of, party to, one of the greatest acts of mass deception in history.

In the US, many distinguished Republicans protested the way they were being railroaded into the war. In the UK, Blair's Government was all but torn apart by internal dissent. And in Australia? Total, abject surrender to Howard's echoing of the White House line; taking us into the first war of the 21st century.

Does anyone reading this column have the slightest doubt that we wouldn't fall for it again? Do it again? We'll do it simply because they want us to do it. Such is their power. Such is our craven weakness.

Tolerance

February 23, 2004

IMAGINE THE MIGHTY word TOLERANCE being spelled out in lights, stretching across Uluru like the HOLLYWOOD sign over Los Angeles. Then watch the globes being shattered one by one. Out goes the T, the O, the L, the N and one of the Es, until all that's left is RACE.

Don't worry. This isn't a political column. God, aren't you sick of politics? At every tier? The mendacity of municipal. The sleaze of state. The humbug at federal. The brutalities of international. The hypocrisies and betrayals that link every level. From local councillors on the take to Presidents who run international affairs for their billionaire mates. So I promise you this column won't be about politicians. It's about us.

We mustn't use politics — or politicians — as our excuse for those broken globes. The fact is that, just before our 100th birthday party, we changed our minds. Oh, we still celebrated the Centenary of Federation with shock-and-awe fireworks, but neither that orgasmic incandescence or the glow of the Olympic cauldron could hide the fact that something had gone very, very wrong. If anything, all that self-congratulatory dazzlement merely deepened the shadows. For the virtues we'd claimed for ourselves, the qualities we saw defining Australia, had gone AWOL.

I was on a COAG committee (The Council of Australian Governments — representing the states, the territories and the Commonwealth) charged with planning the birthday party. Members covered pretty much the entire political spectrum and our first duty was to tell COAG what Australians felt about themselves, what they wanted to celebrate.

We decided to ask everyone who talked to us the same question. "What is it that makes you proud to be an Australian?" Before interrogating the RSL, the CWA, the Boy Scouts and hundreds of other community organisations, I put the question to David Malouf, who predicted that people would talk, first and foremost, about the landscape. And he was right. The spirit of Dorothy McKellar was alive and well. Even if insufficiently expressed in environmental activism, it was as if the immensity, the physicality, of Australia was a metaphor for freedom, as if our vast distances contributed to a special quality in our democracy.

So I'd point out that all this and more had existed long, long before something called "Australia". What had 100 years of white settlement — by no means a total blessing for flora, fauna and landscape — achieved? There was a brief silence followed by ... the T word. Tolerance. Without exception — and I mean this literally — everyone who made submissions praised Australians for their tolerance. Even people speaking on behalf of organisations with intolerant track records insisted that tolerance first and foremost, was our defining characteristic.

Tolerant? Us? An odd choice, given certain difficulties with the indigenous population. Given almost 70 years of the White Australia policy. For generations, Australians had been tolerant to people provided they were identical to them. That is, white. They turned their backs on the black and slammed the front gate on the brown and the yellow. Nonetheless I was disinclined to argue. For, since the late 1960s our attitudes and behaviour had been somewhat redemptive. There were the Referenda in the late 1960s that had opened the possibility of Reconciliation — passed by an unprecedented majority of people in a majority of states. Then there'd been the quiet, bi-partisan agreement to dump White Australia. Yes, every new wave of post-war immigration had provoked hostilities but, by and large, we'd sorted them out. To such an extent that the Australia we'd be celebrating with all those fireworks displays would have appalled the Founding Fathers for its inclusiveness. That's not what they'd had in mind.

Consequently, the theme of tolerance was central to the COAG Report. Even our most conservative members signed off on it.

Then it all went wrong. Because this column isn't about politics I won't identify the pollies who most enthusiastically spread the anthrax of prejudice — you won't read names like Graham Campbell, Wilson Tuckey and Pauline Hanson in this column. Nor the names of far more powerful figures who appropriated their momentum. But the truth is the phenomenon wasn't created by politicians — simply intensified by them.

Thus Reconciliation didn't make it to January 1, 2001 and whilst we cheered and clapped as the international athletes marched into the Olympic arena, we were disinclined to tolerate the poor bloody reffos who turned up in dribs or drabs. Nor did we express much in the way of grief when over 300 drowned in local waters in SIEV X.

But you know the story. You know how badly we've been behaving lately. You know what an issue race has become, once more, in Australia. And you know, in your heart of hearts, that we've got to do something about it. We've got to start replacing all those broken light bulbs.

Politicians won't do it for us. First of all, each of us has to fight the bigotry in ourselves — and I rarely meet anyone entirely free of it. I'm not. During my childhood I was pro-grammed for prejudice and, ever since, have had to deal with it. It's a bit like trying to eliminate a computer virus.

We've got to tackle it in our families, amongst our friends, in our neighbourhoods, in our schools, even in our sport and our places of worship. Tolerance is not something that Australia has ever truly achieved. But we have, during our better moments, worked towards it.

If you're sick of politics, so be it. Make this issue personal.

Blockbuster

March 1, 2004

I'D SPENT ANOTHER scorcher in the shearers' shed, wading through the residue of what's left of 'my papers'. Already the bulk of them: a couple of hundred boxes containing documents, manuscripts and hundreds of thousands of letters have gone to the National Library in Canberra. Forty years of correspondence with readers, film-makers, friends, fanatics and people who confuse me with the Ombudsman. Amongst today's discoveries? The first draft of a film script David Puttnam and I commissioned from Bob Ellis, two 'lost' screenplays by Peter Carey and Ray Lawrence, the original MS of an unpublished novel by Geoffrey Dutton. Plus a flurry of memos from John Clarke about a proposed film called *Blockbuster* ... and a hand-written note from Grace Kelly, containing her home number and an invitation to call in for a cup of tea.

Grace, Elizabeth Taylor and Kim Novak were among the famous names desperate to appear in *Blockbuster*, an idea that came to me at my first Cannes Film Festival. I was trying to flog *Don's Party*, starring the likes of John Hargraves, Graham Kennedy and the bloke who decades later would write his biography, Graeme Blundell. The wider world knew little and cared less about Australia and its films. Whilst my director, Bruce Beresford, would go on to make two Oscar-winning movies — *Tender Mercies* and *Driving Miss Daisy* — and our writer, David Williamson, would be invited to Hollywood to script the life story of Malcolm X, there were no names to conjure with in the credits. Our Don wasn't invited to their party.

Sipping coffee on the Croisette, watching the paparazzi swarm at the merest hint of a suggestion that Clint Eastwood might be about to emerge from his suite at The Carlton, I came up with a bittersweet idea. A devious Australian would announce a film starring Paul Newman, Peter O'Toole, Robert Redford, Gregory Peck, James Stewart, Shirley MacLaine and Julie Andrews — and sell it to international distributors on a hit-and-run visit to the world's most powerful film festival. Only when he'd laughed all the way to the Bank of New South Wales would the truth emerge. That his megastars were merely Australian namesakes, picked from capital city phone books. In other words, it would be a scam movie, the sort of thing that, down the track, Mel Brooks would do for Broadway with *The Producers*. I remember sitting there, adding to and embroidering the idea, making it more convoluted and baroque, and wondering whether I shouldn't actually do it. That is, not simply make a funny film about the idea but make the film itself.

I had a crack at the script but couldn't get the funding. But when I started Adams Packer Films, John Clarke and Andrew Knight — both destined for greatness — took the idea and ran with it. It was all in one of the bulging files I found in the shearing shed, albeit the worst for wear, having been nibbled at by rats.

"Hal Burstyn is another in the increasingly long line of Australian movie geniuses," wrote John and Andrew in the treatment. (The name Hal Burstyn parodies the names of

Tim Burstall and Hal McElroy and other characters would be thinly disguised parodies of major figures in the industry or the Film Commission.) "He makes what the *Rockhampton Nut and Screwmaker Monthly* describes as a 'touching and beautifully shot epic' called *The Drover's Blanket*. It wins a hatful of Australian awards and sets off to take Cannes by storm. With the assistance of a bevy of government-paid marketing whiz kids, Hal watches the international film buyers reject it to a man. In favour of films starring Sylvester Stallone.

"This experience triggers an impulse in Hal to beat the international market at its own game. He returns to Australia determined to make a blockbuster containing big stars and aimed at runaway box office success. His vision, however, is thwarted at every turn. He loses control of his picture to Alex, an investment accountant not principally known for his understanding of the film business, and the Government Film Board appoints a lunatic Hungarian, Anton Krankovitch, to direct."

In summary, when Hal couldn't sign a single megastar he rounds up a few dozen namesakes, planning to have the film destroyed in fire at a laboratory before his malfeasance is revealed. Krankovitch, suspecting sabotage, flees to Los Angeles to screen what he sees as the most savage indictment of celebrity-obsessed American culture. But Hollywood loves it! And Hal becomes a national hero.

I can't recall why we didn't make *Blockbuster*, but after a dozen other films we closed Adams Packer down. Whatever became of young Kerry?

The file is full of namesakes we'd tracked down: Steve McQueen, Elvis Presley, Mohammed Ali, George Washington, Marie Antoinette, Roy Rogers, John Wayne,

Susan Hayward, a Mona Lisa and, cross my heart, a Donald Duck. Plus two Peter Sellers, three Gary Coopers, four Clark Gables and a Marilyn Monroe living in Coogee. And that lovely letter from Grace Kelly of Gratton Street, Carlton.

Perhaps there's a delicious irony in that, these days, Hollywood comes to Australia for famous names. So the joke's on them.

Global warning

June 28, 2004

DURING THE Second World War the US, believing Nazi Germany well advanced in its plans to build nuclear WMDs, poured millions into the Manhattan project which, under Oppenheimer's leadership, gave the world its first three mushroom clouds. Later, the world would learn that Germany's nuclear weapons program had been a bit of a fizzer. As were Japan's. Yes, Japan destined to have two of its cities evaporated by atomic bombs, also had nuclear dreams. Years back in Tokyo, I heard a Japanese General admitting to a little Manhattan project. "Would you have used them if you'd had them?" to which his response was an explosion of laughter. "Of course we would!"

The war ended and the Cold War began. Both sides developed H-bombs and massive delivery systems. The world held its breath as the policy of MAD — mutually assured destruction — kept pushing us towards the apocalypse.

Even now that the Cold War is over, or at least dormant, and leaving aside the nuclear weapons of France, the UK, China, Israel, India and Pakistan, there are still 18,000 missiles ticking away in US and Russian armouries. In the missile silos. In the submarines. Still aimed at each other's cities. Yet even if there was to be a nuclear war between nation states — or a nuclear attack by terrorists on a major city — that would not represent the greatest threat to planetary survival. That comes, and it's coming closer and closer, from global warming.

Decades back, one of Australia's greatest scientists told me about the Greenhouse effect, how every day in his laboratory ("and in laboratories of colleagues all over the world") there were ominous changes to the atmosphere and a growing probability of climatic catastrophe. "Greenhouse" had been identified and named in the late 19th century — but it would take another 100 years for "global warming" to enter the political vocabulary. And what it threatens, what it promises, though less spectacular and immediate in its effect than nuclear explosions, will destroy more lives, more cities, more forests, more everything, than any nuclear war.

A couple of scientists, usually with connections to the coal and oil industries, still mock the notion of Greenhouse. By and large they're the same sort of scientists to be relied upon to dispute any connections between smoking and lung cancer. The overwhelming majority of researchers in every related discipline agree that we're now conducting the largest and most dangerous experiment in planetary history. And what people fail to comprehend is that we're not simply talking the melting of the ice caps, though that will be disastrous enough, but massive deforestation, accelerating desertification and the greatest obliteration of species since the climatic catastrophe that wiped out, amongst innumerable other species, the dinosaurs. Scientists might disagree on the speed of the process, on the meteorological mechanics. There is, however, universal agreement that we have made a very bad mistake in the way we've burnt our fossil fuels. Yet it's a mistake we continue to make today, tomorrow, next week, next decade.

Global warming won't stop when Sydney's harbourside mansions have been drowned, along with a few small Pacific nations and pretty much the entirety of Bangladesh.

The waters will keep rising — as will the temperatures. They won't level off in a few years and give us decades to make adjustments. The temperatures will keep rising. As the scientist told me 20 years ago, "We're going to cook ourselves."

Tim Flannery is the latest scientist desperate to alert us to this slow motion suicide, to an event that will make the fire-bombings of Dresden and Tokyo and the atomic bombings of Hiroshima and Nagasaki seem like minor events. Like others who've looked at the scenarios — even the optimistic ones — he sees, for example, Perth becoming uninhabitable. And there will be a lot of Perths all over the world that will face equally implacable fates.

And what are we doing about it? Bugger all. The US, far and away the greatest global warmer, (though its pre-eminence will soon be challenged by the growing might and concomitant pollution of China) refuses to sign Kyoto. Hardly surprising, given that so much of Bush's financial backing comes from the coal and oil industries, whose continuing denials about global warming are as insane, nonsensical, absurd and hypocritical as, for example, the Vatican's stand on contraception and the condom.

And in Australia? In the same breath as the Prime Minister proudly announced a long overdue and under-whelming plan to save the Murray Darling, he unveils an ecological policy that boggles the mind. We won't, of course, be signing Kyoto. Dubya wouldn't approve. Nor will we pour money into alternative energy, into anything vaguely sustainable. Instead we'll be encouraging increased use of diesel and shoving money at, yes, coalminers.

I do not exaggerate the risks. It's impossible to do so. Not even *The Day After Tomorrow* does that. While it's overly dramatic in its reliance on digital tsunamis, on the sort of spectacle and drama compulsory in a good disaster movie, the real thing will be far more sinister and incremental. But it will lead to consequences beyond even Hollywood's imaginings.

As you read these words you'll probably sigh deeply, brush them aside as hyperbolic or shrug them off with a feeling of surrender and helplessness. Or perhaps you've turned the page already. But just as you can prolong your life by giving up smoking, even at the age of 60, we can begin to ameliorate what lies ahead — by acting now. By listening to the likes of Tim Flannery and by placing pressures on politicians who, notoriously, think in the time frames of election campaigns, if not in 10-second grabs. We're discussing nothing less than the survival of our planet, at least in some recognisable form. We're talking about the survivability of our species and of the lives of billions of our fellow creatures. And Australia has a special responsibility in all this — as one of the world's greatest producers and exporters of coal. While it isn't wildly radioactive and tends to just burn rather than produce mushroom clouds, coal will prove as deadly as anything that derives from uranium.

I've been studying Greenhouse and global warming since the 1980s. I've lost count of the books, articles and papers I've read, the conferences I've attended, the debates I've chaired. And I firmly believe that our acquiescence to global warming is our greatest mistake. Even greater than the wars we've waged upon each other.

And if you don't know that yet, it's because you don't want to know.

Cattle dog

July 26, 2004

"THERE'S A WILD DOG under the shearing shed," said
Aurora.

Whilst we've feral everything else — pigs, goats, cats, you
name it — we've been spared the problem of dogs. But I'd
spotted our first dingo a few days earlier and, with lambing
beginning, went looking.

He was hard to spot. Moving fast and low to the ground,
he concealed himself in the grass, the shadows, but fleeting,
fragmented images started to form a picture. Not of a dingo
but a kelpie cross, dragging a metre of chain from its collar.
Odds on the chain would get caught under a shed or in the
barbed wire of a fence — and the dog would die of thirst,
hunger or strangulation.

Our prime concern was to protect the lambs from attack,
so we tried to lure it out with profferings of food. But it
seemed suspicious of the dog bowl, preferred to raid the
dustbins, scattering rubbish everywhere. Then Aurora came
running. "Dad, he's IN a bin." And he was. Trapped, the
chain snagged.

All fangs and snarls, he presented both a danger and
a dilemma. What to do? I managed to free the chain and
started to tug at it, fully expecting an explosive attack.
But what emerged from the dustbin, like a tortoise from

its carapace, wasn't aggressive. It was the most terrified animal I'd ever seen.

The broken chain suggested it had escaped from a neighbour's property or jumped off the back of a passing Ute. We started phoning around: "Are you missing a cattle dog?" and we added another "Lost Dog" to the noticeboard at the local store.

Then we stopped phoning and removed the notice. How could we return the dog to an owner who'd clearly brutalised it? It cowered when you attempted to touch it. It reacted to the gentlest pat as if it were a beating. And we couldn't let the dog go free without a home, without a name, off the chain. Already a wild dog it would clearly get wilder.

If released, it would do its best to hide, to disappear. And it could only survive by attacking the sheep. Or the dustbins.

For days the only time it stopped shivering with terror was when Timmy, our cattle dog, would come bounding up, all licks and tail wags. Timmy's third-party endorsement of me seemed to reassure the refugee.

But it still snarled at Patrice, growled at Aurora and savaged Gavin's hand when we tried to worm it — its appetite was enormous but it remained appallingly thin. So the consensus was that I should take it to the vet. Have it put down. Put out of its misery — the accumulated misery of its abused life. Reluctant to do so, I kept talking to it, trying to calm it and, after three days, had a breakthrough. For the first time it actually inched towards me, just a couple of feet, without me hauling at the chain. A day later, it began to nuzzle me. And if I sat beside it, would try to climb into my lap.

Little by little it has decided to trust me. And to love Timmy. Now I let it off the chain and it follows me everywhere, obediently heeling. When I go out on the motorbike it runs beside me. And I can pick it up and plonk it in the back of the FWD when heading off to cut firewood.

Trouble is I spend three or four days a week in Sydney. When I leave, it immediately reverts to being terrified. No one can get near it, let alone chain it up at night. And once again, it heads for the dustbins. On my return, usually at 3am on a Friday morning, it appears slowly, tentatively, out of the darkness. It takes a lot of reassurance to persuade it to creep forward for a pat.

Nonetheless, as I mumble these words into the Dictaphone, it's got its head in my lap, looking up at me with the saddest eyes you've ever seen. Understandably, the family's consensus remains that the situation is untenable. You can't have a dog that's domestic three or four days a week and feral the rest.

But I find the poor little bugger irresistible. More than any of the dozen dogs I've owned, he has encouraged my maternal instincts. So I miss him when I'm in Sydney and can't wait for 3am Friday mornings. Today he let me pick him up and carry him around, giving me some affectionate licks. It's taken an inordinate amount of time and effort to get this far but few tasks have been as rewarding.

For no particular reason Patrice has christened this escapee, this asylum seeker, this mad, sad, little dog ... George. And I've had to promise to replace the wrecked plastic dustbins with a couple of strong galvo ones.

Come on, George, stop frightening the family. And wag your tail at the readers. Look! He did. Only a couple of little wags, but that's progress.

Graduation speech

July 27, 2004

*From an address given to a Graduation Ceremony
at the University of South Australia.*

HUMAN BEINGS ARE driven by a variety, almost an infinity, of fears, needs and desires. The greatest fear, that of death, leads to the desperate desire for eternal life. This in turn has piled up the pyramids and created our cathedrals whilst driving many into the most destructive of fundamentalisms.

But preceding our desire for life after death is an urgent appetite for life itself — which requires a diet of food, sex and information. And the most insatiable of our appetites is ... curiosity. We thirst and hunger for knowledge, for the answer to those big questions that are both our curse and our inspiration. Indeed, curiosity is a more powerful appetite than lust which after all it precedes, beginning at birth and lasting after the fires of lust have subsided.

Inside your noggin, smouldering beneath your mortarboards, is a very curious organ. Science remains somewhat mystified as to how the damn thing works — but while they're sorting that out we must acknowledge that it is a curiosity machine. We're told there are more neurons and synaptic possibilities in the average head than there are suns in the heaven. And that's saying something, given there are more suns out there than grains of sand on Earth.

So here it is, the brain, questioning away, endlessly, insatiably curious. My partner, our 12-year-old daughter and the latest dog went for a walk the other day, along the most remote fence line at the back of our farm. As usual, Patrice was looking closely at plants, botanising with every step she took — a habit that, from time to time, leads to the discovery of something that has rarely, if ever, been recorded. And whilst her mother looked down, our daughter looked up, searching the treetops for koalas or watching eagles swirling on the thermals. I was looking at the ghosts of old post-and-rail fences, dating back a century and more, often going straight up the mountainside. How the hell had they done it? With only axes and crowbars and pack horses.

The cattle were curious, too. Moving quietly through the trees to study us, calves clustering around their mothers, gazing at us with their huge eyes. In contrast to their long attention span there was our dog. Nothing is more curious than a dog, but it's short-lived and as narrowly focused as a lecturer's laser pointer. Timmy is fascinated by anything that appears in front of his nose, from dragonflies up — but would bound off, barking rapturously, in pursuit of any passing kangaroos. Whilst cow and canine are curious, they're insufficiently self-conscious, too lacking in memory, to make sense of what they observe. Whereas humans are like vacuum cleaners on legs, hoovering impressions and observations into the dust bags of our brains.

I never attended a university. My formal education lasted a few short years and was utterly mediocre. What little I've learnt came as a consequence of the curse of curiosity. And if I resent life's brevity it's not because of a fear of death so much as my curiosity in everything. Because everything is interesting. Plants, old fences, eagles, kangaroos, cosmology, geography, quantum mechanics, religious beliefs, diseases, politics and other people. As I get older I realise that I know less and less about more and more.

So I'm here to tell you that your education begins — or begins again — after you leave this fine institution. Be grateful to the university for the opportunities and knowledge you've been able to access here. If, however, you allow your curiosity to be sated, as too many do, by sitting dumbly, numbly in front of the television set, allowing your mind to be turned into cold porridge, or if you yield to the narcosis provided by either narcotics or shopping, then you should hand back your degree and donate your organs, including your brains, for medical experiments. For the curiosity that's been kindled at the uni has to be kept glowing, blazing, for the rest of your life. If only in a desperate attempt to try and keep up with what is, by any measure, one of the most fascinating times in history.

Devote your life to curiosity, to the questions. Even when that question has no simple or known answer. And remember that every answer we've ever found has created more questions.

It's a rare day when I don't learn something interesting, principally because I'm privileged to be able to talk to countless thousands of remarkable people on my wireless program. But each of us has the same unlimited access to reading. Or to learn things simply by thinking. Or trying to think. By looking up at the stars on a cloudless night and feeling that sense of the numinous — the mixture of awe, wonderment and dread that any human being should feel when contemplating the eternal and infinite sky.

Congratulations on your degrees. But more than that, congratulations on your curiosity. They say it killed the cat although, I suspect, it helped save us from the sabre tooth. Curiosity is our greatest asset. With the possible exception of a sense of humour.

The brain

October 4, 2004

I'VE BEEN THINKING about thinking. The way the brain sorts, sifts, spirals and associates. The constant Google-searching it does whenever you prompt it. Think of a word, any word. A place, any place. A name, a face, a time, an anything. And the damn thing starts to ... well, to think! And that seems to begin with, to depend upon, making connections. Echoing the physical reality of synapses, making connections between neurons. They talk about firing these minuscule electrical circuits.

So let's use firing as a demonstration. The firing of pistols, rifles, canon, employees, oneself. I remember Rupert Murdoch firing me years ago, the firing of a 21-gun salute in London and the firing of a few canons in Central Park to dramatise an open-air performance of Tchaikovsky's 1812 Overture. In a nanosecond, the mind recalls footage of missiles being fired from silos, submarines, shells from aircraft and others aimed at aircraft from battleships. The firing of arrows at Agincourt during Olivier's adaption of Henry V. The firing of arrows at cowboys in the crappy Westerns I used to see at Hoyts matinees on Saturday afternoons. And as fast as all these weapons are fired, the mind keeps firing.

The brain also cross references to words that sound like firing, like flying, frying, filing. Do you remember watching the widening ripples when you tossed a pebble into a pond? That's the brain for you. A single pebble leading to an infinity of ripples that overlap and interact. A whirling, eddying vortex of hundreds, thousands of fragmentary thoughts that, even whilst forming an image, an idea, a word, are also running out of control, randomly, in every direction. So fast, so amazingly, that you can start with anything, from a dinosaur to a teaspoon, and feel the mind, or rather the minds, because we seem to have dozens of them living inside our skulls, creating the chaos that, in turn, creates our consciousness.

I remember the late Carl Sagan scooping up a handful of sand in Cosmos, and letting the grains trickle between his fingers. "There are about 10,000 grains of sand in the average handful," he told us. "And there are more suns in our universe than there are grains of sand on all the beaches on Earth." These days we know that there are trillions upon trillions of suns, more than numberless grains of sand in all our deserts. Yet I've heard it said that just one human brain contains more synaptic connections than all those suns.

Odd, that the brain within our skulls, as grey and unlovely as the snail within its carapace, is capable of such complexity. Oh, those into AI insist that they're on the way to replicating and improving upon it, but it sounds like hubris to me. At very least, it's going to take a long time for human science — created by the brain — to catch up with the brain which, after all, has created everything from the wheel to the Voyager Spacecraft, from the stone axe to the cruise missile, from the Gothic cathedral to Hard Rock cafes, from the Gods to the Theory of Relativity. Though, sadly, most of us choose to waste most of its capacity on the most trivial of pursuits and distractions and the mental counterparts to junk food.

"The mind is its own place," thought Milton, "and in itself can make a heaven of hell, or a hell of heaven." While an even greater philosopher, A. A. Milne, said that the "third-rate mind is only happy when it is thinking with a majority ... and the first-rate mind is only happy when it is thinking."

Given the brain's capacity and how we waste it, it's like having a Ferrari that you leave parked in the garage or a Stradivarius violin you strum like a ukulele. Or like using the Mona Lisa for a tea tray.

Brain. The enlarged anterior end of the spinal cord, which co-ordinates the instinctive activities of the organism necessary for life; in higher vertebrates it is also the centre for learning. The brain of an adult British male, I've been told, weighs approximately 1,409 grams whilst that of a female is 1,263 grams. But when compared with an average body weight, the size and weight of both brains is proportionately equal. The cerebrum in humans, the centre of thought and conscious activities, is about 80% of the brain's weight. Tall persons have heavier brains than short persons but, relative to their height, short persons have larger heads and brains than tall ones. But statistical averages show there is only a slight correlation between a large head and a high intelligence.

But the facts are nothing compared to the fantastic abilities of what is, after all, a never ending fireworks display between your ears. If only people cared to use it instead of letting it bog down in bigotries, get doldrummed in dogmas or, just as bad, habit. I know people who haven't had a new, let alone original thought in decades — who think the same things over and over again. And there are others who are so bored with what their brain reveals to them that they seek 'altered states' through various forms of narcosis. When, in fact, all you have to do is close your eyes for a few seconds and follow your thoughts — which will immediately take you into realms more extraordinary than Alice's Wonderland, Kubrick's Space Odyssey or the maelstroms of LSD. In fact, you don't even have to be awake. Try dreaming.

Years ago, Bruce Petty drew a marvellous cartoon of a family sitting in front of the telly. On the screen were written the words, "Have your emotions lived for you tonight by American experts". I reckon it's only a matter of time until Hollywood, the dream factory, starts mass marketing dreams; until they are piped to your digitised pillow via the professional imaginings of a Steven Spielberg; until your dreams are provided by Dreamworks as another service of Pay TV.

Another interesting thing about the mind is that I don't believe that, finally, it forgets anything. Decades ago, I sat with a group of people whose names I no longer remember — except for one, Bob Ellis — and we tried, as an experiment, to recall a particular year in our life. And what happened was extraordinary. Goaded, provoked, stimulated by each other, we started to develop a sort of fractal memory, which kept revealing moments, details, experiences that none of us as individuals had had for decades. It was as if our synapses and neurons were intermingling — and the experience was funnier than any séance, wilder than any chemically-induced fantasies of a Timothy Leary. We weren't on anything, we weren't even drinking. What we discovered, with a little bit of help, was the brain, the mind, becomes fissionable material and there's an explosion of memory. In that case simultaneously astonishing and hilarious.

It's all in there. Choose a specific time in your childhood. Go back to a classroom at primary school. Look at the blackboard. See the teacher. Hear the voices of the kids around you, behind you. Lift up the lid of your desk; take out your pencil case and slide open the lid. Open your exercise book or look out the classroom window. It's all there, or at least far more of it than you can imagine. All the experiences of thousands of other mornings, almost as vivid as what's happening around you on this Saturday morning as you read The Oz. Whereas Google searches for words, your brain searches for the taste, flavours, textures, colours, pains, hopes, shapes — and can find everything from inexpressible joy to the most profound of sadness. And it's all in your head. Between your ears, at the top of your spinal cord. In that grey, snail-like organ that makes us conscious of ourselves, our lives and yes, our mortality. You only have to hear a couple of notes of music to remember a song you mightn't have heard for 30, 40 years. You've only to see a few seconds from a film you might have seen in the 60s or 70s for it to come rushing back. You've only got to do a Proust and dunk a bikkie in a cup of tea for the taste of it to bring back the totality of a long-gone time or experience. And yet we think nothing of it. We don't think about our thoughts very much at all, preferring to marvel at the tiny tricks of technology. Or to go ooh, aah at the capacity of a new laptop. Yes, IBM has built a computer that can beat Karpov at chess, but it was the human brain that built the computer and, for that matter, conceived the game of chess.

Check mate!

2005

Dreaming about drugs

April 16, 2005

ALL ABOARD, all aboard for the Theme Park of Mind Altering Substances! Roll up, roll up to the Disneyland of Drugs! Welcome to the Darryl Lea of narcotic confectionery! Wallow in Willy Wonka's wonderful world of things to inject, smoke, sniff or swallow! And laugh your heads off at the greatest folly in the history of public policy. Yes, the ludicrous attempt to wage, let alone win a war on one of mankind's most enduring appetites. The sad, sorry, silly attempt at prohibition and interdiction of demonised substances from the endless hit list of pain-killing, aphrodisiacal, fantasy-producing pharmaceuticals.

The US began experimenting with prohibition long before the Civil War, when factory owners were concerned with the high incidence of workers falling into the machines in their dark satanic mills. It wasn't the death and mutilation of gin-soaked employees that worried them, but the effect the accidents were having on production and profits. In the 1830s legislators, obviously affected by liquor, passed ludicrous laws to ban the bottle — finally repealed a hundred years later. The affects of prohibition are well known — the culture of illegal stills, speakeasies, violence amongst the distributors and retailers of illegal hooch and the corruption and debauchment of the entire system — from the politicians and the police to the judiciary. And everyone remained plastered.

Learning nothing from history, and determined to repeat it, Washington's war on drugs has been a far greater disaster, nothing short of a global catastrophe. As you read these words, the economies of many Central and South American nations are totally dependent on growing the raw ingredients for the ghettos of the US and Hollywood parties. The black economy of drugs has an appallingly high percentage of young blacks crowding the prisons that can't be built fast enough, and an entire pop-culture (mass-marketed by Time Warner) continues to advertise and celebrate the pleasures of addiction and killing cops. And thanks to another unwinnable war, the War on Terror, the production of heroin in Afghanistan is now back to the level it was before the Taliban took over.

By acquiescing to the US model of prohibition and interdiction Australia condemned itself to the same sort of problems — the creation of new categories of criminality, the clogging of our courts, the crowding of our prisons, the further corruption of our cops (as if the prohibitions on gambling and abortion hadn't been profitable enough!) and the escalating violence amongst the importers, pushers and pedlars.

I've always argued this sad truth: that we'd be no worse off, perhaps far better off, if we not only decriminalised but legalised pot, heroin, amphetamines, the whole surreal and sometimes suicidal smorgasbord. After all, the real killer drugs, responsible for over 90% of drug deaths are not only legal but also respectable. Check the who's who of directors sitting on the boards of Australia's brewers and tobacco companies. Grog and smokes are so much part of the culture that governments are addicted to the revenues.

(The increasingly successful campaign against smoking — a combination of twenty years of propaganda campaigns, punitive excise and public shaming shows that you can have a significant effect on addiction if the drug is legal.)

It wasn't so long ago that drugs were legal and the body count was a fraction of today's. Then addiction was seen as a medical condition rather than an issue of criminality. Yes, much addiction was caused by prescribed drugs — a problem vividly described by Eugene O'Neill in the portrait of his mother in *Long Day's Journey into Night*. And that remains a major problem in the 21st century, one dealt with by doctors, rehab clinics and public understanding. But if you're poor — and black — it's off to the slammer. Three strikes — and some pot can give you a life sentence. Or, in Australia's neighbourhood, a death sentence.

If every ounce of heroin were to miraculously disappear, would addiction disappear? Of course not. Equally lethal and perfectly legal alternatives abound. Apart from alcohol and cigarettes, there's petrol. It kills billions of kids' brain cells in indigenous communities, and can't always be replaced by Avgas. Glue, too, can be deadly, but no one suggests banning Tarzan's Grip.

No matter how profound society's disapproval or harsh its punishments, humans remain human. Thus forbidding abortions doesn't save the unborn. It kills women. And laws against pornography, even death sentences for adultery or sodomy do little to change human behaviour, except to make it furtive.

Yes, forty years ago I did inhale, but these days my only drugs are tea and coffee. Nonetheless I've seen what damage addiction does, whether it's to heroin or money. And I'm convinced that decades of moral panic about this or that drug is not only worse than useless but comes about because populist politicians are addicted to moral panic.

Hon Doctorate, Sydney University

April 29, 2005

THERE'S AN OLD Frank Sinatra song, beloved of inebriated businessmen in karaoke bars. 'I Did it My Way'. Given his uncouth behaviour and flirtations with the Mafia, Frank's way was, frankly, problematic ... it certainly offers no role modelling for high quality humans like yourselves. Nor does the example of drunken executives singing it out of tune — a song that is a hymn of praise — of self-praise — to rampant individualism ... a sort of advertising jingle for neo-conservatism. So much so that I expect it to replace 'Hail to the Chief' whenever George Bush walks into a room — or 'Oh say can you see by dawn's early light', as the US National anthem.

I mention the song here, today, because a few lyrics came to mind as I thought of the improbability of the honour this great institution is bestowing on me today ... and perhaps you'd all join me in singing them ... or perhaps not. The words? "Regrets, I've had a few, but then again too few to mention." Sorry Mr Sinatra, you're not singing my song. Regrets?

I've got a lot. Far too many to mention here. Enough to fill volumes, or this splendid hall. And one of them is this. I deeply, deeply regret never having attended a university. The thought, the possibility never entered my head. Neither of my parents suggested it. Nor did my teachers. The subject simply never came up.

No one in my family had ever gone to uni ... I don't think we even knew anybody who had ... so the nearest I got was passing Melbourne Uni in a Lygon Street tram.

To some extent it was a class thing. We'd always been working class ... and a financial thing ... no money ... but it was deeper than that ... there was no sense of entitlement. Rather, an overwhelming sense of mystery verging on the fearful ... unis were like secret societies, like monasteries, the Masonic Lodge, the Melbourne Club, not for the likes of us ... and that wouldn't change much until the early 70s when Gough Whitlam put out the welcome mat. So I left school midway through my secondary education, itself spectacularly mediocre, and got a dreadful job ... learning what little I could from second-hand books, a brush with what was left of bohemia — and a brief skirmish with the communist party ... in other words, what's known as the university of life. But as the years passed I realised more and more what I'd missed and was missing. Sometimes people are kind enough to suggest that I've done alright without uni ... but whatever success I've had is, I know, I feel certain, far less than what I could have, would have, had I been able to attend a place like this. And learned how to research, how to really read, how to run the intellectual marathon. I know it four nights a week, when, for the last twenty years, I've discussed every imaginable topic with Academics and scholars from scores of universities, from Sydney, Harvard, Cambridge — and others not so firmly positioned on the A-list. I've interviewed more Professors than you've had hot breakfasts or hamburgers.

At last count, I'd talked to over 10,000 of the best and brightest on the planet. This doesn't mean I'm entitled to an honorary doctorate, but probably means I deserve a place in the Guinness Book of Records. Hardly a day passes when I'm not confronted or simply delighted with another discovery from the realms of scholarship or by the delight of a new idea or a new angle on an old idea. I'm privileged to be in close contact with a world that, all those years ago, was denied to me ... or at least seemed closed to me ... and am constantly reminded that the work done in a place like this still drives (for good and sometimes ill) the great engine of human thought ... and fights the good fight against the armies of the night — still recruiting from the ranks of the bigoted, the dogmatic and the fundamentalist. And the armies of the night have rarely been more powerful, more dangerous than they are today ... you'd have to go back to Europe in the 1930s or the US in the 50s to find a time as perilous as our own. And at this time, the universities are under unprecedented attack and, yes, financial pressure ... and the campuses are not as given to spontaneous cultural and political combustion as in the past ... the mood is changing — and I detect similar moods in other places, in other institutions, from the United Nations to the High Court to the ABC to what's left of decent newspapers.

But to hell with it. There are no greater pleasures than thinking, learning, writing, arguing ... with people in this sports' crazed nation — the only arena where elitism isn't a dirty word — cannot know that tossing or kicking ideas around is far more fun, yes FUN, than tossing a Frisbee or kicking an inflated bladder. And more important. No one can remember the name of the captain of the Pope's soccer team — but we all remember who painted his ceiling ... and we treasure the books, the ideas, the inspiration of his scholars. And the defiant heresies of the Galileos. Indeed, we still write books about their books and argue about those venerable arguments.

I am greatly privileged to be here today ... but so are you. You worked harder for your degree than I worked for mine ... but you have been given an opportunity still beyond the reach of most and even, as in my case, beyond their dreams. Thank you for inviting me here today — and let me issue an invitation in return. Come and let me interview you at the ABC.

All you have to do is write the book. So leave here today and get stuck into it — into the wildly improbable gift of life.

Then, in 80, 90 or 100 years' time, when you're facing Frank Sinatra's final curtain, when it comes to regrets, you might very well finish up with too few to mention.

Dog days

May 1, 2005

DUE TO THE unprecedented level of complaints about this column from conservatives, both Christian and secular, I've decided, for one week only, to avoid any mention of religion or politics. Jesus will not appear on this page. Nor will Howard, Bush or the Pope. Instead I'll return to the safe subject of ... dogs.

It's been months since I last reported on George, the asylum-seeking kelpie we captured when he snagged his broken chain whilst raiding our dustbins. I've told of the weeks spent trying to sooth this terrified, traumatised stranger, of persuading it that an extended hand might proffer a pat, instead of a blow. Of how, little by little, he came to trust me although he remains disinclined to trust anyone else. Only my thirteen-year-old daughter is permitted to touch him, and even then George flinches.

Nonetheless he's now rapturously happy, provided other humans leave him alone. And he has two friends for life in our other cattle dogs, the matronly Rosie and Timmy, the eternal puppy. They've welcomed him to the farm and shown him the ropes. And the rules, principally: no chasing of sheep, chooks or trucks. This energy, this instinct is better employed mustering cattle.

In the morning the dogs are dancing on the chains, bundles of joy. Once released, they pee on the shrub or tyre of their choice and then come hurtling at me. I sit on the garden bench for this encounter, so that they can climb on and over me. Timmy is the most skilled in this daily exercise. Like a ruckman after a mark he clambers up the other dogs and knocks my hat off. It is crucial to avoid affectionate licks from tongues recently employed in rectal ablutions.

Then it's time to run to the ute for the daily trip to the Gundy Store for the papers. Timmy's first to jump onto the tray, followed by Rosie who, despite her ample proportions, can still leap like Nijinski. But George? He flattens himself to the ground and looks up pathetically. So I've got to lift him. Given that he eats mountains to make up for years of malnourishment, this takes effort. And like the other two, he likes to roll in dirt and cow shit, so he's dusty and he pongs.

They bark all the way to the store. Not at anything. Just to register approval with life. Timmy, the tenor, barks the loudest. Rosie is a contralto and George a counter-tenor, providing the descant with an occasional yipe.

Then it's down to business. Thanks to the endless drought that can't possibly get worse but does, on a daily basis, we've got to move 150 cows with calves from the River paddock into Spring Paddock. The river's empty, the spring dried up years ago, but we've rigged up a trough and there's a bit of dry grass to nibble. The cattle are scattered all over, up the hills, in the scrub, in the gullies, and Gavin and I need the dogs' help. As usual, Timmy is worse than useless, getting in front when he should be behind, and George, whilst he tries, is scared of pretty well everything on Earth, from chooks to cattle. Only Rosie earns her keep. She loves nipping at hooves and when a cow turns on her, holds her ground. At the end of the day, when the other dogs are just covered in dust, she's covered in bruises.

The dogs take a dip in every dam. Which means they sink deep into mud and ooze, the only moisture left. Which means they have to be actively discouraged from jumping on you. Mind you, by then we're all stinking to high heaven.

Pretty buggered after three hours of persuading recalcitrant mooies to form a coherent mob and head in the right direction and through the right gates, which is as difficult as that biblical reference to camels, rich men, and the gates of heaven (no, this is nothing to do with religion, as I've promised to stay off the topic) we head for home only to discover there's a problem at the other end of the property. So it's onto the ATVs, the four-wheel bikes, for a 25km on and off-road ride. Rosie's not interested. No hooves to nip. But Timmy and George volunteer, and by the time we get back, we will have covered perhaps twice the distance, given that the eternal pup takes the refugee on huge detours chasing kangaroos.

Come sunset, I tie them up and feed them. If I'm not careful Timmy will eat his tucker first, then George's, who's so subservient he won't even complain.

A final pat. A 'see you in the morning'. A last wagging of tails and an entire column free of controversy! Though there'll probably be a few letters from angry vegetarians.

On bullshit

May 14, 2005

THERE'S A LOT of bull in metaphoric and colloquial language. A Hereford herd of bulls at the gate also wreck china shops and thunder down Wall Street — to lock horns with the Angus, Longhorns and Brahmins that provide bullshit, bulldust and bullshit artists. And now bullshit is the subject of a serious philosophical enquiry in a little publication called *On Bullshit* published by the highly respected Princeton University Press.

Surprisingly the words of wisdom on this improbable subject come from a 76-year-old moral philosopher. Professor Emeritus in Philosophy at Princeton, has been studying bullshit for over twenty years and has come to the conclusion that bullshitting is at least as bad and probably worse than lying.

Talking the other night he made the point that a liar has some respect for the truth. Otherwise he wouldn't feel the need to lie about it. Whereas a bullshit artist doesn't care about the truth. What he cares about is what you think about him.

To demonstrate, Harry G Frankfurt cites the example of a humbugging politician giving a Fourth of July address. (You may like to transpose what follows to Australia Day or Anzac Day.) He drones on about "our great and blessed country," and how the Founding Fathers enjoyed God's guidance in providing the world with "a new beginning for mankind". But he doesn't really care what the audience feels about founding fatherhood or God or manifest destiny.

First and foremost, first and last, he wants to make the right impression, to be seen as a patriot. Frankfurt agreed that echoes of such humbuggery could be found in almost every speech given by an incumbent or would-be president. It's only when the humbugger starts making claims for, for example, WMDs, that we move from bullshit into lying.

But bullshit is bad enough. The bullshitter does not reject the authority of the truth, as the liar does. "He pays no attention to it at all," says Frankfurt. "By virtue of this, bullshit is a greater enemy of the truth than lies are."

"It is impossible for someone to lie unless he thinks he knows the truth," says the Professor. Thus the liar and the honest man are linked by a common if not identical regard for it — for both the truth is a real concern. But not for the bullshitter.

Yet while the liar is disapproved of, even despised, the bullshitter is effectively forgiven. He gets away with it. And profits from it. The professor agrees that that's because the bullshitted are often complicit. Though people insist they can pick it a mile off, they hunger for it. The audience for a political stunt speech know it's bullshit but clap all the louder; the audience for some ranting buffoon of a televangelist send him donations and. women viewing nonsensical cosmetic commercials run straight from the telly to the Chemists. While bullshit is hardly a new ingredient in personal and social lives, it seems to be growing in magnitude and stench with our communication technologies, and the public can't get enough.

We probably take it lightly because we know the bull-shitter knows he's talking bullshit and he probably knows we think it's bullshit. So what's the harm?

Trouble is, says Frankfurt, that it gets harder and harder to "know how things truly are". Matters of substance become impoverished and tawdry. At least lying has its standards.

So Frankfurt believes that the bullshit artist can be, already is, a threat to democracy.

We talked of pre-war speeches by Bush and Blair, how bullshit crossed the line into lies, but was bad enough without them. Frankfurt factors in contemporary views — post-modernism comes to mind — where truth and falsity dissolve, where nothing can be claimed as a certainty. Is this an environment which encourages, or at least tolerates bullshit?

What was it that Marx said about everything solid melting into air?

On one level, the book is great entertainment. But that doesn't entirely explain the way it's selling. Readers, it seems, share the good professor's anxieties about the problem. Writing without jargon, Frankfurt has a reputation for trying to get 'to the bottom of things' and has struck a chord by examining something that we've taken for granted, something short of a sin and outside the commandments, that nonetheless undermines our public lives. "Even the most basic questions about bullshit," he says, "are not only unanswered but unasked."

He's right. And bullshit is getting thicker and thicker in our public and political lives. Before we get bogged in it, let's fight fire with fire. There's only one antidote.

Whenever and wherever you hear it, call out:

"BULLSHIT!"

Sub-conscience

May 29, 2005

IN THIS LAND of the blind Judi Moylan is queen. She's one of the handful of Liberal dissidents belatedly demanding her party's policy of mandatory detention be modified. No, not abandoned but made less of an ethical cesspit. After campaigning quietly backstage and getting nowhere, she went public, receiving 2,000 supportive emails in a single day.

Moylan was astonished. I wasn't. When Phil Ruddock threatened any Australian harbouring an escapee from Woomera or Villawood with a ten-year jail term (more than you're likely to get for murder) I invited readers willing to take that risk to join a campaign of civil disobedience. Thousands volunteered, to be joined by thousands more at the time of Tampa. Finally 10,000 people, a significant percentage of the newspaper's readership, helped me form 'Australians for Just Refugee Policies', providing almost $1,000,000 to fund it. In my fifty years of journalism I'd never seen anything like it.

"I am ashamed to be an Australian." Those words appeared in every other letter as readers expressed as much distaste for the compliant Beasley as they did for Howard.

The great refugee hoax was and remains one of the boldest political stunts since Joe McCarthy waved his laundry list at a press conference, claiming it held the names of '200 communists in the State Department'. With voters already convinced there were Marxists beneath every mattress, McCarthy's fraud triggered one of the US's darkest times. Exploiting a similar climate of fear, Howard's imaginary invasion of asylum seekers tipped Australia, with its lingering White Australian phobias, into a comparably shameful era. Whilst, as Howard now admits, tipping him into power.

(Let the record show that over recent decades we've averaged less than 1,000 boat people per annum, scarcely a drop in the refugee bucket. Yet so successful was the Howard scam that the Lib's Lynton Crosby exported it to the UK to help the namesake leader of the Tories. But the Brits, to their considerable credit, refused to be stampeded, and Michael Howard is on his way out.)

Again Beasley has backed Howard on this most divisive of issues, refusing to endorse the suggestion of a conscience vote on the private members' bills that Petro Georgiou and Moylan propose. Why are we not surprised? Kim's conscience is as guilty as the PM's.

Despite moral horrors from the Tampa to the SIEV X, few on either side of the house dared rock the boat. So refugees from Saddam Hussein, the Taliban and Iran's mullahs, whose right to seek asylum is guaranteed under international agreements to which Australia is a signatory, were demonised as criminals and, after September 11, branded as likely terrorists. We put them in concentration camps (don't splutter with outrage at the term before you've checked the accepted definitions) and threw away the keys. Even for the kids.

Dramatising the bigotry that the Howard-Ruddock-Reith campaign manipulated, it took a scandal involving a blonde Australian woman to shock white Australia into looking again at this pornographic policy. Thanks for that,

Cornelia Rau. Now more of the brutalities perpetrated on Ruddock's watch are being revealed. (Not for the first time in her career, Amandatory Detention Vanstone is cleaning up someone else's mess.) But note: the focus remains on wronged Australians.

Not on wronged refugees. Bugger them.

Meanwhile the perpetrators of the refugee hoax have been generously rewarded. As you may have noted, Howard is still Prime Minister, Peter 'kids overboard' Reith has his cushy job in London and Ruddock was promoted to Attorney General with deafening rumours he's heading for the High Court! And Beasley? Having whimped out on the greatest moral challenge of his career, he's regained the job he finds most congenial, as the Opposition Leader who rarely opposes anything while specialising in gracious concession speeches.

Howard's smartest move, from Tampa on, was not so much to demonise as to 'anonymise' the refugees. To make sure the media couldn't get close enough to see the faces, learn the stories. While Ethey were no more than dots on the Tampa's deck the asylum-seekers remained ciphers. They could be slandered at will. But now, as we get closer and can recognise them as human beings, the politics get tricky.

Not just Beasley was complicit in this filthy policy; Latham's gut instinct was to criticise Ruddock for being too soft. Thus the ALP is as mired in the mess as the Coalition. So it's past time for Labor to listen to the 10,000 readers of this column who, having rallied to the asylum-seekers' cause, are still waiting for a hint of moral leadership.

At very least Labor MPs must demand a conscience vote in Caucus, lest the prime function of Her Majesty's Opposition passes to braver souls on the other side of the despatch box ...

Kennedy

June 4, 2005

WEEKS AFTER the event, I've finally watched a tape of the Kennedy funeral. Every bit as under-rehearsed and amateurish as the 1950s television the service recalled and celebrated; it was simultaneously naff and charming. Yes, Graham deserved a state funeral, and many would have expected or preferred something glitzy and glossy, but that thrown-together effort, in a small country theatre, with things going wrong, was a perfect fit. Noelene Brown, Tony Sattler, Mike McColl-Jones and the rest did him proud.

When I first met Graham we were just kids. I was a 15-year-old office boy and he, 19, was already well on his way to stardom. After delivering copy to his Melbourne radio station I'd stand outside the studio to watch the pioneering double-act. The front-end of 3UZ's panto horse was a gentle-voiced gent called Nicky with the skinny kid bringing up the rear, doing the high kicks.

And boy, was Graham skinny. Later in life, he'd thicken up — but then he was awkward, shock-pale and gaunt. Add those startled eyes and he recalled a freshly shorn sheep. Clearly comedy wasn't so much a calculated career choice as something imposed by physical reality. As with the diminutive Dudley Moore or the hyperthyroid Marty Feldman, it was a survival technique, a way of coping with playground ridicule. And for the rest of his life Graham would use humour as both weapon and shield.

Long before television you could see the mixture of anxiety and brilliance in Graham's performance. He made it seem and sound so easy but he'd finish the programme drained, exhausted. And right from the outset, he had the same ambivalent attitude to the public affection he earned in abundance.

Years later, when I was broadcasting on 3AW, we got him out of early retirement for a rare interview. The switchboard lit up with people calling in to tell him how wonderful it was to hear his voice again. Graham would turn off his microphone and scream abuse at them! And if a caller expressed affection he'd writhe in pain.

Memories, memories. Stuart Wagstaff MCed the funeral, and I suddenly remembered hearing him, the toffee-voiced actor on a local version of Desert Island Discs. Stuart did everything he could to prevent the programme becoming a psychiatrists' couch but, finally, the interviewer nailed him. And it turned out that the Benson & Hedges man had been brought up on a dirt-poor farm in England and brutalised by his father. Later I'd remind Stewart of his answer to the question "does that make it hard for you to love?" "No," he said, "but it makes it almost impossible to be loved."

Any abused child — I was one — understands that feeling. Certainly the funny man in the coffin knew it well. As John Mangos said at the service, it's a tragedy that someone so loved couldn't have loved himself at least a little.

During the long run of *IMT* I'd often watch Kennedy rehearsing, and see the difficulties endured by those around him, principally Bert Newton, who'd often bear the brunt. That on-air brilliance came at a great price to Kennedy, and to others. And afterwards? After a night of transcendental ad-libs, risk and riffs Kennedy would, as I've written before, just fold himself up like a ventriloquist's doll, put himself in a case, close the lid and go home. Usually a lonely one.

You could see his ambiguous attitude to fame in the house itself. On one visit to the cliff-top eyrie, with Graham characteristically quiet, he opened a door to show me the entire wall of a room covered in a huge 24-sheet poster — proclaiming him "The King". Yes, but he would abdicate every night.

At the time of *Don's Party*, with Australian film stars few and far between, I got the appalling idea of casting big names from television. For example, I wanted Mike Willessee to play the cuckold dentist, and negotiated with Paul Hogan to star as an ocker sexual predator. (Paul finally refused on the grounds that 'Hoges' [and he always spoke of himself in the third person] couldn't possibly behave in such a vulgar fashion.) Only Graham, as the voyeur-pornographer, Mac, survived this casting process, though Bruce Beresford, David Williamson and most of the cast were either iffy or sniffy about it. Graham was iffy too — didn't think he could do it — but I knew that no one could fill a screen like that human Muppet. Naturally, he finished up stealing the picture. I loved giving Graham the overseas reviews, from New York to Tel Aviv, almost invariably singling him. Graham rejoiced in the fact that the kudos came from critics who'd never heard of him, but in the same breath despaired of finding another part for 'an ugly little bugger with bulgy eyes'.

Well, Graham, Australia found a very big part for you. You. And only you could play it.

The death of George

June 16, 2005

GEORGE IS DEAD.

For months readers have been asking 'how's George getting on?' And he was getting on fine. No longer cowering when you reached out to pat him, he was even conducting tentative experiments in tail wagging. For the first time in his miserable life he was having fun.

And that's what killed him.

Over the years so many dogs have come and gone, but George's death is the most wrenching. It's not that we haven't lost dogs under equally dramatic circumstances. Annie, the Jack Russell, came off second best in a fight with a snake, dying beside me as I drove like crazy to the vets. Timmy, a kelpie, got run over by a neighbour. Willie, another Jack Russell, kept running under anything with wheels — trucks, tractors, ATVs — until he ran out of luck. But whether dying of misadventure or old age, like dear old Rosie, they'd had happy lives.

But not George. I won't tell the story again. Suffice to say that he arrived in our lives, snarling, terrified, feral. A refugee escaping abuse and seeking asylum. Ignoring advice as to the hopelessness of the task, I spent hours, days, and months trying to teach a dysfunctional dog to trust. If no one else, at least me.

And it worked. Wherever I walked, he'd trot at my heels. When I went riding around the farm, he'd run behind. Twenty, thirty kilometres, it didn't matter. The only time he'd leave me was if Timmy, his new best friend, would take him chasing kangaroos. Barking ecstatically they'd be gone until dark.

Last week we'd yarded two hundred head, cows with calves, for weaning. It's always a sad day on the farm, with the mums loudly protesting the separation. We'd also rounded up thirteen bulls. Time to separate them as well. It was a bedlam of bellowing, all dust and drama. The trick was to put some distance between them. Cows from calves. Bulls from cows and heifers.

For the last five years we haven't had much feed or water. Though we've plenty of paddocks, many will be useless until the drought breaks. If it ever does. So with limited options, we pushed the bulls across the sad little creek that used to be our river and watched them pushing and shoving as they lumbered over to a trough. Trouble is, they kept shoving and managed to wreck it. Water gushed from a broken pipe — and our biggest water tank began to rapidly empty. Disaster.

The bulls' paddock was only a few hundred yards from the homestead. So, because of the drought, there were a few dozen kangaroos, munching away in the olive grove. And while I was trying to save the water supply, the dogs started chasing the roos. Just for fun. They've never caught them, any more than Timmy catches the dragonflies he likes to hunt. But for the first time ever, the dogs managed to trap a whopper between the last remaining stretch of water — always known as 'the billabong' — and a twenty-metre cliff. I could see the big roo sitting back on its tail, towering over the dogs as they lay panting in front of him. With all three motionless it looked like a religious tableau, as if the dogs were worshipping a superior being. I yelled at them to leave the roo alone — but was too deep in mud to pay more attention.

As well as watering the bulls, the tank also supplied troughs for the calves and cows kilometres away. By the time I'd fixed the pipe, I was choc-coated in mud. And so was Timmy, who'd come bounding back ages ago. But where was George? In that instant I knew the roo had killed him. I searched and called for an hour but he wasn't coming home. I looked in and around the billabong for a drowned dog then walked the gullies to find his body. I've known a male roo to kill another with a couple of mighty kicks, the loser hopping away to die from internal bleeding. So killing a dog's easy. And I've heard many stories from neighbours who've lost a favourite dog to a kanga. Either kicked to death or drowned in a dam.

There's still no sign of George's body. Probably eaten by feral pigs. Poor little bloke. For the first time in his life he was having fun. Can't tell you how sad it is without him. But at least his death had an epic quality. Killed by the national symbol.

And his ghost may be heard as you pass by the billabong.

Those bloody abos

June 19, 2005

THOSE BLOODY ABOS! Cost us a bloody fortune. Spend millions on the buggers. Straight down the gurgler.

Yes, a lot of taxpayers' money is allocated to indigenous communities, much of it absorbed in whitefella bureaucracy and some of it wasted in corrupt or incompetent blackfella businesses. Nothing like as much as whitefellas waste on shopping, for example, buying everything from junk culture to obscenely overpriced luxury goods: cosmetics, cars, the entire cornucopia of crap. Or as much as shareholders allow to be squandered on the salary packages or payouts of those international nomads, the modern CEOs. But, yes, too much.

If, however, the indigenous population 'cost' white Australia ten times as much, it would still be the biggest bargain in history. Ours, not theirs. Put it down as twenty billion, give or take. That's just pocketknives, mirrors and beads for what we've got in return. Just about the biggest and best country on earth. It's chicken feed. A steal. All we've really paid for, in terms of market price — quids per acre — is an area the size of Tassie. We got the mainland thrown in for nothing.

Before Mabo, before a grudging return of a few bits and pieces, allowing the Abos little more than visiting rights, we'd mustered them like cattle and dumped them far from home, in the most useless land we could find. Later we'd realised that these bleak vistas hid goodies like iron ore, uranium, even diamonds, so we mustered and moved them on again.

Talking about herding indigenous communities like cattle recalls the time when the pastoral industry was totally dependent on Abos herding cattle. At slave labour rates. In the late 19th century in Western Australia, when cattle properties were being marketed, the bills of sales would list, along with the size of the holding and the miles of fences, how many 'niggers' were included with the stock.

Then we started kidnapping their kids, to use as domestics in white homes.

For centuries, the indigenous population has paid dearly for our generosity and taxpayer. In desperate poverty, illness and abbreviated life spans. But most of all in the destruction of the world's most ancient culture — which we belatedly celebrate by hanging Abo art on museum and corporate walls.

Pity about everything else. The reason Abos cost us a lot of money — in belated attempts to deal with third-world life expectancy, drunkenness, petrol sniffing, domestic violence, vandalism and sundry minor crime — is because we smashed 100,000 years of tradition — of learning and language — into smithereens. We treated an entire race with a mixture of contempt, cruelty and catastrophic paternalism.

The other day I met a great young bloke trying to do something to help. Victor Steffensen is working with Kuku Thaypan elders in Cape York — Tommy George Sr (79) and George Musgrave (85) who are living archives of tens of thousands of years of traditional knowledge. Though Victor's from an entirely different community he's helping them preserve — on video — what they're desperate to pass on. Trouble is, the kids in their community are either alcoholic or absent or dead.

Their country covers mangroves, estuaries, grasslands, woodlands, floodplains and sandstone escarpments — a vast area full of sites associated with occupation, ceremonies, spirits. Prior to European settlement local clans spoke at least eleven different languages, now mostly lost. Tommy and George, who were saved from being stolen by being hidden in a couple of mailbags, are the last fluent speakers of their clan language, and Victor is recording it, putting it on a data base; along with the videoed secrets the old men are showing him, and the sacred places they're visiting together.

Already the old men have taught environmental scientists traditional and therapeutic fire management. It's now being used in the Lakefield National Park for the first time in many decades, with official agencies looking on. And Victor is convinced that this is just the beginning of what the elders can teach us all.

Best of all, he believes the mere act of being interested in what these old fellas have to say is having restorative effects on the community, giving people a renewed sense of dignity. Clearly, we need more Victors talking to more Tommies, more Georges. While there's still time. It's the best way to preserve the past while, at the same time, serving, and rehabilitating living communities. Which means it's another way for whitefellas to get more than their money's worth.

Trouble is Victor doesn't have any. This truly exceptional human being is doing the whole project on a non-existent budget — equivalent to what a CEO would blow on lunch in a three-star restaurant.

Everything Victor's learning is being preserved and cross-referenced on a database that's already a treasure house. The data is remarkable in its breadth, depth and detail, the project a model for wider and urgent application.

Joke for
humour edition

June 29, 2005

WHAT IS THE evolutionary purpose of humour? Seems to me that it's to compensate humans for the mixed blessings of consciousness, in particular a unique sense of mortality. Faced with oblivion, humour keeps some of us, some of the time, from going mad. When pondering its function, Darwin focused on the smile, that "contraction of the great zygomatic muscles and the raising of the upper lip", leading to the upper front teeth being commonly exposed and to the formation of the well-marked naso-labial. Less concerned with superficial appearances, Freud dug deeper, seeking the relationship between the joke and the unconscious. "Anyone who has at any time had occasion to enquire from the literature of aesthetics and psychology what light can be thrown on the nature of jokes," he complained, "will have to admit that jokes have not received nearly as much consideration as they deserve."

My partner and I have been forced to think seriously about humour. Over the past dozen years we've collected thousands of jokes for a dozen Penguin collections and, as you can imagine, it's been a thoroughly depressing experience. Jokes come brimming up from Freud's unconscious seething with ethnic and religious bigotries, with every sort of warped sexuality and, most of all, with an unhealthy obsession with lawyers. Yes, it's been dark and lonely work, but somebody had to do it.

However, we've made some significant discoveries. Firstly, and in this I'm perfectly serious, we now know what causes the primal smile and the first laugh. It is purely and simply a shock response. To demonstrate, grab a very young baby and toss it into the air. This is something that proud daddies do to the tiniest kids. On the way up, the child is understandably alarmed, its concerns intensify as it accelerates downwards. When the parent catches it — and the child is caught in the majority of cases — the little creature lets out a gasp of relief. The zygomatic contractions of the grimace somewhat relax and, lo and behold, you've achieved the grin. Whilst the gasp becomes the laugh.

For the rest of the child's life he'll continue to grimace in terror and smile in relief, whilst laughter will remain his response to mild shock. Take the shock any further and it will become a scream.

Hence the importance of black humour. You see it most clearly amongst people under pressure — millennia of persecution have produced the deep, rich ironies of Jewish humour, and you see the same thing in gallows humour and amongst those who deal with death on a daily basis. Ambulance drivers, surgical teams, ALP pollsters.

If the prime purpose of humour is to help us deal with the dread of death, jokes are, quite clearly, little acts of exorcism aimed at dealing with the other things we fear or hate. Like mothers-in-law, lawyers, politicians, and, for musicians, viola players. (Over the years we've collected even more anti-viola jokes than we have savage indictments of the legal profession.) Sexuality of course rears its ugly head in the form of penis jokes which narrowly outnumber bum jokes. Variations on sexual dysfunction and, latterly, Viagra, outnumber jokes about defecation and doctors. And all carry the heavy baggage of distaste, fear and resentment.

Show me a joke and I'll show you an assault, conscious or subconscious, on something that causes you anxiety. The more shocking the example, the louder the laugh. Within nanoseconds of the first Challenger disaster, NASA was heard to say: "Need another seven astronauts." When the Boeings hit the World Trade Center we were receiving the first appalling jokes within ten seconds. Then came Bin Laden jokes, Saddam Hussein jokes and George Bush jokes. Judging by the number devoted to Dubya, he's less popular than Saddam or Bin Laden.

In Australia we had Lindy Chamberlain jokes by the tonne. A few weeks ago, there were scores about Schapelle Corby. Of course, many of these jokes are mere updates. I told Paul Keating, when he was Prime Minister, that most of the best/worst jokes about him had started their career as anti-Hitler jokes. We'd tracked them down to a couple of comedians in Munich who'd ended their days in Dachau. And that's no joke.

What people do is update the political insult, reattributing it to Keating or Thatcher or Reagan. Or Alexander Downer.

And jokes are frequently relocated, in geographic terms. When he was Prime Minister, Bob Hawke told me a beauty. "There are two corpses on the Hume Highway. One's a dead kangaroo and the other's a dead politician. What's the difference?" When I confessed I didn't know, Bob said, "There are skid marks before the kangaroo."

We then discovered this was a universal joke that, in its American version, involved Route 66 and a dead skunk.

Patrice and I have retired from the joke business. We've suffered enough. For finally there's nothing more serious than a joke. And you get to the point where every smile looks like a rictus. We've got to the point where, whenever we hear a scream of laughter, we scream.

My favourite joke? One that seems unequivocally and uniquely Australian. Two farmers' labourers have completed a fencing job and received their cheques. They consider their immediate future:

"What are you gonna do?"

"I'm gonna go down to Sinny."

"Yeah, I hear Sinny's a pretty good place. Which route are you taking?"

"Aah, I thought I'd take the missus. She stuck with me through the drought."

Growing pains

July 1, 2005

IT IS THE BEST of times, the worst of times. It usually is. And this is particularly true for our kids. On the positive side of the ledger, they look forward to life-spans that, having doubled in the last century, promise to stretch beyond the horizon as the biological sciences pull so many rabbits from hats that we've got a plague. Of medical rabbits and scientific hats. So much so that if it wasn't for a few small problems like global warming, global dimming and global terrorism, the globe would be aglow with optimism.

But with the evolutionary apocalypse upon us, not to mention a few score wars with more in the offing, you'd have to be wildly optimistic not to be a pessimist. Fortunately our children have a smorgasbord of narcotics to intensify their pleasures and dull their pains, whereas the only drugs at our place were Grandma's laxatives and a stale packet of Aspros. Of course, if you were totally delinquent you could try a ciggie behind the shelter shed or a furtive sip of the family's flagon of special occasion sweet sherry.

Today kids enjoy a legal autonomy and a freedom from adult control that permits them to enjoy and/or wreck their lives without much interference. Or parental interest. In my era such freedoms from constraint would have made Utopia seem derelict. Moreover, they know all sorts of things that we couldn't have imagined. To my mates, apart from the ones with big sisters, girls were — as Dylan Thomas put it — 'blurs below the waist'. The only nude women we'd ever seen were members of African tribes coyly depicted in *National Geographic*, which we only read for the articles. Now even the pre-pubescent are on intimate terms with every nook, cranny, position and deviation, thanks to that wonderful educational tool, the Internet. The low down via download.

Then there's the corporate paedophiles who mass-market the pornographies found in movies, on television or, interactively, in video games. Truly, the cup of today's child runneth over, with muck reminiscent of the broken sewer. So much so that childhood has all but disappeared, and kids force-fed on the mix'n match pornographies of sex and violence become kidults at ever-earlier ages. Some miraculously survive the War Against Childhood, like the kids hauled from the rubble of a tsunami or earthquake days after all hope is lost. But few escape unscathed.

Lucky little buggers. We had to put up with Perry Como, Johnny Ray and the banalities of hit parade pop. Instead of doggies in the window, they've got rock, rap, hip-hop and crap — more idioms than we had hot breakfasts. Not that they get hot breakfasts, unless they go to that plastic place, Macs. In our day a plastic Mac meant a rainproof coat, not an entire politico-cultural package, which also provides about 25% of Australia's teenage employment. Come to think of it we didn't get hot brekkies either. But we did have a choice of truly indigenous forms of nutrition. The Rice Bubble or the Cornflake.

And this reminds us that it is no longer necessary or desirable or even possible to have an Australian cultural identity. At Eltham High we had a vocabulary full of words like drongo and wacker, whereas today's kids speak fluent US ghetto, the lingos of Los Angeles and Silicon Valley. US movies get 95% of Australia's cinema box-office — a situation echoed in pay-TV, DVD sales and video rentals. Yet we can feel really, really proud, because most of the American characters are now played by Australians, whereas when I was a kid, you had Australians played by Americans. Like Robert Mitchum in *The Sundowners*. Believe it or not, that made us feel proud too.

Today's kids enjoy high-tech toys with IQs higher than their parents. Giant companies produce and retail cornucopias of kiddie clobber, whereas we had hand-me-downs. Entire industries are predicated on the induced desires of mini-consumers, previously known as children. And knowing things of which we were totally or mercifully ignorant, our kids have an unprecedented familiarity with death.

This is a consequence of violent entertainments and increasingly candid news coverage. We were protected by a mighty armada of censorships that have long since been scuppered. Trouble is, five-year-olds see the scattered body parts from a suicide bombing on the telly news whilst having their dinner.

Every kid, given half a chance, wants to be kid. At least some of the time. My thirteen-year-old, very mature, well read, widely travelled and politically progressive, regards her Dad with the familiar teenage mixture of amused tolerance and mild embarrassment. Yet in a flash she'll revert to the little girl who loved to giggle, clown, be scared by ghost stories, climb trees. There's still an innocence and, equally precious, a sense of wonderment. We should fight to protect them. The kids, the innocence, the wonderment.

London Bridge

July 10, 2005

IT'S A QUIET, ho-hum, run-of-the-mill day in Iraq. Just a few bombs will explode in Baghdad. Only a few dozen will be killed or maimed. Fifty or sixty max. With the victims predominantly locals — only a couple of US soldiers amongst the casualties — they'll hardly rate a mention. Won't crack it for the Nine Network or ABC news. Perhaps a brief para in tomorrow's broadsheets.

Oh, almost forgot. There'll be about twenty kidnappings today. This has been a major racket in Iraq for a year or more, with thousands of locals snatched off the streets. Nothing political about it, nothing religious. Just a grab bag of business people and school children to be held for ransom. So many kids are kidnapped these days that parents are keeping them home.

Will these incidents be reported in the US, UK and Australia? No, they won't. Not news. Just further symptoms of a totally dysfunctional society. Unless, of course, if one of the kidnapped is one of us. Then all media hell will break loose.

Yes, what happened in London was appalling. But it happens every day in Iraq. Has ever since the Coalition of the Willing, of which Australia was such a willing member, came thundering in. Things were crook before but have been far worse since. Pinned down by sanctions, inspections and fly-overs, still licking his wounds from Gulf War 1, Saddam's greatest crimes were long behind him. The mass graves were history. But since the Coalition? Cemeteries are booming again.

Mind you, you don't read much about the local death toll. The body count for Iraqi troops, let alone Iraqi citizens, is censored. Washington only allows us to know — and then reluctantly — that around 2,000 Americans have died.

Unlike those humdrum bombings in Baghdad, the slaughter in London was very big news. And let's be clear about it: the people who died in the subway tunnels and on the bus were victims of the Iraq war. They died because of Blair's London Bridge, the one he built from the Thames to the Euphrates. Had he not misled his nation — and all senses of the word misled apply — into that murderous folly of an invasion, the people would have walked off the trains instead of being carried off on stretchers. Or had their body parts collected in bags.

Blair's response? The same rhetoric, the same mock-heroics, a renewed commitment to the political and strategic idiocy of George Bush. You can hear his spin-doctors thinking: "If we play this right, we'll improve in the polls." And you can hear the same thoughts from Howard's people, who will rely on the new political correctness of conservatism — that it's uncouth to link terrorist attacks in London, Madrid or possibly Sydney — with the chaos unleashed in Iraq.

As many in Britain are pointing out, they didn't need some Islamist loonies to focus attention on Blair's sorry role in the Iraq fiasco, that a clear majority have long deplored his duplicities, his misleadership. His bridge too far. But Number 10 still says the same things, day in, year out, as if hoping through Pavlovian repetition to wear the public down.

Ditto down under, as our Prime and Foreign Ministers try to blur the linkages with Iraq. They stress that Islamists are attacking our values, our way of life, our love of freedom in these murderous stunts. And everyone, most of all Howard and Downer, knows this is twaddle. The selection of targets is largely based on involvement in and enthusiasm for Bush's new world order. The PM tells the truth when he says he cannot promise that our cities are safe from terrorism. He tells the truth when he confirms that an attack on Australia within Australia is not only possible but probable. But he lies when he denies it's his policies that have made our lives more dangerous.

The great divide between those who supported the invasion of Iraq is as wide as ever. We seem to live in different universes, with both sides using the London bombings to support their positions. The Coalition forces in politics and the media look at the mayhem and say 'told you so'. The critics of the war, and the way it was conflated with the War on Terror say 'told you so' too. They say the latest brutalities prove their case, that the Iraq war had to be fought to light the flame of democracy in the Middle East, and that our efforts must be renewed. We say that what's happening in Baghdad and now London was inevitable, that the invasion has not liberated democratic forces but detonated more hatred, much of it directed against US hegemony and hubris. And against those countries, like Britain and Australia, who rushed to Washington's colours.

But Howard can't see it. He can't afford to.

Spielberg

July 23, 2005

SPIELBERG'S FIRST effort, and still his best, was that film-of-few-words, *Duel*. One of the simplest features in cinema history, it's Little Red Riding Hood on wheels. A harmless bloke in a little red car encounters the Big Bad Wolf in the form of a monstrous black tanker with an unseen driver. Brute force sets out to destroy Mr Harmless. The tanker first running him off the lonely road, then into the path of an oncoming train, next by ramming the booth when he tries to phone for help. This lowest of low budget efforts is close to the perfect film, almost a silent movie. It tells its story in simple, elemental images without need of dialogue or digital effects. The only sound on the track that really matters? When the truck, tricked into driving off a cliff, emits a great groan of defeat, like the moan of a dying dinosaur. A sound we hear again, decades later, in Spielberg's *Jurassic Park*, based on the same central proposition. Vulnerable humanity versus an implacable enemy, with another incarnation of monstrousness that can neither be reasoned with nor placated.

It's no criticism to say that Spielberg has effectively made the same film over and over again. In *Jaws*, the unsuspecting swimmer is doomed by a giant shark. It's the tanker with a dorsal fin. You can't negotiate with it. It has no conscience, just wants you dead.

Even the sentimental *Sugarland Express* has its echoes of *Duel*. Poor Goldie Hawn, not pursued across the country by a single truck but by an endless convoy of police cars with their flashing lights. And in *ET*, which has an extra-terrestrial in the garden shed substituting for Jesus at Calvary, the young disciples have to deal with the might of the American State, substituting for those grim ancient Romans. In *Close Encounters*, similarly theological in its subtext, a prophet without honour has to contend with the ruthlessness of both Washington and the Pentagon. For a variation of all *Close Encounter* themes, and many of the images, see his current TV series *Taken*.

The *Duel* duality reaches its peak in *Schindler's List*, where little Red Riding Hood (and Spielberg gives a single character, a young girl, a red costume in an otherwise monochromatic film) confronts the biggest, baddest wolf in history, the implacable, unreasoning force of Nazism. Here humanity, at its most vulnerable, falls victim to the tanker, the shark, Tyrannosaurus Rex and every other incarnation of monstrousness rolled up in one.

There's an argument, proposed by at least one intelligent US critic, that *War of the Worlds* (WOTW) is a remake of Schindler's List, in that it makes the entire cinema audience feel like Jews in 1930s Germany, that Spielberg gives us all a hint of the horrors of the refugee experience. The Nazis have morphed into the intergalactic invaders and no matter where you run, there is no escape. That's a stretch, but *WOTW* is certainly a Dolby'd, digital *Duel* and those thinking about the story, rather than just having fun at another horror film, might detect a few useful messages. Like the unimportance of human disagreements in the face of an eternal, infinite and unfriendly cosmos.

WOTW is Spielberg's third crack at alien invasion, with *Taken* the fourth. In *ET* and *Close Encounters* the visitors come bearing gifts of both science and spirit. Only in the H G Wells' epic are they unequivocally awful, wearing ginormous jackboots. And it's said that the attentive audience member may even pick up a hint of criticism of President Bush.

So let's give Spielberg the benefit of the doubt and see this film as akin to *Schindler's*, effort to make us aware of humanity's vulnerability to tyranny, be it in the form of space invaders or fascism. Of course, young Stephen insists on happy endings — humanity usually wins out. (Let us hope that's true with the Bush administration. When it ends I'll be happy.)

Half the reason for Spielberg's success lies in the demographics of his dramas. Not for him the Transylvanian castle. His horrors haunt ordinary people living in new subdivisions with schools and shopping malls. His films star the very people who see them at the local multiplex. Capra, another great US storyteller, sets his films in small town America, others in LA or New York. Spielberg is the first suburban storyteller on the big screen — learning the trick from the television sitcoms that moulded his sensibility.

(And we must never forget that it was ordinary people in ordinary houses who unleashed Hitler.)

Let *War of the Worlds* be a useful parable, an all-purpose warning against anything you don't fancy. Use the aliens as metaphors for political terrorism or GM food, whatever turns you off. For John Stone the aliens could be Muslim immigrants or the very thought of multi-culturalism.

Personally, I found myself worrying about sharks, dirty tankers, Tyrannosaurus Rex and fascist tyrannies. Oh, and George Bush.

The deer

August 1, 2005

WE HAD A RAM that wasn't and wouldn't. Not one of your ramrod, rampant rams he showed not the slightest interest in, if you'll forgive the expression, ramming. At the first sign of a ewe, this one-word oxymoron would do a U-ie and head in the opposite direction. Despite the sort of pedigree that promised insatiable lust and lots of lambs, he was more metaphysical than physical in his inclination, recalling Ronald 'St Trinian's' Searle's immortal schoolboy, Nigel Molesworth Jr. Nigel did not serve his school well when playing cricket. Instead of chasing the ball, Nigel would recline and make daisy chains whilst being heard to murmur 'hello clouds, hello sky'.

Ram n. 1. Uncastrated male sheep. 2. the zodiacal sign. 3. battering ram. 4. pile driving machine.

I rest my case. That's what being a ram is all about. Ramming involves hammering away, as in 'ramming home the argument' or 'squeezing or forcing into place under pressure'. As Oxford's famous lexicographers insist, to ram is to 'dash or violently impel'. It's not about saying hello to the sky but about rampaging and rambunctiousness. Why do you think Sylvester Stallone chose the name Rambo for those silly, ultra-violent films?

But our ram was more Rimbaud than Rambo. The rambling, poetic type. Rather than the requisite gleam in the eye, he had a dreamy expression, switching to alarm in the presence or at the approach of females.

And that was only the beginning. As time passed he not only neglected his duties, forcing us to call in reinforcements, but he gave up even being a sheep. He became a cow.

There was no cross-dressing, and he never learned to moo. But he abandoned the flock for the herd. He started hanging out with the cattle. I'd chase him back to the sheep, but he'd jump the grid or wriggle through a kanga hole in the fence and once more, insist on that company of the genus Bos of ruminants. He was so bovine that we called him Bovril.

Bovril has long since gone to God. He's up amongst the fleecy clouds where the Lord is his shepherd. Now we've an even odder transgenic oddity. Another creature in denial.

We were out the back of Elmswood, as far from the homestead as you can get, checking on a few hundred weaners. Making sure they had enough feed and water, by no means certain in this endless drought. Nearing the Hut , a remote and derelict slab-building, once used by overnighting stockmen, and now providing shelter for feral pigs, we came across about half the herd, all looking relaxed and happy. So it seemed safe to leave them there for a few months, mustering them come January.

Whereupon I noticed something. Something very strange. In the middle of the calves, standing head and shoulders over them, was an animal that wasn't a calf. I did a double-take, a treble-take. What I was seeing didn't compute. So I asked for second and third opinions. And we all came to the same conclusion. Running with the weaners was ... a deer. A dear little deer. A young buck with knobs on its head that would, in due course, produce antlers.

I walked quietly towards the herd. The deer was right in the middle trying to remain invisible. When the calves moved off, it moved off with them. When they stopped, it stopped. Clearly it thinks it's a calf.

I've been back a few times and it's still with the cattle, getting on famously. It butts them, they butt it, but entirely in friendship. We can't account for its presence on the place. Only seen one wild deer in twenty years. Must have been mislaid by Santa.

Paw Note. Thanks to an insane and sadistic stepfather my childhood was a nightmare. Having driven his own daughter to suicide, he turned his attentions to me — and my only consolation was a bitzer dog. My stepfather's most ingenious cruelty? He forced me, an 8-year-old, to drown her puppies. I told of the trauma in the first animal story I ever wrote, and it's reprinted in *Adams' Ark* along with happier memories of assorted dogs, kangaroos and other animals. Now I've received an anonymous letter from a reader who, oblivious to a kid's misery, attacks me as "a puppy drowner, a dreadful human being". With entire websites devoted to attacking me I get used to abuse — but this was hard to take.

Fortunately there've been many great letters from readers telling me their dog stories, including $30 cheques for the book. (We want to send some money to the seeing-eye dog people in memory of poor little George, my refugee kelpie killed by a kanga.)

Rights Australia

August 3, 2005

BACK IN THE early '90s, the Government asked me to Chair the National Australia Day Council, about the smallest commonwealth agency, but one with a big brief — to encourage Australians to explore and celebrate our national identity. At the time, Australia Day was a big daggy — lots of re-enactments of Arthur Phillip setting foot on shore. To blackfellas, it was offensive, at best a day to celebrate survival. To most, it was just the last weekend before the end of the summer holidays.

We decided to make the day about the present and the future rather than the past. We talked about the core values that were Australian — about the sort of country we could become. Reconciliation was a big item on the agenda then, promising a lasting solution to indigenous disadvantage. Both sides of Parliament had given it their support. My Board's first Australian of the Year, Mandawuy Yunupingu, showed the new direction. We had hundreds of public meetings underway in town halls across the country.

And at every meeting there was a clear consensus. Australia was about 'a fair go'. The fair go was the article of faith. Sadly it's becoming a mythical creature. Hiding in a billabong somewhere in the bush with the bunyips.

But the 'fair go' issue came alive at the time of the Tampa when 10,000 readers backed me in establishing 'A Just Australia'. And we've just gone through a five-year struggle to get kids out of detention, to stop housing thousands in detention camps in Nauru, Woomera, Manus Island, Christmas Island, Curtin and Port Hedland. Our government is still 'processing' the people who fled terror regimes in Iraq and Afghanistan, as their 'temporary' refugee status is reviewed, getting on to four years since the last of them arrived by boat.

Finally, 'A Just Australia' has got some promises of solutions for long-term detainees. We've seen children moved out of the detention centres and have built up a coalition of forces to break bipartisanship of support for bad policy. We've seen the campaign broaden from just the left and the churches, creating divisions in the government to achieve change. But there's no guarantee that if another group of asylum seekers headed our way, we wouldn't do it all again.

Where was the 'fair go' in all of this? What practical difference did it make that Australia was a signatory to all the major human rights treatises? That even chaired the UN Commission on Human Rights during this time? Where was the protection of the courts for the most vulnerable people in Australia?

The fair go, it turned out, wasn't guaranteed by the High Court. As Justice McHugh said, "It's not for courts, exercising Federal jurisdiction, to determine whether the course taken by Parliament is unjust or contrary to basic human rights."

Our kids get the idea of rights from watching American TV. It takes a while for them to realise that they don't have constitutional rights in Australia. The Bill of Rights is there for Americans — and for Canadians there's a Charter of

Rights and Freedoms. Britain joins with the rest of Europe in the European Convention on Human Rights.

We don't have these protections. And we've seen the results. Attempts to bring even a limited bill of rights through a referendum were defeated, with the main argument being "the courts will protect". There's a few Australians like Cornelia Rau and Vivien Alvarez who would dispute this — and thousands of new Australians who've had grim experiences of our human rights protections when they've arrived.

Yes, we've got a Human Rights and Equal Opportunity Commission. It was a body born of compromise and is now neglected and ignored. Our Government still goes through the motions in reporting to UN Treaty bodies on our observance of key international instruments, but dismisses any criticism in offensive terms.

There's a host of other issues that have gone off the boil. The mentally ill still walk the streets or are institutionalised in our jails, rather than getting the treatment they need.

And we've got new challenges — a Government that can't even tell the truth about the connection between our involvement in Iraq and the prospect of terror attacks is asking us to trust them with new 'anti- terror' laws. And the industrial relations 'reform' may well leave millions of Australians unprotected and vulnerable.

We need a stronger voice for human rights now.

Ferrari fever

August 10, 2005

OVER THE DECADES my vices have not been regal. Unlike Her Majesty, I do not frequent the race track and despite a physical similarity with the late King Farouk, have rarely been sighted in a casino. True, I've popped the odd corks on Bollinger 75 but these days alcohol rarely touches my lips. Neither do I sniff nor inject narcotics and the only pot to which I'm addicted contains Elmstock, my favourite tea. Moreover I observe a majority of the Ten Commandments and a wide variety of laws and road signs, particularly those saying KEEP LEFT.

I admit, however, to a momentary lapse. It lasted 20 years and involved a flirtation, almost a fatal fascination, with the internal combustion engine. Forget Chanel. For me it was a hint of petrol in the breeze that triggered my particular form of promiscuity. Compared to me, Mr Toad was a model of self control. I had an affair with a Ferrari.

The Ferrari is, of course, a vehicular embodiment of all things Italian. Mine was cardinal red, and upholstered in deep, luxurious lasagne. It had a 12-cylinder engine made of two giant Gaggia coffee machines. Lift the bonnet and there it was, gleaming and steaming, with carburration provided by two high-pressure cappuccino frothers. The tyres were Fellini radials and just in front of the prancing horse were papal bull bars. Turn the key and the giant exhausts emitted the thunder of Roman legions tramping through Gaul. Press the accelerator and you heard the roar of the crowds at the Colosseum.

The only problem was that it hardly went anywhere. Ever. Like all good Italian cars, like all the best affairs, it involved the tempestuous and the unpredictable. And my Ferrari was an 'off road' model. Not in the 4WD sense (it was so low-slung that you could barely clear a Melbourne tram line) but in that it was rarely ON the road. It spent most of its time and my money with the mechanic. It had a habit of breaking down every morning. In the driveway. Between the garage and the front gate. The family's dustbins travelled further, at least on Tuesdays and Thursdays. There'd be a roar from the Colosseum crowds, a few thuds of the legionnaires' boots and then it would splutter and die.

The Ferrari people were helpful. They'd send out a priest from the factory to pray with me or, on one memorable occasion, to give the car the last rights. I'd dropped it off at a Valet Parking service at Tullamarine Airport and, on my return from Sydney, found that the mighty motor had all the power of an Austin 7. On the way to parking it, some prick had taken it for a hammer down the freeway and blown the engine.

(You have to understand that these high performance engines have to be nursed, cajoled, treated with deference, tenderness, respect. And some brat who was probably used to hammering V8 Monaros had broken it.) I couldn't prove it, of course. Forensic tests revealed no teenage fingerprints. The CSI team found no incriminating mud on his Reebok or my accelerator. But the damage was done. The priest suggested I Hail some Marys. Instead I hailed a cab.

I managed to track down a replacement engine. It belonged, scout's honour, to the Sultan of Brunei and was surplus to his requirements. So I remortgaged the house, sold the children for medical experiments and had it shipped out. Same engine, same model, same everything. But being built by Italians, it didn't fit. Nothing in or on an Italian car ever really does. Whilst the build quality of British cars is notorious, whilst Jaguars were becoming junk and most Rolls Royces were failing to proceed, and Range Rovers leaked more oil than an Iraqi pipeline, Italian cars only looked superb. In truth, they were put together with the erratic brilliance of a meal by a drunken Italian chef.

I'd had enough. I joined Autoholics Anonymous and to this very day remain on the 12-stage program. Though it has to be admitted that I'm still struggling to make it to Stage 3. The sight of a Lancia or even an Alfa Romeo can still cause delirium tremens and if I see a Ferrari I'm a goner. So I rush off to my AA meeting, say "My name is Phillip and I'm an autoholic" and, when things are really bad, seek a priest to confess. No, not Ferrari's priest. He was the devil in disguise.

Behind me Satan! Now the Ford is my shepherd.

Barnaby Joyce

August 20, 2005

YOU'RE A WHITE-COLLAR crim doing time for insider
trading or for being a celebrity's accountant. To save you
from being the sex slave of a gigantic Hell's Angel who's
serving five to ten for making amphetamines in his garage,
your lawyers persuade His Honour to send you to a low
security prison. At first, it's not too bad. Reminds you of the
Club Med where you once took the wife and kids. But the
screws won't let you manage your share portfolio — and
they find you're concealing buy/sell instructions in your
son's homework. So you plan to escape. And do so, in a
laundry van and a blaze of publicity.

Now, where to hide? They're watching the airports, so
you can't fly to a picturesque tax haven where you've squir-
reled away a few mill. Do you head for the hills? Or seek
to lose yourself in a crowded city? Given that you're scared
of snakes and have no credit cards, neither option appeals.
Instead, in a stroke of genius, you'll pretend to be a newly
elected National Party senator. Or a Liberal Party back-
bencher in the Reps — one of those quiet blokes who are
never heard at Question Time, never speaks in a debate and
just does what they're told.

It's perfect! Nobody will notice you. You'll be in the lap of
luxury. Lots of grog, good food, a comfortable back bench

to drowse on. And the superannuation is fanbloodytastic. It's daylight robbery but it's LEGAL.

For decades our Federal parliament has guaranteed hundreds of MPs and Senators total anonymity! Whilst many go to Canberra with the famous baton in their luggage, others go for the quiet life. It's as good an escape as the Foreign Legion and nothing like as dangerous. Provided you keep your mouth shut you'll be invisible and nobody will suspect. Not the press gallery and certainly not the PM. As long as you put up your hand at the right time in the Party room, you'll be right for life.

There are scores of serving pollies on both sides of the house who nobody's heard of because nothing's ever heard from them. They're the also-rans, the extras in the political dramas who murmur 'rhubarb rhubarb' in the background, or who get quietly pissed in the Member's Bar. Oh, they might yell some ritual abuse at Beasley, or laugh too loudly at Costello's jokes. But that's about it. And it's even better in the Senate because most of the time no one gives a stuff about Senators. Unless, of course, it's time to push through the sale of Telstra.

Then there's Barnaby Joyce, who the Libs regard as worse than criminal. Anything but quiet, determined that his light will shine through every bushel the bastards try to bury him in. In ten seconds flat he got to be more bloody famous than 90% of the Senators who've been there for decades. He went from total anonymity and utter inconsequence to political stardom quicker than you could say 'cross the floor'. In the entire annals of Australian politics, no one has managed such a dramatic debut. It took the likes of Howard years of grinding away before he got noticed, it's taken Beasley three or four goes at the Labor leadership to achieve his current unimportance, but young Barnaby is faster than Chris Chattaway or Ian Thorpe. This is the political counterpart to the four-minute mile. This is gold medal!

Yes, it's a measure of Barnaby's quick learning curve and his consummate opportunism. It's also further evidence that Her Majesty's opposition is found WITHIN the Coalition rather than the ALP.

But it's also a demonstration of how fast you can become a celebrity.

I remember being at a dinner in New York hosted by Jack Valenti, the consummate Washington insider who'd served as Uriah Heep to President Johnson, candidate Hubert Humphrey and for a time, the Kennedys, listening in fascination as he and his heavyweight mates discussed whom the Democrats should run against Reagan. Valenti insisted it had to be Dale Bumpers. Dale Bumpers? Once heard, it's not an easy name to forget. But I'd never heard it before (or for that matter since). Surely, I suggested, this represented a marketing problem. Everyone laughed. "You can make anyone famous in this country in about two weeks!"

But making Bumper famous would require lots of money and a talented team. Whereas the Queenslander did it all on his own. In an instant. Didn't cost him a penny. (It's not exactly on the cheap as it'll cost the taxpayers billions.) But let the record show that Barnaby's spreading across Australia quicker than the cane toad on roller skates.

Not that the PM needs to worry about flogging Telstra. Let Barnaby cross the floor. You see, there's another new Senator, recently escaped from prison, who's hiding behind him. Right up the back. And his vote can be relied upon.

Meteorological terrorism

September 11, 2005

WHEN THE COALITION of the Willing was winning the Iraq War so convincingly, vanquishing terrorism and causing democracy to bloom throughout the Middle East, when Saddam's stockpiles of biological, chemical and nuclear weapons were being revealed to the world, thus silencing all the Doubting Thomases who'd opposed the invasion, I wrote a column admitting to taking not one but sixty WMDs on an interstate flight.

My WMDs were invisible to Mascot's weapons inspectorate, showing them to be as hopeless as Hans Blick. Max Moore-Wilson's X-Ray machines didn't even blink as an entire boxful passed along security's assembly line, and past the little machine that sniffs for explosives.

I am referring to a box of Redhead matches. In the wrong hands, a few matches can cause more damage to this country, more death and destruction, than most political terrorists can imagine. Trying to put the risk of some suicide bombings into perspective, I wrote about the terrorists who, each summer, set large tracts of Australia ablaze, wiping out scores, even hundreds of homes — and threatening cities as large as Canberra. Even if few human lives are lost, thousands of millions of birds and animals can perish as the result of a single act of arson. An act undertaken by someone living quietly amongst us. All too often, the member of a voluntary fire brigade. And, yes, fire fighters risk and lose their lives as a consequence. Few of these terrorists are caught and even then are let off with a stern admonishment.

Why is there no War Against Arson? Why are there precious few discussions about an on-going crisis? TV programs or newspaper reports on the who's and why's of this form of terror, dwarfing anything that Australia has had to fear or bear from Islamic extremists are rare. Yet like the London bombers, these terrorists are born here, live amongst us, and give few clues to family, friends and neighbours. How can our fellow citizens, our children do this to us? They ask that question in London when there's a bomb on the tube. Why don't we ask it more in Australia, when bombs come in boxes of sixty, cost a few cents and are available everywhere?

Now we face another threat, even greater in scale than arsonists in the Australian bush or bombers in Bali, one that has less to do with any clash of civilisations or religious conflict. While it involves power politics more than the War on Terror, only one member of the Coalition of the Willing shows concern. Tony Blair. Though the crisis is immense, as dangerous as nuclear war, both Bush and Howard ignore it at OUR peril.

We got a hint of it in New Orleans. Sea temperatures in the Gulf have risen beyond the limit and hurricanes will increase in scale and frequency. Bush not only failed to prepare for an act of meteorological terrorism that was utterly inevitable — not merely predicted but guaranteed — but still refuses to deal with the cause. He refuses, as does an obedient John Howard, to ratify Kyoto. Instead both men protect and encourage coal burning and actively discourage alternative sources of power that could at least begin to tackle the problem.

A senior executive in one of Australia's major electricity providers, anxious to embrace alternatives, to add them to the grid, told me that investment in sustainable power ventures has stopped dead since Howard's latest policy announcements. "It's over before it began." Yet we're already on the receiving end of climate change, with far worse to come. That considerable scientist, Tim Flannery, sees Katrinas galore heading our way — as surrounding sea temperatures reach the boiling point that gets hurricanes and typhoons bubbling.

Right-wing lunatics still ridicule global warming, and encourage the tendency to see environmentalists as zealots, fools, subversives. In the US the campaign is so effective that a majority, responding to surveys, tick the 'extremist' box to describe those warning of global warming.

Flannery doesn't see the same pathology here — though he's astonished by the pseudo-scientific propaganda put out by some of our conservative think-tanks. He also stresses that Howard is light years ahead of Bush in his response to some environmental issues — citing the Tasmanian forests and the Murray Darling.

But the problems we face, of which events like Katrina provide an early warning system, are so profound that nothing short of a War Against Warming, led by a sane US president, will do. And even then it might be too late.

The social breakdown we saw in New Orleans will become increasingly common as the world cooks itself. Internal and international refugee crises will overwhelm us.

Terrified by religio-political terrorism? The odds are over-whelmingly against you or your family being harmed. With meteorological terrorism, no one escapes.

Billy Longley

October 9, 2005

I'M STANDING IN a small cage in Pentridge Prison's notorious H Division. A few feet away, in an identical cage, stands Billy "The Texan" Longley, the enforcer for the Painters and Dockers,

Australia's most criminal union. A hard man with a soft face, Longley is fifty years old and serving a life sentence for a murder he says he didn't commit. That's why I'm there — he's put his case in a letter. On that day, thirty years ago, Billy and I began our long, strange friendship.

I'm in a small lounge room in a little brick house by a railway line. Billy, now 80, sits beneath a framed photograph of Marilyn Monroe — the famous 'over the grate' shot. He's not too well these days — has had to give up ballroom dancing. This column is about what happened in between.

I've received scores of letters from prisoners over the years, confusing me with the ombudsman, asking for help. As it happens, two more this week, protesting the writers' innocence. What made Bill's different was the quality of expression, impressive from someone whose skirmish with formal education was even briefer than mine. Hence the visit to 'Coburg College', to a man with a contract on his life. Hence H Division and the cages.

Forget the Sopranos. Bill's the real thing. In a childhood of desperate poverty, which had him going door-to-door begging for food, young Longley learned to fight who took him on. First up, he belted a teacher for bullying his little sister, then graduated to blues about girlfriends, religion, payback, control. His mates were into sly grog and debt collection for illegal bookies and he was soon on the receiving end of cops' boots in police stations. It wasn't long until he'd graduated to guns. The legend of 'The Texan' had begun.

By the time we met he had an impressive CV. His house had been bombed twice, he'd been charged with the murder of his first wife (in what he insists was an accident) found guilty of manslaughter and acquitted on appeal. He'd been acquitted of six counts of wounding with intent to kill or cause grievous bodily harm, then found guilty of receiving money from Australia's biggest armed robbery. And guilty of the murder he'd written to me about.

After our meeting in Pentridge, I talked to people involved in the case — prosecutors, defence, someone close to the Judge. "Well, he mightn't have done that one, but it's hardly the Dreyfus case. He did plenty of others."

I got permission to give Bill a typewriter, so that he could start tapping out his story. Later he asked me for a set of golf clubs. When moved to a country prison he was allowed to practise his putting. And we've continued to correspond ever since, to see each other from time to time. Now Billy's whole story's been well told by Rochelle Jackson in *In Your Face*, including an account of our friendship. And Jackson's researches have recovered a lot of memories I'd lost — and goes a long way to explaining why I've always liked this disturbing, dangerous yet almost endearing bloke. Because I found Bill to be highly ethical. In his own terms, honourable. Certainly courageous. It's just that he lived in another universe, working in a union that was home to men on their way to Pentridge and on their way out again. An organisation that the police quite liked, not only because of the cash flow in their direction but because they liked knowing where everyone was. It became a clearinghouse for crime and corruption and the dead were many.

Given that the cops were by and large indistinguishable from the crims, the moral and even legal judgements of our world seemed to me, all but irrelevant. Our world hardly intersected with Billy's. We're talking of a parallel universe with its own rules and laws that Billy obeyed and, yes, enforced. It had its own rough justice, recalling Aboriginal law that can, from time to time, overlap with what happens in our courts. But, more often, cannot.

My friendship with Billy would lead directly to the Costigan Enquiry — Frank Costigans' Royal Commission that began with the Painters and Dockers and turned into a search for the "Mr Big" of Australia's organised crime. This would embroil another of my close acquaintances in a nightmare of rumours and accusations.

Jackson's book is both an anthropological study of both criminal and police cultures; and an intensely personal portrait of, believe it or not, a sensitive and deeply philosophical man. Unlike the media industry that swirled around Chopper Read, there's no glamorising of Longley. He wouldn't want it. You may, however, end up liking him. Like me.

Costigan

October 9, 2005

LAST WEEK, I told you a little of my strange friendship with a convicted murderer, the 'enforcer' for the Painters and Dockers Union, Billy "The Texan" Longley. At the same time, I had what might seem an even stranger friendship with Kerry Packer.

This week? How those friendships collided.

Although I'd worked for his father, Kerry and I had never met. But we disliked each other from a distance, on principle. Then he invested in a film I was producing, *The Getting of Wisdom*. Over the course of a few meetings, I found myself liking him. I'll leave the details to the auto-biography I'll never write — suffice to say that Packer was highly intelligent and very lonely. And we were more alike than we'd expected, both half educated, both having survived harsh childhoods. Most of all, I liked Kerry's curiosity. He's not the sort of bloke who reads books, so we'd talk for hours on end about anything and everything — from black holes to ancient history — passionately dis-agreeing about politics.

Having visited Longley in Pentridge — in Rochelle Jackson's biography of Longley, *In Your Face*, I describe Bill as a 'charming, avuncular gentleman with violence swirling around him like a mist' — I'd started to learn about his life with the Painters and Dockers. A very dangerous world. And by complete coincidence, I'd be visited by a young journalist, David Richards, who was determined to 'go underground' in the Union to get the story of their racketeering.

I warned him he'd be killed. Whereupon David pulled up his trouser leg to show the gun holstered at his ankle. Not common equipment for an Australian journalist. His initial plan? To use an empty shipping container as a 'hide' and to photograph 'ghosting' — the pay envelopes being handed out to fake workers. Graft from the shipping companies.

David wouldn't be talked out of it. But why tell me? Because he needed the backing of a newspaper. At the time, having been sacked by Rupert, I was writing for *The Age* so drove straight into town. Halfway there, I changed my mind — I'd had a blue with the editor the previous week — drove back to the office and phoned Trevor Kennedy, then the editor of Packer's *Bulletin*.

In five minutes flat, Trevor agreed to back Richards — and Richards delivered! He also saw Longley in prison and, in return for an undertaking to push for a retrial — the same request he'd made of me, Billy gave Richards loads of dirt. "They are a bunch of criminals," he told him. "Everything they do stems from the barrel of a gun ... the private sector is open slather to graft and corruption. You can simply name your price ... millions have been made ... from ghosting, slings, robberies."

Richard's first cover story appeared in the *Bulletin* on 11 March 1980. Others followed. They were remarkable. Kerry phoned a few times to thank me — the *Bulletin*'s sales were soaring.

And there was growing pressure for a Royal Commission. As *In Your Face* reports, Frank Costigan agrees the articles were the trigger. Despite a distinct lack of enthusiasm by the Victorian government, Costigan began work.

Then, in a twist of fate, Costigan turned his attention from the union to Packer. Soon Kerry was caught in Costigan's net. Incredibly, the *Bulletin* stories had led to ever-wilder accusations that its publisher was Mr Big in organised crime. Kerry, a teetotaller who'd threatened to sack a Playboy editor John Jost over stories even hinting that marijuana wasn't so bad, was being accused of pushing heroin! And worse. Money found in his car boot, used by Kerry for his gambling addiction, was seen by Costigan as returns on drug sales. The stories got sillier and sillier, with tonnes of leaks from the Commission appearing in Fairfax's *National Times*. Until Trevor Kennedy, Malcolm Turnbull and I persuaded Kerry to identify himself as "the Goanna" — the code name chosen for him by the *Bulletin*'s main competitor. That decision turned the tide. Little by little, one by one, the accusations were denied and finally dismissed.

Kerry's fair-weather friends had deserted him in droves — he would never forgive many of the most prominent, particularly in politics and he'd learned what it was like to be on the receiving end of a relentless media attack.

When Billy finally got out of jail, and resumed his ballroom dancing, he still needed to make a quid. So he went into debt collection. As Billy told me at the time, things went pretty well. "I just leave my business card in the letterbox. People always pay up." These days, at the age of 80, it's all in the past. And in Rochelle Jackson's book, *In Your Face: The Life and Times of Billy 'The Texan' Longley*.

Danny Boy

October 22, 2005

GAZING AT A birthday cake, many candles ago, I felt like Hamlet contemplating Yorick's skull. Far from feeling happy, as the all too familiar family chorus urged, the iced sponge was an intimation of mortality, the thirty-odd flames a bonfire of the vanities. Which you're expected to extinguish with your life's breath. As that fatal cake and morbid ceremony move you ever closer to your last breath. Another bloody year up in bloody smoke.

To make matters worse, to intensify the bleak symbolism of a cake that turns to ashes in the mouth, was that effing song. Crook tune, rotten lyrics: Happy Birthday to you, happy birthday to you. Et bloody cetera.

Not even God Save the bloody Queen, the most god awful anthem in the history of patriotic propaganda, is as mournful as Happy bloody Birthday. Not even the Death March, March Funebre by Chopin is as bloody depressing.

But there's a worse one. Joan Didion, who's been writing a lot on mortality, following the deaths of her daughter, Quintana, and her husband, John Gregory Dunne, says of "Row, Row, Row Your Boat, that ostensibly cheerful round sung by so many families on Sunday drives, that this is "the most terrifying verse I know: merrily, merrily, merrily, merrily, life is but a dream".

I've always thought that. Profoundly depressing because it's profound. Spot on. As utterly accurate as an arrow through the heart. More than depressing, it's desolating.

But there's an even worse one than that worse one. The saddest song of all, redeemed by its utter beauty. Though reduced to kitsch by endless repetition and the mawkish sentimentality of most interpretations, it rises like a phoenix, like the moon, as soon as you hear it sung simply, by, for example, Sinead O'Connor. Or my dear dead grandmother.

About life and death, it is amongst the most beautiful songs ever written. Perhaps it's THE most beautiful song. It certainly sounded so when my Grannie, Maud Smith, used to sing Danny Boy to me when I was three, four, five years old — and it would reduce me to tears. It still does.

Oh Danny Boy, the pipes the pipes are calling, from glen to glen across the mountainside ... words of love and loss, of times passing. A simple hymn to human mortality. I couldn't bear my Grannie to sing of her own death — let alone of how I'd leave her to return too late. Yet that's exactly what would happen a dozen years on. To my eternal regret.

"For I'll be here in sunshine and in shadow ... oh Danny Boy, oh Danny Boy, I love you so."

The bleak and beautiful power of that old Irish song came back when I was interviewing two survivors of the Burma Railway. Tom Uren and Arch Flanagan. Arch, ninety years old, and his son Martin, have produced a book called *The Line* about the horrors of the railway. Subtitled 'a man's experience; a son's quest to understand' it's a fine effort, crowded with characters Arch remembers — like Weary Dunlop and Mickie Hallam, who died a brave and dreadful death.

In his foreword Martin writes: "Mickie Hallam's favourite drinking song was Danny Boy. A lot of years later, Dad saw a documentary on the song, and was much taken with guitarist Eric Clapton who refused to dress up the tune in any way, since to do so presumed that he could improve it. Instead Clapton played it plain but true. That was more or less Dad's philosophy of writing when, in his seventies, he wrote the first of his pieces ... that make up this book. He wrote with a pen in his small curiously crafted hand, Mum typing it up on the kitchen table ... the apex of his life is clear, the event by which he stood to judge all others."

I played Clapton's Danny Boy before we started to talk, and read that paragraph. There's good advice for every writer in that call for simplicity. Keep it plain and true. And you read it in the writing of old Arch, and in his sons, Martin and Richard Flanagan.

But any excuse. Twenty years ago I played it on air at 2UE, and then re-read the lyrics and talked of the song's place in my life and Maud Smith's death. I don't think I've ever received more letters in response to a broadcast. And it happened again when, a few weeks ago, I played it for Arch.

There are lots of songs about death. Like Happy Birthday To You. Like Chopin's Death March. Like Row, Row, Row Your Boat. But no other song I know tells so purely, so truly the story of the generations, of the way the young leave, of how the old die, of how we return home too late. That happened with Maud Smith and with her daughter Sylvia. My mum. Who was waiting for me to come before she died.

And the plane was delayed.

2007

The windmills
of his mind

January 7, 2007

FOR ALL SORTS of personal and political reasons Max
Whisson is one of my most valued friends. We first made
contact at the beginning of the AIDS epidemic when this
most ethical of men was a principal guardian of our Red
Cross blood supply. More recently he's been applying his
considerable scientific skills to the flow of another precious
fluid. Water.

Does this country have a more urgent issue? Will the
world have a greater problem? Whilst we watch our dams
dry, our rivers die, our lakes and groundwater disappear,
whilst we worry about the financial and environmental
costs of desalination and the melting of the glaciers and
icecaps, Max has come up with a brilliant and very simple
idea. It involves getting water out of the air. And he's not
talking cloud-seeding for rain. Indeed Max just might have
come up with a way of ending our ancient dependence on
rain, that increasingly unreliable source.

And that's not all. As well as the apparently empty air providing us with limitless supplies of water, Max has devised a way of the same empty air providing the power for the process. I've been to his lab in Western Australia. I've seen how it works.

First of all, there's a lot of water in the air. It rises from the surface of the oceans to a height of almost 100 kilometres. You feel it in high humidity, but there's almost as much invisible moisture in the air above the Sahara or the Nullabor as there is in the steamy tropics. The water that pools beneath your air-conditioned car — or the brimming tray beneath an old fridge — demonstrates the principle. Cool the air and you get water. And no matter how much water we took from the air we'd never run out. Because the oceans would immediately replace it.

Trouble is refrigerating air is a very costly business. Except when you do it Max's way. That involves the Whisson windmill. Until Max's inventions are protected by international patents, I'm not going to give details. Though Max isn't interested in personal profits — he just wants to save the world — the technology remains 'commercial in confidence' to protect his small band of investors and to encourage others.

But even without its ability to turn air into water, the Whisson windmill would be a considerable achievement. It seems that, in essence, windmills haven't changed in many centuries. The great propellers that are producing power for the generation of electricity are direct descendants of the rusty galvo blades that creak on our farms' windmills — and the vanes that lifted Don Quixote from his saddle. Usually three blades face into the wind. Whereas the Whisson windmill has many blades, each as aero-dynamic as an aircraft wing, each employing 'lift' to get the device spinning. I've watched them whirr into action in Whisson's wind tunnel, at the most minimal settings. They start spinning long, long before a conventional windmill would begin to respond. I saw them come alive when a colleague opened an internal door.

And I forgot something. Max's windmills don't face into the wind like a plane's propeller. They're arranged vertically, within an elegant column.

The secret of Max's design is how his windmills, whirring away in the merest hint of a wind, cool the air as it passes by. Like many a great idea, it couldn't be simpler — or more obvious. But nobody thought of it before.

With three or four of Max's magical machines on hills at our farm we could fill the tanks and troughs and weather the drought. One small Whisson windmill on the roof of a suburban house could keep your taps flowing. Biggies on office buildings, whoppers on sky-scrapers, could give independence from the city's water supply. And plonk a few hundred in marginal outback land — specifically to water tree-lots — and you could start to improve local rainfall.

This is just one of Whisson's ways to give the world clean water. Another, described in this column a few years back, would channel seawater to inland communities. A brilliant system of solar distillation and desalination would produce fresh water en route. All the way from the sea to the ultimate destination, fresh water would be produced by the sun. The large-scale investment for this approach hasn't been forthcoming — but the 'water from air' technology already exists. And works.

Australia needs a few Whissons at the moment — and the Whissons need initial government funding. For the price of one of John Howard's crappy nuclear reactors, Max might be able to solve a few problems.

2013

The vote ...

January 17, 2013

WHAT HAVE THE Romans ever done for us? You'll recall John Cleese posing this rhetorical question in *The Life of Brian* — leading to a number of concessions about the benefits of Roman roads, aqueducts, sanitation, irrigation, medicine, health, public baths and public order.

When given the job of encouraging disinterested youth to register for the vote I plagiarised that scene for a TV spot. Cleese's blundering revolutionaries were replaced by teenagers dismissing our democracy as a waste of time — only to reluctantly concede that Australia wasn't such a bad place. And that the Commonwealth of Australia HB pencil, dangling on its string in the polling booth, might have some sword-like might.

The current debate, if a few recycled mutterings can be dignified by that term, argues that the half-hearted pencil wielding at state and federal elections be made non-compulsory. Instead of mustering people to the polls with the cattle-prod of a threatened fine, we make the vote voluntary.

There are those in Western democracies who take this further by making voting damn near impossible. You'll recall the US Republican Party actively discouraging the Hispanic, Black and youth votes in the Presidential election by legalistic chicanery. Perhaps inspired by Republican dirty tricks, that great political thinker Bronwyn Bishop has revived the voluntary voting issue in the belief that this would add to Labor's woes. And it certainly would. But it might cause the Libs some problems of their own — in that the next federal election involves choosing between two of the most woeful and unpopular leaders in living memory. The once sacred HB pencil will be a heavy burden and, without coercion, the polling booths of Australia might be as empty as phone booths in this era of the mobile.

Of course it's not just our pollies who are viewed as surplus to requirements. Almost all our once admired institutions, even our churches and certainly our banks, are on the nose. The media is not held in the highest regard. Yet by any objective measure Australia remains, warts and all, a paragon of societies. Having frequently needed its help at times of crisis, I'm here to say that even our much maligned health system remains a remarkable achievement.

Despite fissures, factions and fractures, Australia has social glue aplenty. I see it in the bush where a voluntary fire brigade system rallies at times of crisis. (Indeed voluntarism across the board is an Australian phenomenon.) And I see it in the generous response to natural disasters, whether ours or our neighbours'. For all our complaints and cynicism we remain communities.

We enjoy freedoms and take for granted entitlements that are beyond the imagination of billions of our fellow sufferers on this endlessly troubled planet. Which is why people all over are dying for the right to vote we not only take for granted but view with indifference or contempt. Let's admit it. We're spoiled rotten.

And most of this has been achieved or enhanced by the HB pencil dangling on its string. Our achievements in all the public sectors — public education, public health, public libraries, public broadcasting and even the public transport we loudly damn — provide some of the measures. (Loudly damning is one of our entitlements.) Even public roads are, I reckon, impressive. All roads still lead to Rome in tiny, ancient Italy, yet thanks to corruption many of their major arterials fall into ruins even as they build them. Whereas an Australian can drive almost everywhere in this incomprehensibly vast and recent nation,

What has democracy done for us? Sanitation, irrigation, public health, public baths — as with the Romans it's a long list. Rather than the deafening denigration of democracy, the worst system apart from the alternatives, we should be proud of our collective achievements and be determined to defend and extend them. And if we don't like our politics the best way to change them is by participation — if only by voting.

What has democracy done for us?

Laughter

February 11, 2013

I RECKON A human's first laugh is a response to the fear of flight and falling. Behold that ancient scene — a father tosses his baby into the air and the poor little bugger inhales with fright only to exhale with relief when caught. That little detonation of breath begins a lifetime of laughter, more often than not triggered by personal or cultural tension.

Just as jokes are little exorcisms protecting us from things that embarrass. When collecting thousands of examples for the Penguin Book of Australian Jokes it became obvious that most were attempts to deal with notions, issues and areas that cause concern — like sex, race, religion, mothers-in-law, politicians and lawyers. It was hard to find a joke that did not originate in a form of anxiety. Or even horror. Which is why even tragedy — especially tragedy — triggers jokes in response. Within minutes of the NASA launch that killed the astronauts or the killing of Bin Laden, bad, brutal jokes were bouncing around. In the sense that they're therapeutic, jokes are deadly serious.

It's no accident that so many comedians are Jewish. A few millennia of anti-Semitism and pogroms have produced the highest form of humour; the Jewish joking that unites Woody Allen, Jon Stewart and Seinfeld with Lenny Bruce and Mo Mackacky. There's something of the same quality in rural Australian jokes, coming from people who have to deal with the ironies of drought, flood and fire. And you find variations of 'gallows humour' wherever people are caught up in terrible circumstances.

What sets us apart from other creatures is our awareness of mortality. We seem to be alone in knowing that we die. Death, this cruel joke of God's, leads to insanity, suicide, cruelty, religion, science, art and, yes, the sense of humour that is the sense and essence of human. We laugh because it helps us cope.

At the same time humour, and particularly jokes, can be utterly inhumane. Many of those we collected for Penguin were appalling in their sexual, religious and racial hostility. As well as Jewish jokes — anti-Jewish jokes, and a great many aimed at 'Abos' — or 'reffos'. Collectors, not censors, we grew weary with answering angry letters complaining about the racist jokes we'd included — many of which had been bouncing around for centuries, with regular changes to settings or dramatis personae. (I remember telling Paul Keating that we'd tracked jokes attacking him back to jokes attacking Hitler, just as Irish jokes had previously targeted Poles.)

The big joke is that we are born to die. What a punch line! The un-funniness of that simple fact can drive us mad. Better to laugh it off, or try to. Along with fantasies of faith, where death is just a doorway to an eternal life, a notion some of us find hilarious, it's evolution's way of dulling the pain. A pity that that sometimes means increasing the pain of others.

Sex continues to inspire a juggernaut of juggernaughtiness of jokes. Infinite variations on jokes about generative members, cuckoldry, farmers' daughters and recalcitrant nuns, dating back way before Shakespeare and Chaucer. Homophobia and misogyny abounds with jokes alleging Irish or Polish stupidity reappearing as attacks on blondes. About the only ancient text without bawdy sexual humour seems to be *The Bible*, where fear of women is very unfunny (Jezebel, Salome, Lot's wife, etc.) In fact there are very few intentional laughs at all in the Testaments, Old or New. Just lots of approving references to God's ethnic cleansing and genocides. Odd given the Jewish authorship.

(Leaving aside the story of Eve's creation the Good Book lacks much rib-tickling, but you find laughs in the oddest places. I recommend Parliamentary Hansard.)

Despite the dark side of humour's moon it is, in the end, a great boon. As a response to whatever foments your fears or frustrations it's far cheaper than drugs or psychotherapy.

Anna K

February 14, 2013

WITH KEIRA Knightley joining the ranks of movie Anna Kareninas throwing themselves beneath cinematic trains, I seek your permission to tell you my all-time favourite story about the consequences of one of my columns.

I was tapping away on a piece about the connections of famous Northern Hemispherical authors with our Deep South, the antipodean encounters of many of the most famous 19th century novelists with white Australia. *Moby Dick*'s Melville, for example, visited us, as did the mighty Mark Twain. Quite a few notables came here when young, sometimes working on ships while gathering material. Others, like Mr Clemens, at the height of their fame, making a few quid from public readings to culturally malnourished colonials. Far earlier, *Gulliver's Travels* was linked to Adelaide — check the latitude and longitude and you'll discover that Lilliput was in South Australia!

Anecdotes about Charles Dickens abound — as do references to Australia in his plots. It wasn't only his characters Dickens sent here but also his sons. Two became jackaroos on the Hay Plains and would include press clippings in their letters home to dad. There's a clear connection between Oliver Twist's Fagin and a real-life convict at Port Arthur, and circumstantial evidence that a story from a Sydney newspaper, about an heiress jilted at the altar, sent to dad by one of his boys, inspired the character of Miss Havisham in *Great Expectations*. Sitting in her decaying mansion in her rotting bridal dress, while rats nibbled at the ruins of her wedding cake.

There I was tap-tapping away, when my fingers faltered. A paragraph short and nought to add. So for fun, I fictionalised a fact. After another row with his missus, I had Leo Tolstoy come to Australia in a huff, move into the Healesville Hotel and have an affair with Anne Kerin, the wife of a minor municipal official and the great, great grandmother of Federal Treasurer John Kerin. It didn't go well as Mrs K threw herself under the 3.30 train to Melbourne. Having completed the novel at the Healesville pub, Count Leo went back to Russia and the countess.

When academics expressed doubts as to the truth of the story, I suggested they write to John Kerin, then the Federal Treasurer. Some did — and John, a highly amusing bloke who could, you might recall, hypnotise chooks — wrote back confirming my scholarship; on official Federal Treasurer letterhead. I have no doubt that there's now the odd Australian don who takes the story seriously.

Years later, a sequel. An expat Russian writer asks me to launch his latest novel set in a seedy holiday resort on the Black Sea. The venue, Gleebooks in Sydney. Though I'd not met him, his wife (and translator) was an old friend so I'm happy to oblige. Standing at the lectern I tell the story of the Kerin-Karenina hoax and am rewarded with polite titters. But when the novelist takes to the lectern, there's a very strange turn of events.

Remember that we'd not met until that evening. That he'd no idea of what I was going to say ...

In thickly accented English he tells the gathering — and me — that he'd read the column while living in Moscow. And that he'd believed the story of Russia's greatest writer and the Healesville Hotel and of what might be described as a kangaroo kookaburra Karenina.

"It was one of the main reasons I came to Melbourne from Moscow. If it was good enough for Tolstoy, it was good enough for me."

Thinking back to the night when I was ghasted so flabberly there are two responses. The first involves the long arm of coincidence, and of unexpected outcomes. The second? Perhaps the novelist, being a novelist, perpetrated a second hoax. He insisted he was telling the truth, but you never know with novelists. Ask John Kerin.

The Pope's Address

February 15, 2013

GOOD MORNING, fellow Catholics. On this, my first day on the job, I'd like to have a bit of a chat. To explain what I'm feeling and considering. Whereas my predecessor was described as God's Rottweiler, I'd prefer to be God's Labrador — a likeable seeing-eye dog guiding the Church from its doctrinal blindness.

First up, I will make no claim of infallibility. That's one of the sillier papal policies. I'm a human being, with all the usual frailties. All I can do is try to take the best advice and think things through. I'll want all my utterances to be discussed and challenged.

Secondly, we've got to sort out our problems with sex. As a 75-year-old virgin I've had no direct experience but it seems to me our faith has a few problems with sexuality. You know: immaculate conceptions, virgin birth, an unmarried priesthood sworn to celibacy and a misogynistic attitude to the role of women. And that's before we look at such reproductive issues as our blanket ban on contraception — climaxing, if you'll forgive the expression, in continuing condemnation of the condom in the era of AIDS.

Until quite recently we were still emasculating thousands of young Italians to keep their voices pure for our church choirs. Unthinkable now. Yet we attempt a form of emasculation by denying members of religious orders the sacred pleasures of sexuality. Most worryingly we refuse to allow our young priests to go through the process of sexual maturation, we create taboos and tensions that lead, inexorably, to child abuse. Time to scrap our fears and taboos. Time, for example, to welcome married priests. And while we're about it, it's time to welcome women to the priesthood. Next time there's a conclave in the Sistine I'd like to see some female cardinals.

While I'm not ready to end our disapproval of abortion it's clear that if we want to reduce its incidence we've got to give contraception our blessing. My Polish predecessor went very close to approving the Pill. I now do so. Along with those funny little rubber things. Apart from slowing out-of-control population growth in so many poor countries condoms can clearly reduce the incidence of AIDS. I may not be infallible, but I'm not stupid. Enough already.

The world looks with disapproval at the governance of China, where over a billion people are excluded from taking part in the election of their leaders — a process that, remains utterly mysterious. In our church another billion are precluded from participation in that more mysterious process that creates bishops, cardinals and, yes, Popes. I'd like that to begin to change. Just as Beijing is nervously experimenting with democracy, at least at lower levels in the system, I think it's time for Rome to take the first steps away from centralisation to democratisation. I don't think Jesus wanted his church to be a dictatorship.

Our church is the world's oldest multi-national corporation. By some measures we are still the most powerful and remain amongst the richest. We've branches everywhere and huge influence in national and international politics.

My cardinals are the company directors of the enterprise and, as of today, I'm the CEO. And I want to make sure we take better care of our billion small shareholders. So after we clean up the Aegean stables of Vatican finances — riddled with corruption — I shall insist on disposing of surplus real estate and loot to better help the poor and needy.

(Cardinal Pell recently spent a vast amount refurbishing a church here in Rome — a case of coals to Newcastle. Couldn't, shouldn't Australian funds have been put to better use?)

So there you have it. As long as I'm not poisoned by the Curia I shall be a reformist pope, reaching out to those of other faiths or no faith and fighting for social justice. Pray for me.

Oscar

February 26, 2013

I ONCE SHARED a double bed with Harvey Weinstein, the pillow-plump movie magnate. We were on it, I hasten to add, not in it. The scene was his suite at the Carlton at Cannes, effectively Hollywood's HQ during the annual horrors of the world's most famous Film Festival and the king-size served as his desk as, one by one, producers, actors and directors paid obeisance to His Majesty of Miramax. The elephant in his own room Harvey seemed to contain within his bulk all the studios he'd outlived or outmanoeuvred — as if he'd devoured Metro's Lion, Rupert's Fox, Rank's bloke with the gong and all the Warner Brothers.

Though I can't remember which film I was trying to pitch, the suite was unforgettable for its total chaos. Film bumph, room-service trolleys, flunkies and mendicants and a cacophony of shouted conversations and ringing phones. While Harvey wallowed amidst the detritus on his bed, doing or denying deals.

The scene returns every year as I watch the Oscars, even if only for a few moments before choosing a less agonising option by stabbing myself in the eye with a fork. For you can bet that from beginning to end of that infernal eternal telecast, winners of the lusted-after statuettes will, after thanking God, their parents and their colleagues, thank

Harvey. Sometimes while kneeling on the stage shedding tears of gush and gratitude. Many will thank him before God, as Harvey's name appears in the credits of an inordinate number of winning films. Not because he's a genius, though that may be the case, but because of his ubiquity. He does a lot of deals.

All that grovelling to Harvey, God and the Academy has me reaching for the remote and thanking God I left the film business. As with our little Logies, the Oscars are shaped like suppositories and should be inserted rather than presented. They represent everything about the movie business that's detestable — brutal cultural imperialism and budgets as big and bloated as the egos. And the egos off-screen are as monstrous as those of the stars. The politics of the Oscars are as mendacious as any in the Middle East or the battles for supremacy as lethal as the Vatican's. And what we called Hollywood is as claustrophobic a community as any convent.

The Oscars are not so much a celebration as an abattoir choreographed by Busby Berkeley — and increasingly the glitz and the gold are little more than coins on the eyes of a corpse. For it's not only newspapers that are in deep do-dos. Born in the late 19th century the US movie business struggled to survive in the 21st. All the cringe-producing in-jokes from the sacrificial objects hired to compere the event cannot conceal the crisis. New technologies win Oscars for SFX — but others are attacking cinemas like wrecking balls. The collective experience of seeing a movie, of laughing, dreaming and gasping together is slowly dying as people watch what they want to watch on Is — pads and pods. And there are more challenges to US dominance than Bollywood's. It's good to see, for example, Asian audiences preferring local product to Hollywood's.

l spent decades helping build an Australian film industry — to reduce the 95% share of our box-office that went to US films — only to see that figure consolidate while many of our best and brightest learn to do ever better American accents and surrender to US seductions. It was only half-joking when this column described the Oscars as 'golden nails in the coffin of the Australian film industry'. Whether awarded to our actors or technicians, all too often Oscars represent the triumph of cultural imperialism. And that's before you factor in the dominance of US material on free-to-air or cable. Our problem? Largely because we speak English. Which means that increasingly we speak American.

The Uncommonwealth of Australia

March 7, 2013

YOU HAVE A NEW female Prime Minister. Me. Gina. Welcome to the Uncommonwealth of Australia.

My decision to take over was made in the best interests of the nation. Well, in my best interests which are, coincidentally, your best interests. No correspondence will be entered into.

My Daddy's motto, embossed on every ingot, read simply "What's yours I'll mine, what's mine is mine". These words will now appear on Australia's coat of arms betwixt roo and emu and on the nation's newly minted cast iron currency beneath my profile. Naturally the right profile. I abhor the left in all things.

For decades my father and his disciples dreamed of secession. Western Australia would become his fiefdom, a king-size version of the Hutt River Province. This was the only issue on which Daddy and his devoted daughter disagreed. His jism for chism lacked vision. Bugger secession I'd say. It lacks sufficient grandeur. Think bigger. Hence my decision to take over the entire continent. After all Western

Australia had long driven the national economy and dominated Canberra politics. As you well know, we organised the coup that toppled Rudd (with a little help from Billy Shorten and my predecessor) and have decided on all significant matters of taxation. So the changes I'm implementing are modest and minimal.

(There was another reason for changing a policy of disaffiliation for one of unification. Western Australia is rapidly diminishing in size because I've been exporting it in great dollops to places like China and India. We have, if you like, been seceding in instalments.)

My new ministry is a remarkable grouping of great men. Virile visionaries one and all. Twiggy Forrest is my Deputy. Andrew Bolt is Minister for the Media — and chair of the ABC. Lord Monckton is Senate Leader — in an Upper House we'll rename the House of Lord. Him. Dear Christopher will also keep an eye — actually two remarkable eyes — on those greenie terrorists as Minister for the Environment. (The rest of the Senators have resigned to spend more time with their families — seen as preferable to spending all their time in the GITMO-style Gulag we're opening in the Nullarbor to accommodate dangerous dissidents.) I welcome Eddy Obeid as Minister for Mining and shall retain all the portfolios that begin with F, like Finance and Foreign Affairs. I was going to announce the new Leader of the Opposition today but, on second thoughts, have decided to dispense with an opposition.

We shall immediately return to the Australian tradition of a basic wage — the one I've been talking about in recent months. $2 a day. You can't get more basic than that. As I'm totally opposed to racial discrimination this will be mandatory for all workers irrespective of immigration status. Yes, whether you were born here or arrive as a temp the same generous remuneration will apply, less of course a small deduction of 50% to cover health care.

In a compassionate policy change we shall also welcome reffos. Boat people will join the others working in my mines — on the same $2. Less shipping costs.

My proposed 'special economic zone' for the North, with its tax-free arrangements, will now be extended a little South. All the way to our base at Mawson. No major corporation will be required to pay tax — and this has nothing to do with the generous flow of their donations to our Party. I deeply resent that insinuation. Oh, did I mention I was going to call us One Nation? It seems another inspiring woman has that registered. So I'm calling my party 'My Party'.

Finally I'm especially proud to announce my decision to dam any and all remaining rivers while constructing lots of new harbours to facilitate mining exports — employing the technology advocated by Daddy. Nuclear explosions. These will be supervised by family friend and ex-Senator Barnaby Joyce, now Minister for A Bombs.

Moral compass

March 15, 2013

ADDED TO THE long list of powerful women who've commanded my destiny (mother, wives, daughters, head-mistresses, magazine editors and ABC producers) has been the digital dominatrix who issues instructions on the GPS. She Who Must Be Obeyed must be obeyed — she does not brook argument.

'Turn right in 400 metres'. And if my response is recalcitrant, if I perform a minor act of motorised mutiny, she'll issue the stern command of 'do a U turn', repeating it until I submit.

Her voice is charmless and implacable. No hint of warmth or fellow feeling. In dread of her, I turn the radio up, but that doesn't silence her. She simply increases her volume and tells me where to go, directing me in directions that I don't wish to go, to destinations that are entirely irrelevant. 'At the next roundabout take the third exit.'

And yet there's something calming about her bullying, like a Mother Superior admonishing a slightly naughty nun. It's simply a matter of surrendering any lingering delusion of free will.

Which is why I agreed to extend the GPS system to provide a wider range of services. To dictate every aspect of my life. To provide all directions, not simply 'turn right in 400 metres', but my moral compass also.

This necessitated removal of my brain (which I donated to fill the cranial cavity of Andrew Bolt) and the downloading of the updated digitised micro-chipped model, based on the HAL 9000. The improvement was instant and dramatic. The amplified voice of the dominatrix was replaced by the inner voice of Hal, syrup-smooth and soothing and issuing completely different and more diverse instructions. Programmed with the Ten Commandments and other prohibitions listed in the Seven Deadly Sins and supplemented by the teachings of both Christ and Pope Frank my in-head Hal functions as a guardian angel and murmurs a constant stream of warnings and encouragements —only audible to me.

Thus 'turn right in 40 metres' is replaced by 'do not covet thy neighbour's ass'. If inflamed by some absurd political utterance I'm quietly reminded 'thou shalt not kill', or 'love thy enemy'. Should I linger by a patisserie and look longingly as the pastries I'm warned about gluttony and given a calorie count. Any sideways glance at a woman provokes a warning about lust. So far it's working perfectly (no HAL 9000 has ever made a mistake.)

So here I am test-driving Tomorrow — a future wherein the old-fashioned human brain, that great dollop of grey porridge, is replaced by a wondrous piece of technology. Not a mere iPod, iPhone or iPad but a wholly digitised I. It thinks, therefore I am.

Some time ago we handed over the world's finances to the billionth-of-a-second trading decisions of computers thus eliminating human error — and we haven't had a GFC for weeks. You may be concerned that HAL-like brains have taken over from airline pilots but Boeing and Airbus can be completely trusted. Pentagon generals are also being retro-fitted so as to better cope with the bombardment of military intelligence thus eliminating the military intelligence of utter nutters like George Patton, Curtis Lemay and Macarthur. Soon our cars will be self-driven and we'll all be wearing Google glasses. So my new brain shouldn't alarm. Others fitted with the same model include Ray Hadley and Tony Abbott. Alan Jones's blew a fuse.

Clearly I am a big improvement on the erratic PA of the past. In proximity to asses, pastries and women I behave impeccably, though I did briefly covet my neighbour's BMW and last week I showed a tendency to worship a graven image of Gough Whitlam.

Asteroids

March 30, 2013

AT A TIME when anxieties about errant asteroids are making news — and movies — I want to tell you about one that is NOT threatening Earth. This "minor planet" is about 20 to 30 kilometres in size and circles the Sun whilst remaining between the orbits of Mars and Jupiter. It was discovered by R. H. McNaught at Sidings Springs in 1990 and named 'Phillipadams' in 1997 by the International Astronomical Union. Why was I accorded this single honour? Essentially because John Howard put us in harm's way.

The citation to the IAU was drawn up by the remarkable British/Australian Duncan Steel FRAS — a space scientist whose right royal studies included stints at Queen Elizabeth and Queen Mary Colleges, the Imperial College of Science and the Laboratory for Atmospheric and Space Physics at the University of Colorado. In Australia he established the first and only southern hemisphere program for the discovery and tracking of near-Earth asteroids. The sort of things that dodo'd the dinosaurs and recently rocked the Russians. At last count he'd discovered a dozen 'minor planets' and has written extensively on the risks we face from the endless game of cosmic billiards. His books include *Rogue Asteroids and Doomsday Comets; the Search*

for the Million Megaton Menace That Threatens Life on Earth
(with a foreword by Arthur C. Clarke).

And here's where our paths crossed. "Adams helped promote the Australian search and follow-up program from 1990 to its cessation in 1996." Which is when, with characteristic vision, Howard pulled the plug. It was, he argued, a waste of money. What was the point of knowing of a threat when we couldn't do anything about it? Overnight studies of the heavens in the southern hemisphere ceased. In the northern hemisphere the studies intensified, as with plans to avert disaster. One might suggest Howard took the same fatalistic approach to the unfolding disaster of climate change. Avert your gaze. Best not to know.

While the risk from asteroids is real, urgent and potentially apocalyptic, Howard chose ignorance over science. In contrast the PM would enthusiastically promote the invasion of Iraq, citing the non-existent threat of WMDs — thus condemning vast numbers of Iraqi civilians to death, wrecked lives, homes and cities. And millions to refugee status in a war based on lies that had nothing to do with Australia. As the conservative scholar Owen Harries asked, "What have the Iraqis ever done to us — except buy our wheat?"

I wrote columns about it, begging Howard to rethink a really bad decision — too stupid to call a policy. Non-existent WMDs? Well worth a horrendous war. Asteroids? Not worth a dollar or a moment's concern. At a time when space science was literally rocketing ahead. NASA worked with Duncan on the issue. But what would they know? John, it IS rocket science.

Any Prime Minister would agree that the first responsibility of a government is to protect the population from danger. Howard saw pitiful refugees in leaking boats as a huge threat to Australia — and won his 'dark victory' by beating up the fears and bigotries that Abbott continues to exploit. But the infinitely greater dangers of a cosmic clobbering? That might well be prevented by Bruce Willis or NASA? What a great leader Howard was. Too smart to listen to a Fellow of the Royal Society who's published more papers than the PM's had hot breakfasts.

Rocks in the sky versus rocks in the head. And Howard never admits to error. Ten years after he urged Bush to invade, Howard says he has no regrets. Which puts him in a small minority with Bush, Cheney, Blair and Rumsfeld. In the event of a southern hemispheric invasion by an asteroid, there mightn't be many survivors to complain.

Howard probably thinks that asteroids are another left-wing plot.

Currently I'm harmlessly circling the Sun, orbiting between Mars and Jupiter — but I am inclined to go rogue and head straight for John and Jeanette. l know where they live.

Homework

April 30, 2013

COME IN, Australia and sit down. It's a pity your mother, Great Britain, couldn't find time to be here today as we review your progress.

Let's deal with your worst marks first. Once the 3 Rs were Reading, 'Riting, 'Rithmatic, recently replaced by Republic, Reconciliation and Refugees. I'm afraid you score Fs. Your homework on the Republic has been slovenly — and you've been bone lazy on reconciling with the indigenous people. Since Sorry Day I've seen no sign of improvement. You MUST try harder. As for Refugees? The UK and Italy, to name but two, have more refugees in a week than we've had in a decade. Yet your thinking on the issue remains, at best, third rate. Full of grammatical errors like 'illegal immigrants'. You will not be promoted as long as you repeat the bigoted nonsense of the past. I find this all the more disappointing since you abandoned White Australia and have been getting on much better with your Asian playmates.

You did well in the GFC. By combining a little Keynes with Kevin you passed with flying colours. I do not take this for granted, though others do. Ten out of ten and a koala stamp.

You've disappointed in your environmental studies — and don't think we don't know that you're still smoking behind the shelter-shed, emitting vast clouds of CO_2 — and have been listening to the sillier kids in class on climate change. Denialists are dunces. Listen to your science teachers.

On the other hand, we remain pleased with your work on gun laws. We're proud that your achievements have been noted in the USA. No more massacres, a sharp reduction in gun suicides and crime rates, although we have noted increased influence of the NRA, particularly via the NSW Shooters Party, with hunters being allowed in national parks.

You lose points for allowing too much of US-style Law and Order to infiltrate our elections — the political counterpart to playground bullying. Yet despite your insatiable appetite for America's pop-cultural violence via media and video games, you have not been tempted to talk up capital punishment. And you've been better behaved on abortion than America.

You continue to show too much enthusiasm for fighting. Despite getting an F on Vietnam you got involved in fights in Afghanistan and Iraq. More Fs and stay in after school and write a thousand times on the blackboard: "I will not get involved in other people's wars."

Where you and your powerful friend part company is, we're pleased to note, in public health. Here, despite all the problems, you remain far in advance of America. An elephant stamp.

You've dealt well with crises like flood and fire. You've shown character by hopping in and helping. You've been generous to your neighbours when they've been suffering. But I'd like to see improvements in your racial tolerance, and more willingness to involve yourself in the political process instead of just complaining and spraying graffiti on the wall.

While the donations from the Tuck Shop have been reduced, in Music and the Arts you've been trying harder. B+ to A-. Sport? Patchy in swimming and some very poor behaviour off-field with your team-mates in Rugby. As to rumours of drug-taking, match fixing and gambling — not the sort of thing we want to hear.

We've noticed on public occasions that you still don't know the words to 'Advance Australia Fair' — just moving your mouth and pretending. Yes, it is a pretty lamentable national anthem, but we must give the appearance of patriotism. Whilst not taking it too far as you did, for example, in your rowdy and loutish behaviour at Cronulla.

But all in all, you seem to be trying. The last time we talked I reminded you that while Australia rhymes with failure, I expect to see you lifting your game. Leave now — and send in your little brother, New Zealand.

Human

May 3, 2013

WHAT A PIECE of work is man, said a particularly clever
example of the species. How noble in reason, how infinite
in faculty, in action like an angel, in apprehension like a god.
True, Shakespeare went on to knock us off that pedestal by
a glum reference to us being the quintessence of dust —
but he was half-way through writing Hamlet and that must
have been quite depressing.

Humans. A lot of humans aren't. Or not very. Human,
that is. Many seem to lack the psychological ingredients that
make being human human. You see it in the way they treat
other humans, or trample on their human rights. I'm not
just talking about baddies like Hitler or Stalin or Pol Pot
or nongs like George W. I'm not just talking about socio-,
psycho- or other sorts of paths who go in for serial killing
or defrauding pensioners of their savings; I'm talking about
the enormous number of angry unpleasant pricks who
won't let you change lanes, who post toxic tweets or who
gain employment as shock-jocks. I'm talking of the people
who write noxious letters to the Editor, or to loveable, harmless old columnists.

Not a lot of humility with humans. As a species we hold
ourselves in high regard. As the highest of life forms, the pin-
nacle of God's creation or the most triumphant expression

of evolution. Whether you go for the deity or Darwin, there's a tendency to forget Galileo and Copernicus and see ourselves as the centre of everything. We are so important that we're on speaking terms with the Creator, and our lives are so precious that when they're over on earth they're just beginning up there. Die? Not us. We will clutter the heavens forever. Hundreds of billions of us. But not other, lesser animals. Not pussies or puppies. Just us. No Noah's Ark for afterwards. No two-by-two to accumulate in the radiant cumulus of Heaven. Just you and me and Auntie Gladys, who'd much have preferred it if she could've taken her old Labrador. But rules are rules. No pets. Just people. Heaven operates on much the same principle as the body corporate.

What with great universities, high courts, cathedrals and museums we build monuments to our accumulated knowledge, laws, religions, history and even our wars which, on closer examination, are monuments to ourselves, reminding us how exalted, devout, heroic, wise and patriotic we are. Blurring over our wilful ignorance, our brutalities, and bigotries. Another William — James, not Shakespeare, dismisses us as just another beast of prey — 'the only one that preys systematically on its own species'.

We are the beasts of prey that pray. And that's another area of confusion. Many of our most devout citizens, including our PM-in-waiting, loudly profess their Christianity whilst, in the same breath that praises Jesus they condemn our very few refugees to outer darkness; demanding they be sent to the unfortunately christened Christmas Island. And you hear the inhuman voices taking up the chorus when they phone Alan or his ilk on shout-back radio. Road rage, it seems to me, is directly linked to radio rage and reffo rage.

Leaving aside the political cynicism surrounding the

Disability scheme — with both sides trying to disable each other — quite a few of the first responders to radio, letters pages or social media seem to think that mass euthanasia would be more cost effective. Compassion fatigue? Clearly many of our fellow humans never had much compassion in the first place.

About 150,000,000 people died in wars and genocides in the 20th century — showing how we prey systematically on our own species. The fight to the death between altruism and selfishness, tribalism and tolerance, will define the 21st and what it means to be human. Our survival depends on humans being more human. My favourite quotation is Pascal's "man is only a reed, the weakest thing in nature; but he is a thinking reed". Hope he's right.

Race relations

June 5, 2013

HUMANISTS ARE people for whom atheism is not enough. They recognise that atheism is not a belief but simply disbelief, a blank slate rather than a philosophy or a plan for action. Atheists see a universe without creator, purpose or meaning — as a vast mystery that simply exists. So they add to the plethora of isms, many of them profoundly dangerous, one of their own. Humanism seeks to find meaning in human existence — and in doing so can approximate religion. Read the recent works of A C Grayling for the details.

Decades ago I was warmly welcomed by an audience of humanists and chose bigotry as my topic. It did not go well. I insisted that few of us are entirely free of racism, that even the most progressive of us is tainted by a variety of bigotries — that what we do is recognise the problem and do our best to overcome it. Instantly. To prove the point I read from a list and asked the audience to honestly evaluate their responses to each word.

Jew. Aborigine. Homosexual. Communist. Trade Unionist. Catholic. Disabled. Feminist. You get the idea — and you'd have sensed the flinching as my overwhelmingly left-wing audience had to acknowledge an inconvenient truth — that their hatred of bigotry required the instantaneous repression of the pollution buried deep in their minds. Each word had its pejorative halo — to which we reacted with a nano-second of shame. And overlaid with our evolved, considered, hard-won progressive views.

The problem of racism lies deeper than reactions to ethnicity or other people's religions. What we have to deal with is another ism. Difference-ism. I learned this in that cruellest of places, the primary school playground, where kids persecuted each other for being, among other things, refugees from war-torn Europe, dark skinned, shabbily dressed, fat, ugly, smelly, Catholic, eccentric. Anything, anyone different was a focus of hostility, all of it ignorant, much of it fearful. I remember with profound shame the way we 'picked on' a child with Down Syndrome.

(Only the beautiful people — and they came in the form of the school's sporting elite — were exempt from one form or another of bullying. They were treated with the awe due celebrities.)

We cannot escape childhood conditioning, with what comes with our era and the territory — with mother's milk or father's prejudices. The hostility to the 'other' is ancient, hard-wired, a part of our evolutionary heritage. I asked the humanists to understand this — and not to treat bigots as alien or evil. That never helps. We must acknowledge that few of us are saints, free of taint. Even Gandhi saw bigotry within himself.

In the earliest stages of human existence the fearful reaction to anything 'other' was, like fight or flight, part of the survival kit. Countless thousands of years later it represents the greatest threat to survival. Tribalism is no longer cohesive. It is destructive. Human progress, hope itself, is now measured in our ability to obey the first principle espoused by major faiths and those of us without faith. Do unto others. The paradox is that in a globalised world, of instant connectivity and protestations of the importance of 'human rights' we see a retreat into tribalism, ultra-nationalism, sub-cultural enclaves and strident religious intolerance. It's hard not to surrender to fear of the 'other' especially when some of that fear is justified, even orchestrated. Tolerance is being tested by the behaviour of the intolerant. All the more reason to reason.

We've got a lot better at dealing with difference. Disabled people are no longer feared and shunned. Gay people are increasingly accepted. Reconciliation is still making progress. But in our treatment of boat people? The White Australia policy lingers on; ruthlessly exploited for political advantage. Time to listen to Lincoln and appeal to the better angels of our being.

Wisdom

June 15, 2013

NOW EVERYONE KNOWS everything. And they know it instantly. Compliments, or curse, of Google.

You want to know something? You Google it. Or ask Siri. Or Wikipedia. No need to waste time, money or effort on primary, secondary or tertiary education. No need to turn heavy pages. As long as you've a smart phone you're smart. It endows you with a sort of universal all-purpose PhD. You are suddenly a promethean polymath like Barry Owen Jones. You are rendered omniscient, god-like.

Not so long ago only the foolish, the pompous, the deluded and a few members of MENSA thought of themselves as well-informed. Now everyone's an effing genius. There was a time 1 concluded that the best definition of wisdom was knowing what you didn't know. And given how little I knew in the A to Z of knowledge, from archaeology to zoology, about aardvarks or Zaporizhzhya, I felt very wise indeed. Maths, languages, biology, chemistry, football (all codes), poetry and both classical and popular musics are but a few subjects of which my ignorance is not so much blissful as abysmal. I am, to this day, painfully aware that I know at most 0.00000001% of what there is to know on any topic. Having left school at 15 I remain properly in awe of anyone who's studied anything anywhere. Which is why

I get so many professors on my wireless program — some of whom have spent decades studying something as tiny as atoms or ants.

Hawke's Minister of Science, the aforementioned Barry Jones set up an outfit (with the Orwellian name of the Commission for the Future), to build bridges between science and the community. He asked me to be its Chair, confident in the knowledge that while I had very little knowledge I'd considerable curiosity. (We tackled, as our first task, the unheard-of topic, 'the greenhouse effect'. Forty years and umpteen name changes later that bridge is now in dangerous disrepair. At our first meeting, a British scientist made an important utterance — which remains a favourite aphorism.

Data isn't information. Information isn't knowledge. Knowledge isn't wisdom.

Consider those wise words. We drown in data. Everything is measured, weighed, rendered statistical. But data is dumb. Unless you think about it, study it, connect it, it's just digital dross. Only then does it become information. And information needs to be processed, value-added, if it's to make it to the next level. But even knowledge isn't much use unless and until it becomes that rarest of elements, wisdom. (Oddly enough I've known humans unburdened by data etc, who've been innately wise — like the farmer grandfather who raised me, but that's a different issue.) We're talking a lot of hard work.

Or were. Now we have all the data, information and knowledge in our pocket, ready to be pulled out like rabbits from a magician's topper. It's too easy. And it gives the illusion of knowing without the need to know anything. No study, no effort, no value-adding of our own. Thank you

Google, Siri, Wikipedia, with your magicians' algorithms.

I'm not saying it isn't remarkable, because it is. Wholly. However the gain involves a profound loss. The loss of earning our learning. It doesn't even require real curiosity. If anything it destroys it. Before you've asked the question, or questioned your own mind, trying to make connections and work it out, you've got the answer. In one ear — or eye — and out the other. You have the data, information and knowledge. But wisdom? It's like refusing to study and cheating in the exam.

Curiosity, the need to question and understand, makes humans human. I suppose being sufficiently curious to ask your iPhone is something. But it's not enough. All learning involves pain. Fall over, you learn about gravity. Burn a finger, you learn about heat. Perhaps iPhones could give us a small electric shock!

Masked men

July 7, 2013

WHAT'S HAPPENING? Masked men are gazing down. Am I a character in a comic? Being studied by Batman and The Lone Ranger? Or am I a hostage in a heist? Neither nor. I realise I'm in familiar territory. An operating theatre. Been in dozens lately, in a variety of hospitals. This time I'm a martyr in the Mater, an atheist at the tender mercies of the nuns.

The first masked man is Mark, a maestro in the dark arts of anesthesia. Dr Rebecca Adams, my psychiatrist daughter, tells me that of all the callings, anesthetists are the most prone to suicide but thus far Mark seems quite cheerful. Let us hope I won't be the cause of any professional disappointment triggering serious depression.

The other mask masks Michael who's about to carry out not one but two surgical procedures. After ten years of intense and constant pain and a decreasing ability to tango I've surrendered to the chop. Hip ops. Not one but two. Hip ops in stereo. Sounds like I'm about to ghetto-blast an African American idiom.

Michael tells me he's performed this procedure 3000 times — and that over 40,000 per annum are carried out in Australia. A vast wobbling, hobbling army, a democracy of the dilapidated. But very few of us opt for two ops at once. Double the pleasure, double the fun.

Instantly, magically, it's six or seven hours later and I'm in ICU. More masks, including the missus. I assume the trance-like quality comes from the spinal injection that Mark mentioned, plus some morphine. (When you're on a good thing, stick to it. No, that's Mortein.) I'm back in the world of the horizontal, staring up at roof tiles, fluorescent lights and nurses' nostrils.

Days in delirium pass — and I'm trundled into another ward where the C isn't quite as I'd like, as I'm still awoken every few minutes for tests — or to be trolleyed off 'to imaging', to check for clots or demonic possession. No nuns in sight — as with St Vinnie's, the other Catholic hospital with which I'm painfully (literally) familiar, the Sisters of Mercy are rarely seen. The nursing is secular and spectacularly multi-ethnic — and one and all are worthy of sainthood.

Another shift. To Rehab. This is very Roman Catholic. Straight out of the Spanish Inquisition. Here's where I'm punished for my atheism and being rude about Cardinal Pell with racks and pulleys and other instruments of torture. I try and tweet a message to Amnesty or the Human Rights Commission. I fail to organise a mutiny amongst my fellow sufferers. It's an S and M parlour, and physiotherapist, Alison, is my dominatrix.

Two weeks pass. And I've been promoted from the Zimmer to crutches to walking sticks. And while I become very attached to my tormentors (a variation on the Stockholm Syndrome) it's time to leave. For Wolper, a Jewish hospital nearer home.

And if you think the Catholics are tough — you haven't been in the Wolper. It's like a kibbutz during the Six Day War. With a hint of the Mississippi slave era. (Tote that barge, lift that bale!) And I'm going to be here for three days a week for months. Yes, I know, I know. They're being cruel to be kind. They're only trying to help. It's for my own good. But I'm starting to wish that I'd had Michael fit me with Shepherd's castors or skate boards rather than these internal prosthetics. I'd even settle for a billy-cart like Porgy. Then I could be out of here.

Having converted to Catholicism I'll now offer to convert to Judaism. Or is there a Hindu hospital? Or one run by Buddhists? Buddhists are supposed to be gentle. I'll convert to anything that offers me more T in the LC. Or more Morphine.

Physio

July 20, 2013

PROMISE THIS IS THE last time I'll mention my post-operative saga, but it's really been pretty funny. If you can stand the pain.

It comes in two varieties, terrestrial and aquatic. The former began in a Catholic hospital and involves a more or less conventional gym with machines based on the researches of the Roman church during the Inquisition, with recent innovations from Guantanamo.

You are first placed on the rack to be stretched and tied in a variety of knots. I confessed all my sins immediately, including many I've only read about in the Marquis de Sade, but this did nothing to placate my tormentors. I invented the names and home addresses of everyone in ASIO and ASIS — and ID'd all the Communists in the ABC's senior management. When this served only to inspire more ingenious torments I blurted out military secrets including troop dispositions and Eisenhower's plans for the D Day Landing. Once again, my cooperative cowardice brought me no respite.

So I checked out and tried the Jews. Imagine my shock when I discovered the Wolper hospital has even more elaborate terrestrial tortures — plus the aforementioned aquatic variant for all sorts of spirit-dampening, up to and including water-boarding.

Trying to get on friendly terms from the outset I revealed Heisenberg's work on the German A-bomb. But did this lead to gentler treatment? No. It led to being strapped into the Heath Robinsonian machines you see advertised in insomnial info-commercials on TV. Machines you're meant to pedal with your useless appendages, with giant weights you're meant to lift. Not just once but hundreds of times. Sisyphus, stop complaining. Compared to this you're a sook.

But now the narrative reaches its climax. In the hydro-therapeutic pool. A human variation on what goes on at Sea World. Into its not-very-depths we dilapidated old buggers descend. If it wasn't a Jewish hospital you might think it was for a mass and belated baptism. (I say old because we are. The oldest of us in one particular immersion was 95.) Once therein the perfectly formed hydrotherapists — whose health is both wildly exaggerated and an affront — take command. We are expected to do tricks, like arthritic seals.

There are lots of cheerfully coloured floaty things from buoyant dumb-bells to foam sausages. There are rubbery inflatables for necks and arms and legs. It all looks so innocent — and so much nicer than the gym with its grim gadgetry. But this is no kindie. Soon you find yourself being Gitmo'd.

You get chummy with your fellow sufferers and com-pare your war wounds: Right knee, left knee, this hip, that hip. I'm 'bi-lateral' — had two hips done at once — which is deemed heroic or insane, but does give me some status. I use this to have myself elected as spokesperson for the downtrodden. I demand that, like the seals, dolphins and whales at Sea World, we be rewarded. If we get the trick right they should toss us a sardine.

Despite my complaints I must admit that, by the end of the session, one does feel somewhat chirpier. Whereas the forces of gravity press down on you in the upstairs gym, here in Wolper's warm waters, you've the advantage of buoyancy which takes the weight off your appendages. Indeed it's so congenial you wonder why life crawled onshore from the oceans in the first place. And understand why the whales changed their minds and crawled back.

Reffos

July 29, 2013

PEOPLE HAVE BEEN seeking sanctuary in holy places from the dawn of history. Their entitlement to do so were recognised by the Ancient Greeks and Egyptians, though it was Good King Ethelbert of Kent who first codified the right to seek asylum in 600 AD. Fast forward to Joseph and Mary in the manger and Quasimodo in the bell tower of Notre Dame. And to the all-too-few Jews people-smuggled from the Nazi's human abattoirs.

Not all refugees cross national borders. In the US victims of the dust bowl and, more recently, Hurricane Katrina — like the millions dispossessed by our interventions in Iraq and the slaughters in Syria — were detritus in their own countries. Think of the history of the Palestinians.

And the GFC has countless 'economic refugees' (a new expression of contempt to add to 'illegals' or 'queue jumpers') on the move, seeking somewhere, anywhere to get a job. Soon their numbers will be drowned by the tidal movements of environmental refugees, driven from their homes by climate change, as rising waters slowly submerge Bangladesh and the Pacific Islands, and by the dispossession caused by drought.

It takes a lot to force people to abandon their homes, villages, cultures. It takes policies of 'ethnic cleansing' and genocide. From an English decision to evict the Scots from their highlands to the machetes of Rwanda and butcheries of the Balkans. Or the simple crop failure of the Irish potato famine. Such unwilling migrations are central to human history and are destined to increase by orders of magnitude in this century. Judging by recent Australian behaviour the world will fail utterly to cope.

For the past twenty years Australians, whose problems with refugees are vanishingly small in the scheme of things, minuscule, have allowed themselves to be panicked and politically herded by politicians into a very dark place. Pauline Hanson fired the starting pistol — and off they went. The Libs, the Nats, and to its eternal shame, the ALP. Turning elections into auctions where each party leader tried to outbid the other in cruelty and stupidity.

For decades we'd kept people of the wrong colour out of this country with a pre-emptive form of ethnic cleansing known as White Australia. In the late sixties and early seventies we decided that we were tolerant — proclaimed that as our national virtue — and scrapped the poisonous policy. Only to bring it back again in our incremental responses to 'boat people'; a term that can be applied to every non-indigenous Australian in this democracy of diasporas.

Howard won his 'dark victory' election after Tampa by throwing compassion overboard — helped by Peter Reith, slandering asylum seekers as terrorists and baby-drowners. Now Abbott wants to repeat electoral history — with shameful rants about a few desperate families being the greatest threat to Australian security since WW2 — one requiring a military response with its own 'three-star general' heading some gimcrack Joint Chiefs. Turn back the boats? What next?

Sink them? Only to find Rudd outbidding him in the auction. Two leaders who make much of their Christianity are advocating policies that would have Jesus, that brown-skinned Middle Eastern, behind the razor wire.

Since Beasley tossed in the towel over Tampa, Labor's history on refugees has been disgraceful. People forget that Latham wanted to out-Ruddock Ruddock — as did Gillard. And now Rudd. Thus continuing to exaggerate the phoniest crisis in our political history — handing over the governing of this country to shock jocks. Reds under the bed? Now it's browns in boats.

Every religious teaching, every ethical precept, every iota of common sense, tells us we're behaving badly. Yet where are the protests from church and synagogue? Where are the leaders willing to risk unpopularity by proclaiming this simple truth? That our approach to the boat people is brutal, bigoted and absolute bullshit.

1988 in the shade

August 7, 2013

JANUARY 1ST 1988. The Australian Bicentennial begins. I'm standing alone in the desert with Uluru looming in the background as only Uluru can loom, waiting for my cue from genius director Peter Faiman, sitting in his air-conditioned HQ in Sydney. It will be my task to utter the opening words for *Australia Live*, the biggest one-off television show in history.

(Not only Australia's. Anyone's. As far as I know it still holds the record for duration and locations: about a hundred across the continent and the world. And off the world — given that there'd be a cut to the Soviet cosmonauts orbiting in their space station. The gargantuan effort was simultaneously broadcast by the ABC, SBS and Nine, by Channel 4 in Britain and across the US.)

While it was a great honour to be recruited, (all the more because the Pitjantjatjara people had asked me to speak on their behalf) it was hellishly hot. As my brain melted I dimly recall taking issue with the Bedouin. They might know the desert better than most but they're wrong about wearing black. My habitual attire wasn't helping.

If Peter didn't give me the word soon there wouldn't be any words, just the entirely appropriate image of another out-of-place whitefella expiring, like Leichhardt and Burke and Wills. In October 1985 this awesome place, as central to Australia as the hub of a wheel, and certainly central to our cultural imaginings, had been 'handed back' to its original owners. The decision was greeted with hostility at the time — a low-flying aircraft violated the ceremony — but I wanted the Bicentennial audience to understand why this place was a profoundly appropriate place to begin a great Australian birthday party.

You couldn't get a better bloke than young Faiman to produce and direct it. Amongst many other epics Pete'd go on to make *Crocodile Dundee* and direct the opening and closing ceremonies of the Sydney Olympics. Had he been around at the time — and hadn't been Jewish — Leni Riefenstahl would have booked him for the Nuremberg Rallies and I'm sure the Vatican is currently trying to contract him for the Second Coming.

We'd had a lot of fun working on the project, a sort of vast relay. If I survived the opening, the baton would pass to a caped Geoffrey Robertson striding along the dock in Liverpool from whence the First Fleet had departed — and he'd hand the narrative on to Graham Kennedy, George Negus, Clive James, Ray Martin, Jana Wendt, Julie Anthony, etc; all the usual criminals — and on to Thursday Island, the Lodge, Kakadu and the Indian Pacific train, somewhere in the hinterland. With a cheery 'goodonyer' from remote Kingoonya, population 6. Equally challenging, a live cross to the Davis Base in the Antarctic.

Peter and I both had a crack at writing birthday greetings from Reagan, Thatcher, HM, the Pope and a plethora of national and international leaders. (How many can boast that on their CVs?) I'd like to think that Reagan and Thatcher mouthed my words, but distinctly remember the Queen preferred Peter's.

The Pitjantjatra people agreed to grant a long-term lease for tourism — conditional on the theme-park climbs of the rock being stopped. They haven't. There've been strip-tease dances atop the rock — and a golf match. So much for cultural sensitivities. Perhaps by the Tricentennial?

Water water everywhere

August 23, 2013

H$_2$O IS HOT STUFF. Despite its abundance it's our most precious resource. And soon we'll be fighting wars over it. Meanwhile there's a war ON water, as if human beings were determined to destroy it. And ourselves.

Yet our parched planet is so awash in water. The oceans, like our bodies, are full of it — 71% of the Earth isn't. It's the wet stuff. And the air has oodles too — another sea of moisture hovers around and over us whether we're in those steamy tropics or standing on a sand dune in the Sahara without a cloud in the sky.

Let's remind ourselves of the statistics: 96.5% in seas and oceans; 1.7% in groundwater; 1.7% in rapidly diminishing glaciers and ice-caps; 0.001% as clouds and vapour. Of the grand total only 2.5% of the total is fresh. And soon half the human population will be facing 'water-based vulnerability'. As a farmer who's lived through many a drought I know what that's like — and 70% of fresh water used by our species goes on agriculture.

Australians have a long history of wasting water. Take our cattlemen in the arid regions where there are, or were, underground aquifers. Fossil water of perfect purity. So apparently inexhaustible that we got it to surge to the surface for stock to drink — and wasted 99% of it. We were as reckless with our crops, using flood irrigation instead of cautious, careful targeting. We let vast amounts evaporate in open channels. The devastation of the Murray Darling tells that tragic story.

Most farmers have learned the lesson. As water gets more expensive we've become miserly. The trees in our orchards are now watered drop by drop. We increasingly care for our rivers and pump more sparingly from them. But where we farm, in the Upper Hunter, our best efforts are literally undermined by the ever encroaching coal mines. The thirstiest of industries — though now challenged by the CSG cowboys — have carte-blanche from government to expand in all directions no matter what the damage to streams and aquifers. Thousands of applications to open, or expand mines are being pushed through, ICAC revelations notwithstanding. And the coal trains thunder night and day down the Valley to Newcastle, the world's biggest coal port and destined to be doubled in size; exporting climate change to the wider world.

I find it odd to have common cause with Alan Jones — but we both fear the arrival of the CSG juggernaut at thousands of farm gates. The unprecedented onslaught on underground water of fucking fracking has the same degree of government support as coal mining. Mining first, CSG second, farming (and vineyards and horse-breeding) a distant last. In the vanishingly rare case of an environmental court saying no to a mine or CSG invasion the NSW government immediately announcing check-mate legislation. Well, at least that support is 'transparent' — even if the transparency of water won't survive. But we'll have the advantage of using the kitchen tap as a gas service.

Wars over water will soon be more dangerous than wars over oil. Along major rivers flowing through nations — from the Niles to the Mekons — attempts will be made to harness and control the flows. With 70% of the world's population already facing 'water deprivation' the one flow that no one will be able to stop or dam will be the flow, the FLOOD of eco-refugees. Will the Carrs of the world attempt to dismiss them as 'economic refugees'?

Water is life. That's not a cliché but a simple and mighty truth. In this driest of continents few policies attempt to protect water while many collude in its waste and pollution. And few city voters seem to care. Count the pages in papers and magazines devoted to wine. Then find the odd paragraphs on water. Soon we'll be wanting to turn wine into water. It'll be more valuable.

Euthanasia

September 10, 2013

IN 2007 John Howard and Phil Ruddock were determined to ban a book — the first Australian book to be banned in this country for thirty-five years. It wasn't porn, or a naughty Norman Lindsay novel — his *Redheap* had been banned in the 1930s and remained forbidden until 1958. The seditious tome was Philip Nitschke's *The Peaceful Pill Handbook*, concerning voluntary euthanasia. Among moves planned by the government — a Suicide Related Material Offences Act that would make it a crime to use email, the Internet, Fax or phone to discuss the practical aspects of ending your life.

As part of the campaign to oppose what might be described as overkill, Philip organised a dinner for supporters at the National Museum — and I flew down to MC it. The audience, who'd filled a few buses, was the oldest I'd ever had. And, strangely, the happiest. There was nothing morbid about the evening, nothing self-pitying .We had a great night — a celebration of what they saw as their inalienable right to seek assistance in ending their life, if that was their decision.

So the so-called slippery slope isn't that slippery. Not everyone in the voluntary euthanasia movement chose assisted suicide. At the end many cling to life, despite everything. So why the cheerfulness in Canberra?

While we have no say in our conception or birth, millions of Australians believe that the final curtain is their business — that no religion or government is entitled to extend an intolerable life sentence. At the same time those of us who see Nitschke as an heroic crusader for dying with dignity do not want to make it compulsory. And we recognise the ethical dilemmas — that many doctors see even using the gentle skills of palliative care on a suffering patient, fear crossing the line — as do many nurses. Others do blur that line, at considerable legal risk.

Mercy killings — for example when a husband helps a beloved wife die — are viewed with sympathy in many courts. But there are other reasons — non-medical — for opting out. The surviving partner who doesn't want to live on alone may choose to die. However, the quadriplegic who's had enough, the ninety-year-olds who cannot see the point of lingering on when all their friends are dead, will not be helped by any proposed legislation. Nor can someone with dementia necessarily give us an informed decision. Even in Switzerland, one of the European nations with progressive policies, requires a patient to drink a life-ending draught themselves. So much for that slippery slope.

A few days ago, launching Philip's latest book — *Damned If I Do* — written in collaboration with Peter Corris, I realised how little has changed here — though even the US with its all-consuming religiosity, has moved ahead. (The laws in Oregon and Ohio are impressive.)

It is not a left-right issue. The conservative NT leader Marshall Perron had legislation passed in 1995 — immediately provoking massive retaliation by Howard, who allowed Kevin Andrews' Euthanasia Laws Bill of 1996 to be debated, confident he had the numbers. Not in the community but in the parliament where the NO side had the backing of religious forces who were powerful politically, financially and organisationally. The YES side failed to unite. But were a conscience vote to be held in the Federal or State parliaments today? One that reflected community views — victory for YES would seem assured. It's the same with drug laws where, it seems to me, the public is way ahead of the policy-makers (sic). Sadly politicians are afraid of speaking out.

We have a profound fear of death. We avert our gaze from it, preferring to have it denied by religion, defied by cosmetic surgery and delayed by medical science. All human civilisation derives from our awareness of mortality. It's time for the community to demand laws on voluntary euthanasia ... so that it becomes a human right.

Burning bunsens

November 7, 2013

"NO, YOU'RE ALL wrong," the scientist said quietly. "The readings I see in my lab every day show a far, far greater danger."

It's 1985 and I'm sitting in the middle of a long table, having dinner with a group of Australia's most distinguished scientists. It looks very Last Supper and I've asked a last supperish question. "How will our world end — with a bang or a whimper?"

A few years earlier, attending a CSIRO conference, I'd discovered that scientists are so fiercely focused on their own research that they're often ignorant of what the team in the next laboratory is doing. This proved to be the case that unforgettable night under the Shine Dome that looms in Canberra like the UFO mother ship in 'Close Encounters' — the HQ of the Australian Academy of Science.

One by one each tribal elder had given me his apocalyptic vision, each mutually exclusive, though there'd been general agreement that the threat of nuclear war was slightly exaggerated: "Cities levelled, millions dead, but humanity would soldier on."

After the mushroom clouds came 'the giant mouse' and there was a collective mutter of concern. While Genetic Modification was yet to gather its head of steam, it seemed a very superior rodent had been produced and augured a very superior human. Imagine supermen with far higher IQs, disease resistance and vastly increased life-spans. They would quickly take over, rendering us redundant. I recall the scientist saying sadly, "But they might keep some of us on. As house-hold pets."

We were thus intervening in the evolutionary process at our considerable risk — though the next voice tried to eclipse that danger with a variation on the theme.

"It's not flesh-and-blood we should worry about. It's the computer and Artificial Intelligence."

As we passed the brandy he outlined an alternative future where, once again, by interfering in the slow process of evolution that had moved with fits and starts over immense stretches of Deep Time, we were doomed to put ourselves out of business. Artificial Intelligence would so quickly outstrip our own that we'd be left in the dust of history. Cognitive conscious self-replicating machines would not only take over the planet but the cosmic neighbourhood. Out of the bottle the genie of AI would spread through the universe.

And so it went, an evening of apocalyptic scenarios and argument — all silenced by the final contributor. "No, you're all wrong." And he spoke of the here and now, not the tomorrow.

"My colleagues all over the world are seeing it loud and clear on their dials; the steady increase of CO_2 in the atmosphere. At this rate the planet will be uninhabitable in a century."

He told us of something called the Greenhouse Effect. Known since the 19th century and now kicking in. It was, of course, entirely new to me, and to most of his colleagues. We listened silently while he explained what was happening, why it was happening and what would happen.

And one by one the giant mice and thinking machines seemed less urgent threats and the group agreed. This was it. The big one.

The dinner had been convened to help make decisions for the Commission for the Future, designed to build bridges between scientists, citizens and politicians in the hope of framing long-term policies in a world subject to the short-term plans of the election cycle. What should be our agenda?

Now, unequivocally, we had one. And we still do. The crisis darkens, deepens. The Greenhouse Effect has long since given way to Global Warming and to Climate Change. Little changes.

The prism

November 18, 2013

ECTOMORPH, endomorph, mesomorph. Symbolised by a straight line, a circle and a triangle, the terms describe basic human shapes. Tall and skinny versus round versus broad-shouldered and narrow-waisted. We all fit somewhere, and according to the argument our lives have predictable consequences — favouring the mesomorphs.

For many years I've used a similar notion when thinking about politicians, thanks to a view vouchsafed by Tony Benn. Benn famously gave up his aristocratic title to become a Labour MP and working-class hero. Whilst being a burr beneath the saddle of Tony Blair, Benn found time to explain his theory.

All politicians, irrespective of party, political system or time in history, come in one of three categories: Straights, fixers and maddies. The definitions are not as judgemental as you might think. Straights might be dull, but they can also be decent and do a good job. Fixers might be drawn to backroom deals in smoke-filled rooms but they can be the most professional and successful members of the political profession. And maddies, despite being dangerous, are the ones that shake things up, even changing history.

A few examples: John Major was as straight as they came, as was John Cain in an Australian context. Boats might not have been rocked or barricades stormed but they tried to run clean governments.

Fixers? The fixer's fixers were Eddy Obeid and Graham Richardson — in the sleazy tradition of America's Tammany Hall. Neville Wran was probably the most successful fixer of modern Premiers — and the portrait of Honest Abe in Spielberg's *Lincoln* was the greatest fixer in Presidential history.

Maddies range from Napoleon to Thatcher, and tend to be the most exhilarating and transformative of leaders. Though looking very straight Maggie's mate, Reagan, was mad enough to help end the Cold War. (Gorbachev, whom I spent some quality time with, was a fixer — a fixer who broke things including the Soviet Union.) I once described Keating as a maddie and got a phone call from the Lodge. Far from abusive, Paul purred.

Let's do some allocating.

Doc Evatt was a magnificent maddie as, of course, was Gough. As an ACTU fixer, Hawke was a fixer as PM. This did not stop Bob making dramatic policies, but they were driven by maddie Keating.

Like Hawke, Gillard had had a career as a negotiator before being an MP — and was a fixer as PM. Not that her attempts at fixings were wildly successful — and the fact that she 'fixed' Rudd would begin a downward spiral for Labor that the maddest maddie would admire. But first and foremost, a fixer.

I regard Rudd, whom I've known well for years, as a straight, though he can justifiably claim to have fixed the GFC. Those who demonise him as a maddie do so in an attempt to justify their coup.

Howard is hardest to slot. With the appearance of a straight and a fixer's rat-cunning he proved to be mad as a hatter when it came to foreign policy. He incessantly urged mega-mad Bush into invading Iraq, leading to the greatest disaster — and death toll — of the 21st century. He took us into that other bloody farce of Afghanistan and his role on refugees remains unspeakable.

Clinton? A fixer. Whereas Barack Obama arrived as a magical maddie intent on transformation. But his presidency has all but died under the onslaught of the Tea Party's certifiable maddies.

Christmas

November 19, 2013

WE DO NOT comment on operational matters. Nor is our primary concern illegals who arrive by air. However, we will choose who comes to our country — and the shooting down of Father Christmas was fully justified.

Though the Abbott government remains mindful that the Rudd-Gillard-Rudd regime did great damage to Indonesian relations with its sudden cessation of beef exports, we cannot countenance the illegal importation of reindeers. The animals employed by Mr Christmas flaunt quarantine regulations and may well have carried exotic diseases. (One of the downed animals was suffering from a serious case of Red Nose, which veterinarians agree might well have imperilled our valuable venison industry.)

No flight plans had been registered with Australian aviation authorities. The rules that apply to Qantas, Virgin and other carriers had been airily ignored by Mr Christmas, who left his Arctic base without advising any of the nations whose airspace he proceeded to violate. Apologists for the late Mr Christmas argue that his flights were, like the habits of Indonesian fishermen, both ancient and traditional, and predate international protocols. But this was not a risk your government was willing to take.

We were also concerned to protect our kiddies from a possible paedophile. Mr Christmas's use of the honorific 'Father' alerted us to this possibility, particularly when no major religion or religious order would confirm an association. ASIO investigations, linking to Interpol files, indicate that this 'Father' has a long history of making contact with vulnerable young children and often sits them on his knee — and seeks to offer them gifts.

Let us now deal with the politics. That Christmas fellow constantly repeated "ho ho ho" echoing the leftist chants of "ho ho ho Chi Minh", alerting us to the fact that this present-smuggler reeks of ideology.

Take his appearance. Modern facial recognition technology shows us that the late Father Christmas was, in fact, Karl Marx. Though presumed dead and buried in Highgate Cemetery, it seems likely that Mr Marx lived on, presumably preserved by the same Soviet technicians who preserved, less successfully, Lenin in Red Square. We believe that lessons learned from the failure to resurrect Lenin were applied to Marx for the purpose of a global effort to market Bolshevism.

If true, and this government believes that remote possibilities are invariably true, consider this scenario. A man in a red-alert red suit (not blue or green or any other primary colour) circumnavigates the planet handing out 'free' gifts, a clearly socialistic or communistic activity — one that undermines the efforts of retail stores to sell them.

This form of distribution bypasses the GST and undermines not only Coles, Myers, Grace Bros, Woolies and Harvey Norman but your government's ability to fill the Rudd-Gillard-Rudd black hole and balance the budget. This is Vladimir Putin waging economic war on the West.

Lt's true that our attempts to listen in to Father Christmas's mobile phone were thwarted — presumably by highly sophisticated shielding technology passed on to Putin by Edward Snowden. (Snowden? Snow? We believe that to be another clue.) Nonetheless circumstantial evidence supports our hypothesis.

In summary: a paedophile communist — and they're the worst sort — intent on undermining our community values had, like the boats, to be stopped. The drones took him and his diseased deer, out. This is the sort of strong action for which the Abbott government has a clear mandate.

Finally we would point out that Father Christmas camouflages his real motives by identifying himself with the birthday of our Lord. And that's another reason he had to die.

Happy Christmas.

Cowvent Garden

February 27, 2014

SKULLS ARE AMONGST the most powerful symbols of mortality. Take warning from the skull and crossbones. Secret societies at Ivy League Unis have the likes of George W. Bush swearing oaths upon them. Alas poor Yorik, says Hamlet, holding one in his hand. Skulls galore appear in classic portraits — as when Saint Jerome contemplates one in a famous daub of Rembrandt's. Bronze skulls weigh down the Hapsburg tombs.

But I was inspired by the Roman tomb of countless dead monks whose skeletal remains are arranged into giant-size mosaics, when deciding to create a large artwork from the skulls of dead cattle; which an old farm like ours has aplenty.

Deaths over a dozen decades — from falls off cliffs, snakebite, altercations between bulls and other natural causes, though some skulls have bullet holes. My bullets. The saddest job ever, shooting cattle during one of the worst droughts — animals too weak to truck out. In any case, nowhere to truck them.

A young friend made a couch (a cowch?) from the huge bones of a beast. Though not particularly comfortable his spectacular piece of furniture would've been perfect for some pagan despot to recline upon — perhaps Caligula or Nero, whilst thumbs-downing gladiators. Whereas Picasso saw things differently, wittily transforming a bicycle seat and handlebars into the head of a bull ...

... while my three-year-old daughter; Rory, an enthusiastic collector, did exactly the opposite to Pablo, memorably and triumphantly emerging from a gully, holding the horns of a skull as if riding a tricycle.

Rory and I collected them for years, mostly cattle, though with the odd (and more elegant) skulls of horses for variety. Plus small skulls of roos, feral pigs and the occasional goat. But it was mainly mooies. And when we had almost a hundred, the artwork began.

We'd found a small, steep natural amphitheatre in a hilly paddock a few miles from the homestead and started to arrange the skulls, row by row, as if their empty sockets were gazing at Ancient Greeks performing Oedipus Rex. It took us weeks, chipping away to make them comfortable. An artwork that very few would ever see, perhaps to be discovered by some future owners in an another dozen decades. That appealed to my archaeological interests, as did possible misinterpretations. A cow cult? Some Australian echo of the Egyptians' worship of the cow-headed Hathor or the Apis Bulls?

Proud of our efforts it was time to give our cowncert venue a name ... Cowvent Garden appealed. As did the Bullshoi Theatre ... and Cownegie Hall. Then there was the Sydney Myer Moosic Bowl.

But a tragedy occurred. The skulls, mostly revealed by a drought, were swept away in huge rains that broke it. As the river flooded and the dams, as cracked and empty as old ceramic bowls, filled and overflowed, water poured down the hill and swept the skulls into a long-dry creek bed. Some were carried for hundreds of yards. More were smashed into rocks or each other, breaking like eggshells. All finished up buried in mud. And then the amphitheatre itself was destroyed, collapsing in an avalanche.

Now Rory — Aurora — is grown up and far, far away. But the ghosts may be heard as I pass by.

I'm writing this at a time that reminds me of the Bullshoi — in the middle of another drought. And I saw a pair of horns sticking out of the baked silt in the gully. Were they the handlebars of Rory's tricycle?

Tic toc

March 21, 2014

TIME WASN'T ALWAYS so terrifying and tyrannical. Go back in time and near enough was good enough. The sun, moon and shadows were the only clocks humans had, apart from the clock within — the beating heart, measuring out their brief lives. But nobody was counting. Now there are quartz watches on every wrist, their tiny crystals oscillating 32,768 times a second.

For millennia we had no need or word for second, minute or year — though on a larger, slower scale there were the seasons. Nothing as abrupt as Daylight Saving, they changed gradually, predictably — and when agriculture arrived, with the need to prepare for planting — or as in Egypt an annual flood — the astronomers came into being. And the pace began to quicken.

I was raised on a small farm by a grandpa who ploughed our few acres with the help of a huge horse. The world outside was changing fast but Grandpa lived in much the same way as farmers had a thousand years before. Our only electrical appliance was the wireless — and we had a single clock, a cricket trophy, that Grandpa allowed me to wind.

For many centuries there'd only been a single clock in a farming village. A clock in a tower. And it had only a single hand, for the hours. Generations would pass until a minute-hand was added, and no town hall or church clock ever added a third hand, for the seconds. Then clocks became domesticated, or were dangled on the waistcoat or worn on the wrist and accuracy became an obsession, particularly with sea-going clocks needed to calculate latitude and longitude.

Like armies marching to the beat of drums, humans began to march to the tick of clocks, which seemed to accelerate. Now we measure time not by the slow swing of a pendulum or the spinning wheels of clockwork, but in nano-seconds, dividing a second into millionths. And we respond to this acceleration by living in a perpetual state of panic, forever demanding faster responses from smart phone or laptop, so that download times are a major political issue. And any delay causes stress that increases the heart and pulse rate. As we wait with frenzied impatience for the lights to change or for the lift to respond to that repeatedly, furiously jabbed button. Road rage has its echo in lift, light and download rage.

And the simpler, slower, quieter world of our little farm has vanished. The slow changing moods of my Grandpa's era are shattered by exposure to a kaleidoscope of emotions that hammer us from TV or computer screen, as images of sad, bad and mad news is interrupted by a barrage of ads with their hypermanic bullshit. And if that wasn't enough a constant parade of words, numbers and ideas march across the screen, distracting, overloading and confusing.

We are now bored, perhaps frightened, by silence. The quiet walk in the park demands buds in the ears, as does the concentration of study. The simple conversation has to be complicated with texting or tweeting. The assembly lines in our factories move ever faster — and so do the assembly lines of human life as we strive to keep pace with the robots, I-things and demands of ambition and employers. Everything accelerates. The time and motion studies of the mid 20th century, designed to speed up production, are now internalised. And what is achieved? A manic, panic society in which we all have attention deficit disorder and post traumatic stress syndrome. Not to mention multiple personalities.

But are we any better off? Anything we want to know can be instantly Googled, but are we any the wiser? My grandpa had virtually no education but what that simple, decent bloke gleaned from the newspaper, the wireless, experience and thought gave him real wisdom.

And he told the time by the sun.

Aphorism

April 28, 2014

A FEW WEEKS AGO Macquarie Uni was kind enough to give this doddery autodidact, whose brief and brutal education ended when he was fifteen, an Honorary Doctorate. "The closest I got to a tertiary education was going past Melbourne University on a Swanston Street tram," I said wistfully to the Vice Chancellor.

Failing to finish secondary education was one of three reasons I'd never dreamt of a uni education. The others? A total lack of encouragement in a family where university seemed as irrelevant as entering holy orders. And its unaffordability.

Protocol required that I say a few wise words to the hundreds of kids who'd worked long and hard and expensively for their degrees. I'll spare you the clichés. But the aphorism I used at the end, my favourite, seems worth sharing with anyone trying to continue his or her education, even if only attending the school of hard knocks.

The 20th century could take pride in two Pablos, both considered impossibly talented. While Pablo Picasso composed paintings, Pablo Casals composed and played music. Picasso's brushstrokes would create the most famous, angriest and unequivocal masterpiece of the century — Guernica, his response to the war crime when Franco had

Hitler bomb his own people — while the strokes of Casals' bow gave the world incomparable performances of Bach and original works dedicated to peace.

Both Pablos were born in the 19th century and lived for most of the 20th. Both hated Franco, chose life-long exile and lived very long lives. Casals, who'd played for Queen Victoria in 1899, was still around to be invited by Kennedy to play at his White House. Towards the end of his 97 years Casals was honoured with a press conference attended by much of Madrid's media.

This grumpy old man told the graduates at Macquarie what that grumpy old man said in Madrid. On reviewing his life and the woes and wars of the world he would, I'm sure, have repeated his belief that 'the love of one's country is a splendid thing — but why should love stop at the border?' ... and restated his conviction that 'each second we live is a new and unique moment of the universe that will never be again. And what do we teach our children? That two and two make four and that Paris is the capital of France. When will we also teach them what they are? We should say to all of them ... you are a marvel ... you are unique ... in all the years that have passed there has never been another child like you. Your legs, your arms, your clever fingers, the way you move ... And when you grow up, can you then harm another who is, like you, a marvel?' And then:

'You must work, we must all work, to make the world worthy of its children.'

But it was his final words that day that I made mine. Having cast a grandfatherly eye over the problems of humanity — so serious in all regards, with crises in the environment, in famine, in disease, financial inequality and human rights; Casals fell silent for a long moment, thinking about his bleak assessment. Then the aphorism. Two sentences that don't seem to fit together. In conflict with each other. Chalk and cheese. Yet they seem to me profound, the quintessence of wisdom.

'The situation is hopeless. We must take the next step.'

Beyond pessimism. Fatalistic, defeatist. And a clarion call to arms.

The kids at Macquarie face a future of both horrors and hope. We have not made a world worthy of our children. It is dominated by the unprecedented and slow motion catastrophe of climate change, and its denial. If we can defeat it the graduates will live in a world where disease can also be defeated, where the average lifespan will be longer than Casals'. We, and the kids, must take the next step.

Newspapers

June 20, 2014

SO SUDDENLY *The Australian* is fifty. Seems only yesterday. Apart from two brief departures — the first at the personal insistence of Rupert Murdoch, the second when lured to *The Age* by legendary editor, Graham Perkin — I've been here for most of that time. Watching the paper head in different political directions, surviving new brooms and pendulum swings.

How come I'm still around? Am I kept on out of sentiment? Has Chris Mitchell simply forgotten I'm here? Or do I demonstrate pluralism? Dunno. But I remain the Oz's licensed left-wing loony, continuing to enjoy an unusual degree of editorial independence.

Taking over from Perkin as *Age* editor, Creighton Burns warned me to reign in my 'tendency to vulgarity' ... or else. My response was to file a column on farting. When syndicated in the Adelaide 'Tiser, the *Courier Mail*, the Launceston *Examiner* and *Sydney Morning Herald*, I was frequently censored — mostly in the SMH. But in the Oz? Only once, decades ago, when I wrote a satire on a stable mate tabloid. That's not counting my sacking by Rupert, a story vividly recalled by John Menadue, his 2IC, in his biography.

But that wasn't political. Rupert had been mauled in an interview with David Frost, then king of British satire. Still seething on his return to Australia he asked then editor, Adrian Deamer if *The Australian* had any satirists. "Phillip Adams," said Deamer. "Sack him," said Rupert.

(That turned out pretty well. Following an unprecedented outcry from the readership, Deamer was permitted — required — to rehire me. I held out for twice the money!)

For years my columns for this paper raged against Ruddock's policies on refugees and the entire Howard government on everything, particularly the invasion of Iraq ... Not a word was altered. When disagreeing with the paper's line on an indigenous issue I had the odd experience of being attacked in an editorial — but I was never censored.

Many see my survival as improbable as the paper's — or our octogenarian proprietors'. More and more mastheads are filling fourth-estate cemeteries as headstones, or linger on in virtual form. Many I've written for have gone to God, amongst them *Nation, Broadsheet,* the *National Times, Nation Review, Australian Business,* Australian *Playboy* (they hired me to interview a young comedian called Paul Hogan) and *The Bulletin.* Other start-up newspapers — including a spectacular failure spawned by David Syme — have come croppers. But not the Oz.

Despite late-in-the-day flutters of interest from the likes of Warren Buffet and the odd internet oligarch investing in tottering US papers, or Melbourne's Morry Schwartz with his newie, *The Saturday Paper,* we will not see its like again.

My career in print began as an eleven-year-old paperboy doing billy-cart deliveries of the *Sun* and *Age* by dawn's early light, then flogging Heralds at night, dangerously weaving through heavy traffic to jump on and off moving trams. A little later — as a fifteen-year-old — I became a film critic for the Communist *Guardian.* At seventeen I started writing for the *Bulletin*, long before Sir Frank Packer bought it (later to be sacked by Donald Horne). But it was this paper that really got me started. Thanks to Bruce Petty persuading Deamer to give me a try — initially as the TV critic. When free-to-air networks seemed as permanent, as forever, as the thunder of the presses.

I was lucky to live and work through the good old days, the golden years when print was unchallenged in setting the political agenda — and as one of the new wave of opinion-ated pundits I benefited from the transition of newspaper to viewspaper. I've seen countless famous editors, by-lines, critics and cartoonists (often the most crucial contributors) come and go. So, after sixty-odd years as a paperboy, let me wish this paper an understandably sentimental Happy Birthday.

UN

June 29, 2014

UN FOR UNnecessary, UNcalled for, UNacceptable, UN-Australian.

I blame it all on that commo Evatt. Signing the UN Charter in 1945. Getting us involved with the UNited bloody Nations, when we already had the UNited States to look after us. What I don't get is why UNcle Sam allowed it to happen. UN-American.

Couldn't we get out of it? Say that Evatt acted without authority? Everyone knows the Doc was off his rocker. UNhinged.

It's caused us nothing but trouble. Take that bloody UNESCO with its World Heritage bullshit. Coming here and telling us what we can and can't bulldoze. Just when we were about to chain-saw half of Tasmania and ship it off for chopsticks, in come these UNreconstructed environmental thugs and stop us. We've an UNalienable right to wreak havoc and were going to leave a few hundred trees for the tourists. And UNESCO? Completely UNaccommodating.

And if they're not talking to the trees they're getting political with the polyps.

World Heritage? UNadulterated humbug. What's so great about the Barrier Reef? It's been a danger to shipping for centuries. Ask Captain Cook! All that cute, colourful coral ripping holes in hulls, damaging Australian trade. I wouldn't mind if it were somewhere out of the way, but for the polyps to plonk themselves in the middle of the shipping lanes? The sooner we've killed them off the better. Three cheers for dredging and crowns of thorn.

And as for that Human Rights crap! It's bad enough that some UN committee is always complaining about harmless water boarding — suggesting that enhanced interrogation is torture — or muttering about 'war crimes'. But then the buggers start complaining about the way we treat Abos or Reffos. For which we are entirely UNapologetic.

Take the reffo bizzo. This isn't party political! Beasley signed up after Tampa. Latham was as gung-ho as Ruddock. As was Rudd. And Gillard! Australians are UNited on these bloody queue-jumping, boat-smuggled illegals — and the UN keeps waving agreements that Evatt and other ratbags signed about the rights of refubloodygees.

Just because a thousand drown at sea or spend years behind razor wire in concentration camps (built, I might add, along the prestigious no-expense-spared lines of Clubs Med) where they go insane, self-harm, kill themselves or get murdered. OK, lots have been sheilahs and there's been a few hundred kids, but they're all crims, even if what they're doing is legal according to some shonky UN document we were tricked into signing when the implications were UNbeknownst to us. Who knew there might actually be some refugees?

It's that World Heritage-type crap all over again. Do-gooding, nanny-state, Bob Browny, green commo bastards. UNbloodybelievable.

And mark my words — that U bloody N will be pressuring us on that climate change bullshit soon. Who the hell do they think they are? Some sort of world govern-ment? It's bad enough having a High Court that sticks its nostrils in the reffo bizzo without a whole lot of foreigners, most of whom aren't white or Christian. And what about our overwhelming mandate?

As shown by the White Australia Policy, the Colombo Plan and World Series Cricket, Australia has a proud his-tory of racial tolerance. We're perfectly entitled to be bigots but we're not. As I said to Alan Jones on 2GB a few days back, while I'm not sorry about not attending Sorry Day, I've got a Nat King Cole CD, a Namatjira print in the office and I went to that commo Mandela's funeral. So to hear sug-gestions that there's even a hint of racism in the way we treat reffos is, quite frankly, quite hurtful — and I'm suing the ABC over UNhelpful and UNbefitting comments on *The Chaser* and *Q&A*.

On the next sitting day, we'll be announcing that the Abbott Government will be adding the United Nations to the list of terrorist organisations.

(UNedited transcript of speech by Foreign Minister.)

Open fire

July 18, 2014

CHOPPED FENCE POSTS, some dangling a few inches of rusted wire. Pieces of fossilised wood dredged from the river bed and left high and dry by the floods we used to have — too heavy to float and hard to burn. Chain-sawed chunks of boughs torn from trees by the hurricane of 2009. Bits of leftover timber from the repairs to sheds wrecked the same day, in the storm that caused more damage in ten minutes than the farm had suffered in a century.

As I ignite the kindling on this bitter winter night every piece of wood tells its story. I know the storytellers well. Having lugged them, sawn them or split them, it's sad to see them burn.

But with the smell of snow and in pain from the cold, it's them or me. As Oscar Wilde complained of the wallpaper in the hotel room where he lay dying, "One of us has to go!"

So the newspaper shrinks at the touch of the match, and the gum-leaves curl as the twigs flare and splutter. And soon the historic woods are ablaze, sending sparks showering, and smoke up the homestead's two-storey chimney in this first fire of the season. Only to be promptly regurgitated. Fifty feet up the flue's blocked by an abandoned bird's nest. It takes minutes to smoulder and tumble down, half an hour for the smoke to clear from the room.

Finally I can look into the jewel-box of the fire, into the flames of many colours, from reds and russets to opal blues. Humans have known this for hundreds of thousands of years, ever since they learned to create and control fire. Every bit of burning wood burns differently.

Lose the skill to kindle fire and you were dead. Humans not only needed its glow to survive, reliant both on its heat and its power to frighten off predators, but also looked deep into this primordial ancestor of the plasma telly. Wherein we first dreamed our dreams.

This first entertainment would become our first science. We learned to burn the landscape before it burned us. Burning fires in the sand would lead to the fusion of its grains into glass, would teach us how to melt ores and make and mould metal. Fire took us from the Stone Age to the ages of pottery, bronze and iron — and would lead us to ignite nuclear fires for bombs and the bottled fire of electricity.

But tonight's fire is from an age of innocence. Fire to flare, to cast shadows, to toast bread on long wire forks. A direct descendant of the fires in Altamira where, so many thousands of years ago, artists created murals as great as any of the Renaissance — their flickers animating the flight of painted animals on the walls of the caves. Our first movies.

Tonight's fire creates more than heat and images. It appeals to other senses as well as the imagination. Like smell. Not only do woods burn in different colours, but each has its own odour, not necessarily fragrant (Iron bark's no Chanel No. 5). In an open fire of many ingredients, the perfumes fight for dominance. Like cheeses in a deli.

In the morning, with only a few red coals glowing in the grey, there's only one smell. From the scents of energy to the apathy of ash. And as I rake it out, an archaeological find: the few inches of barbed wire freed from the ancient fence post. Ashes to ashes.

There are easier ways to keep warm. With gas or an electric radiator. But nothing comes close to the open fire. Complex, labour intensive and messy, coating everything in the room (including one's lungs) with its dust. But I love the ritual. I throw on another log and prod it with the poker.

It's been hard
to laugh lately

August 1, 2014

WHAT WITH GAZA, MH17, Syria, ASIS, AIDS, Ebola, child molestation, genital mutilation, Libya, the Nigerian abductions, Manus and Christmas Island and even Rolf Bloody Harris, laughter languishes. It cannot provide its best medicine.

I once despised those disinclined to read the papers or watch the news. These days I sympathise. As the MSM competes with social media our world's violence, from the domestic to the genocidal, is more in-your-face than ever before. Everything everywhere is on Candid Camera, but who can smile? Let alone laugh.

Yet laughter is evolution's attempt to provide an antidote to the pain and problems of existence. Up to and including mortality itself. You can't defeat death, but you can laugh at it. Mock the Reaper. Remember Heller's *Catch 22? M*A*S*H?* History records there was even dark humour in the death camps.

When introducing *our Penguin Book of Australian Jokes* I argued that laughter is born as a sudden detonation of breath, as a release of fear — citing the ancient and familiar ritual of a dad tossing his baby into the air — and hopefully catching it. On the way up the child fills its lungs to protest, to cry in terror — only to issue a relaxing, relieving gasp when it escapes the force of gravity. The first laugh of a lifetime.

And we keep laughing, or trying to, in defiance of all that frightens or threatens for the rest of our lives. We laugh at what we dislike or dread, at those things that make us anxious. That's why we've so many jokes about sex (itself a joke, evolution having a laugh at our expense), mothers-in-law and, yes, those unloved lawyers. New fears, new illnesses, produce new streams in humour. Consider the popular genre of Alzheimer's jokes.

Politicians are about as popular as piles. Introducing PM Keating at an Australian of the Year ceremony at Admiralty House I told a few anti-Paul jokes from the Penguin book. (He took it in good grace but Anita, like Queen Victoria was not amused.) And I made the point that jokes about pollies had long histories — that we'd found the anti-Keating jokes of the 1980s had their origins in anti-Hitler jokes told by comics in Munich in the early 30s — and they'd ended up in Dachau.

Other animals fear death as 'fight or flight' attests or as anyone who's heard pigs screaming in an abattoir cannot forget. And creatures from dogs to elephants can be seen to grieve. But humans are, as far as we know, the only creatures on Earth that comprehend the abstract idea of our own mortality — who dread the idea of ceasing to exist. We alone KNOW that we die. To dull the terror of what we perceive as eternal darkness we invent lives after death, but that primal knowledge remains universal and definitive, our blessing and our curse — motivating not only the creation of an infinite number of faiths but our art, music, medicine and science. Much of most human effort is an endless struggle to deny death, to defeat it, or at very least to delay it. And our fear of death drives our humour.

Few issues or events are beyond the reach of jokes. Hence the sick jokes about dead astronauts within hours of the explosion of NASA's Space Shuttle Challenger — or after 9/11. Sick jokes? Yes. But in an evolutionary sense their purpose is to protect our mental health. To laugh off the horrors.

At their worst jokes can be rancid with racism. When collating the Penguin book we found many jokes aimed at Aborigines — just as other cultures had produced jokes aimed at other racial targets. The Irish. The Polish. The Jews.

But at the moment the world seems to be holding its breath.

The Fiddler on
the Roof

September 11, 2014

THOUGH MY CRITICISMS of Israeli policies towards
the Palestinians have had me branded an anti-Semite in
both correspondence and the *Australian Jewish News*, I'm
more accurately described as a philo-Semite — someone
totally in awe of the Jewish contribution to human civilisation. This is out of all proportion to their small population
around the world — a population greatly reduced by the
Holocaust. Had that vast obscenity not occurred there'd be
many millions more Jews, both religious and secular, in the
diaspora. And far fewer in Israel.

As performers, the contribution of Jews to classical
music is incomparable. The fiddlers on the roof become
stars playing the Stradivarius at Carnegie Hall, the members of exalted string quartets and instrumentalists in the
noblest orchestras. (Though Simon Rattle told me that
when he took over the Berlin Philharmonic he was assured
it was "Jew free".) As composers Jews have been pre-emi-
nent — Mahler in the concert halls, Gershwin and Berlin on
Broadway. And Jewish contributions to Jazz is second only
to the African American.

Jews are equally conspicuous in literature. As with playing the violin, and dealing in diamonds, the ability to write a novel is portable —something very important to a people threatened for millennia by pogroms culminating in genocide. And it's endless fear and suffering that get the words — and music — pouring out.

Comedy too. Koestler described the Jews as 'the exposed nerve-ends of humanity' — and the paradox of pain producing humour has given us many, if not most, of the world's greatest humourists and comics. From Mo McCackie to the Marx Brothers and Mel Brooks, Lenny Bruce to Joan Rivers, Woody Allen, Peter Sellers, Jerry Seinfeld, Larry David, Sacha Cohen, Jon Stewart.

'Jewish humour' is so universally recognised that Chaplin, the most famous comedian who ever lived, was wrongly assumed to be Jewish — attacked as such by American anti-Semites. Knowing all too well the connections between misery and mirth, Chaplin declined to deny it.

(Hollywood itself was and remains a Jewish town, movies are a Jewish industry — energised by great and glorious talents fleeing persecution in Europe. In the Dream Factory Jews effectively dreamed America into existence.)

Science? You can sum it up in one word — Einstein. Who, fearful that Hitler would soon have the A-bomb urged FDR to build it first. Thus anti-Semitism hastened the nuclear age, the ultimate weapons created by Jews in the US — and as we'd later learn, in Stalin's Soviet. On the other side of the coin ... medical science. Almost all the doctors, specialists and surgeons who've been keeping me alive are Jews. Many being exiles from apartheid South Africa.

Despite Hitler branding modern art decadent and something else to blame on the Jews, they're under-represented in the visual arts. Not a lot of famous Jewish painters. (Chagall certainly and perhaps Modigliani?) Perhaps this is a consequence of a religious prohibition shared by both Jews and Muslims — the dogma disapproving of the depiction of God or Allah and of the 'grave image' in general. And I can't think of too many Jewish sporting heroes, if you leave out David's gold-medal skills with the sling-shot. Hard to think of a Jewish golfer on the US circuit — Jews weren't welcome in the posh golf clubs.

Footnote. This atheist christened (pun intended) his firstborn daughter with a Jewish name. Twenty years later, aiming to join that most Jewish calling of psychoanalysis, Dr Rebecca Adams travels to the US and converts to Judaism in a progressive synagogue. Whereupon my second daughter, Meaghan, discovered in an old family bible, that her Dad seems to have had a Jewish great-great-grandmother on his mother's side and is, as a result, almost certainly Jewish.

Now that this is public I predict my next criticism of Israel will have me called a 'self-hating Jew'.

Shalom.

The dealer

September 24, 2014

BEFORE BECOMING an antique, I used to buy them. Spent endless hours wandering in and out of the antique shops of Melbourne. And thinking back I realise that as well as collecting antique furniture, bric-a-brac and sundry tat, I also collected antique dealers. Almost all of whom were mildly or wildly eccentric.

In the heart of the antique district, up Malvern Road, was the most imperious of dealers who didn't like selling his things. His very posh, first-class things. Invariably ill-tempered he was rude to everyone. A snarl of 'not for sale' was his usual response to nervous enquiries. Which only made would-be customers all the more determined. No matter how preposterous the price. And if they succeeded in persuading him to accept payment, he'd decline to deliver. Weeks would run into months. Business boomed.

Some from that era survive, notably the wildest eccentric in antique annals, Armadale's Graham Geddes. Indeed my old friend may well be the most intriguing antiques and antiquities-dealer in the known universe. I say this based on personal experience from Los Angeles to London via Paris and Amsterdam.

The stock dazzles in its quality and eclecticism but you enter GG's premises at your own risk. If he doesn't like you he won't sell you the Ancient Grecian urn or the Indian soothsayer's cart. Or he might punish you by doing something strange to the asking price. Or by being physically violent. For example, I recall GG being annoyed by a particularly pompous customer and taking him by the scruff of the neck and giving him the bum's rush into Malvern Road. The customer was Melbourne's Lord Mayor.

Today, however, concerns a different dealer, now deceased, whose antiques were as unremarkable as they were overpriced. Godfrey. Not to be confused with a nearby retailer of vacuum cleaners. It was Godfrey's floorshow, not his furniture, his patter not his porcelain, that made me a regular.

As camp as the proverbial row of tents, Godfrey was gay in the classic, Oscar Wildean tradition who, I suspect, would have been discomforted in the modern era of sexual tolerance. His shop was in Richmond, just prior to its gentrification and he'd a handmaiden of unknown name and dull demeanor whom he'd rechristened Ruby Glitters — insisting that the silent, sullen woman with the feather duster had once danced naked on the tabletops in Bendigo pubs, her naked body gilded in gold dust tossed by drunken miners. Ruby (Gladys? Iris? Ivy?) utterly ignored her employer's fictions and just kept dusting.

What I loved was witnessing Godfrey sell awful furniture to pretentious dowagers. Case in point ... the crap couch. Utterly mediocre and unmemorable, a rickety two-seater in what pretended to be mahogany with two deflated, defeated cushions.

I was sitting in a dark corner with Godfrey sipping Earl Grey from cracked cups and reading Sotheby's catalogues while Ruby shifted the dust from place to place when the

Toorak matrons came in. (Think of two Hyacinth Buckets.) Their eyes swept over the stock and they were — quite understandably — underwhelmed. But Godfrey was one jump ahead. "Mrs Bucket — how do you do it? Every time you visit you immediately spot the best thing in the shop." And he gestured to the crap couch, which neither lady had noticed. "Very rare. Museum quality."

And he instantly faked a provenance that had the couch coming from: A. the golden age of Chippendale, B. the dacha of a Russian aristocrat and C. more recently from a stately home in England. The Mrs Buckets were hooked and Godfrey reeled them in.

"But it's the cushions, of course, that make this piece so important. Stuffed with swans' down. Swans from the lake in the Petrograd Gardens. The very swans that inspired Tchaikovsky to write *Swan Lake*."

Game, set and match. The Mrs Buckets fought to be first to produce a cheque book.

Suchet

September 29, 2014

DAVID SUCHET seemed puzzled at my suggestion that he resembled Charles Chaplin. So I explained. It wasn't in their appearances or bodies of work — but in their very similar approach to the profession of acting. In particular the way they'd created their most famous characters. The Tramp versus the dapper Belgian detective.

Some actors begin to build a role with a voice. Others with a wig. Laurence Olivier frequently employed a putty knife to create a distinctive nose — most famously (and controversially) when making up for Shylock and Othello. Whereas Chaplin and Suchet, both Brits to their very different bootstraps, began with walks. In the former case a waddle, in the latter a mince.

David took his clue from Agatha Christie's text, coming up with Poirot's prim style of perambulation. Chaplin chose to walk like a penguin. Their gaits were emphasised, exaggerated, by their choice of footwear. Hercule's shoes were prissy and over-polished, with spats. The Tramp's, oversized-and buggered boots.

Both concentrated on preposterous moustaches — Poroit forever fussing over his glossy, trimmed and wax-tipped extravaganza and the Tramp's little more than a silly smudge — accidentally anticipating Adolph Hitler's. (This would become very useful when Chaplin was making *The Great Dictator*.)

Though weird and wonderful Hercule's wardrobe was impeccable, from top (an expensive and perfectly positioned chapeau, via various exquisitely tailored coats and suits) to bottom (his spats). Whereas Chaplin chose the Tramp's accoutrements from Sennett Studio's cast-offs — an ill-fitting bowler hat, a very under-sized coat and baggy trousers (held in place by what? a tie used as a belt?) Poroit liked to flaunt a fresh orchid in a tiny silver vase pinned to his lapel. The Tramp? Most poignantly a bloom stuck on him by a blind flower girl.

Finally came their choice of canes — Poroit's is a very elegant number with the silver head of a swan, while Charlie's was a humble and overlong cane. And voila! The two inventions, American tramp and Belgian detective, became huge superstars. Suchet's Hercule blew dozens of earlier interpretations — from Charles Laughton's to my old friend, Peter Ustinov's — out of the water making him perhaps the best known and most loved character in British television. Previously silent movies like *Modern Times* and *City Lights* gave the world the most famous, and the most famous man, and persona, in the world.

There's one more parallel with both men being comparably obsessive. Suchet is known to take infinite pains with his performances, with Chaplin notorious for endless retakes, often reshooting a single scene month after month. And there the similarities end, or almost.

Chaplin was born into dire Dickensian poverty, Suchet into the comfortable middle-class. With Lithuanian Jewish heritage, Suchet's original family name was Suchedowitz, Yiddish for kosher butcher. (David talked to me of being raised without religion, of his conversion to Anglicanism and surprised us both by announcing his recent decision to join the Eastern Orthodox.) Also raised without a faith the superstar Chaplin was held to be Jewish, particularly by American anti-Semites who didn't like his politics, which he defiantly refused to deny.

Both Chaplin and Suchet sought to escape the gravitational pull of a single character. Chaplin would play a variety of roles including the aristocratic Monsieur Verdoux, while Suchet portrayed Sigmund Freud, Edward Teller, Leopold Bloom, Robert Maxwell, Antonio Salieri and played opposite Diana Rigg in *Who's Afraid of Virginia Wolfe?* But for me his greatest triumph, exceeding his Poroit, was as Augustus Melmont in *The Way We Live Now* — based on the Trollop novel about a 19th century GFC with the monstrous Melmont, a predecessor of *The Wolf of Wall Street*.

David also specialises in Cardinals — first playing Wolsey, and now, marvellously, Benelli in *The Last Confession*. In this role he has no need to create a costume. It comes from Vatican Fashions in the form of a red frock — with a smoking handbag.

Gough at Cannes

October 23, 2014

WHITLAM WAS, of course, a megastar of stage, screen and radio. His "It's Time" rallies nudged Nuremberg's, lacking only a Leni Riefenstahl. But he gained specific movie-star status by completing the vision splendid for a revived film industry that Barry Jones and I'd initiated with John Gorton, plans briefly derailed by Bill McMahon.

And as well as transforming the nation, Gough brought another mega-star into being. Gorton had played himself in the original Barry McKenzie epic, the film version of David Williamson's play about John pipping Gough at the post. The great man, however, would appear in the Bazza sequel, famously upgrading Mrs Edna Everage, humble Moonee Ponds housewife, into a monstrous panto dame.

(Dame Edna! Instantly added to the ranks of Dames Nellie Melba, and Beryl Beaurepaire. Edna's anointment was a Whitlam ad-lib, anticipating by decades — and perhaps inspiring —Tony Abbott's equally unexpected elevation of Quentin Bryce.)

The story of Gough's efforts to revive Australian film is well known — but perhaps not his graciousness in regard to Gorton — whom he'd invite to share the spotlight at every galah occasion involving film. Nor, I suspect, do the official histories record Gough's walk-on part at the Cannes Film Festival.

At the time Gough was in semi-retirement in Paris, serving as Australia's representative to UNESCO. He was ensconced with Margaret in Harry Siedler's big, brand new and brutalist embassy, with a young Mark Latham as his aide-de-camp. I was back in Cannes as chairman of the Australian Film Commission, with my young CEO Kim Williams, trying to flog, yes, Australian films. As I recall, it was the year I co-signed Australia's first co-production agreement — with the French, whose Minister for Culture was improbably named Jack Lang.

The harbour at Cannes was, as usual, crammed with billionaires' yachts of vast vulgarity hired by the US studios for influence-peddling parties. Imagine the fit of pique when, suddenly, they were dwarfed by the arrival of the most famous yacht in the world. The Royal Yacht Britannia, carrying as cargo stars that shone brighter than any Hollywood could offer.

Charles and Di. There to flog English films. Charles's mum might be Australia's head of state, but the kids weren't there to help us colonials. They were on British business.

How could we possibly compete with this bullying by Buck Palace? Kim, later to become Gough's son-in-law, suggested we invite Gough and Margaret to fly up from Paris. Margaret couldn't make it but Gough was happy to oblige, arriving at Nice Airport on an airline called TAT. (Gough pointed out that TAT had a special offer — free tickets for spouses. "Tit for TAT" said Gough, an ad-lib he'd proudly repeat to me decades later.)

No one in Cannes knew who the hell he was. But he was obviously important. As we strolled along the Croisette,

Gough's towering and imperious figure caught the attention of the paparazzi who followed in train with fusillades of flash bulbs. Moreover starlets in bikinis, entirely ignorant of Gough's history pushed each other aside to pose beside him, including two who were topless. I've got the photos somewhere.

Gough did us proud that year. With the star quality of Bonaparte — and twice the height — he intimidated the French, nonplussed the Americans and gave great encouragement to the young and sizeable Australian contingent. He probably could have signed a contract with Broccoli to play the new James Bond. At very least his performance deserved a Palm D'Or.

I've a fond memory of the drive back to the airport at the Festival's end. Gough was wallowing in luxury in the back of a stretch limo and, as was his wont, grilling me for gossip about any sexual goings-on involving the comrades. (One of his all-time favourites involved Cairns who, when acting PM, got to stay at Kirribilly House. There staff beheld Jim and Junie cavorting naked in the moonlight amongst the shrubbery fringing its voluptuous hills.) En route to Nice I told Gough of more recent hanky-panky involving a ministerial friend and he began to roar with laughter. Louder and louder. So much guffawing that he slipped off the seat and got himself wedged on the floor. It took three of us to haul him out and get him back on TAT.

We didn't always get on so well. Shortly after winning the leadership Gough spat the dummy and, in his legendary 'crash through or crash' approach demanded caucus re-elect him with an increased majority. My life-long friend, Jim Cairns decided to stand against Gough, not with any hope of winning — indeed not wanting to. (Jim well knew he'd be electoral poison — his motive was "to give Gough a kick in the bum".)

Butcher's hook at the time Jim couldn't get out of bed to campaign — so it would all boil down to the letter he'd send caucus members. Lying in the bedroom of his Hawthorn home, fussed over by Gwen and surrounded by pill bottles, he read me the draft. It seemed to me excessively polite — "Mr Whitlam" this, "Mr Whitlam" that. I began a rewrite that was far more aggressive. Out with the Mr's and in with a phrase that remains famous in party annals. Speechwriter to Calwell and Gough, Graham Freudenberg called it 'one of the most powerful sentences in our political history'.

"Whose party is it — his or ours?"

Our letter had much more than the desired effect. The kick in the bum almost kicked Whitlam out of the leadership. To Jim's astonishment, and mine, and certainly Gough's, the result was not the vindication he'd expected but the humiliation of a photo finish. Had just three people changed their minds, Gough's brilliant career would have ended before it began.

"We never exchanged a cross word," Gough said of he and Cairns in subsequent years. That's because they never spoke to each other again. And for years Gough rebuked me for being "Cairns' campaign manager!"

Yet it remains the one election I'm glad we lost.

Friends

November 10, 2014

NOW THAT THE death of EGW fades into memory, a few last words on the wondrous Whitlam Wake.

Prime Ministers are supposed to pass slowly through the political process, like sands through the hourglass or pigs though a boa constrictor. Their terms are not meant to be cruelly abbreviated by feral Governor Generals while co-conspiratorial contenders lurk in a Yarralumla cupboard. Nor are they meant to be overthrown mid-term by ambitious colleagues. Not-directly-elected in our brand of democracy Prime Ministers are meant to be chosen or confirmed post election by their caucus — leaving office when, like Menzies, they've had a good innings or until they're shown the door by mutinous voters.

But not any more in Australia. Here PMs have the shelf life of yoghurt. To take residence in the Lodge and/or Kirribilly is to find yourself on democracy's Death Row. Hence the extraordinary collection of PMs present and past at the State Wake of Whitlam. Excluding a few PMs from PNG and Whitlam himself (though Gough was emphatically there in spirit) we had Tony, Malcolm, John, Bob, Paul, Kevin, Julia and Kevin. Gorton and McMahon sent apologies.

As well as those who'd climbed the greasiest of poles I spotted a few who thought they should have been PMs.

Crean, for example. Latham didn't turn up — once amongst Whitlam's nearest and dearest there'd been a falling out. Was Turnbull there? Hewson? Big crowd, might have missed them. But it was easy to see another dozen with aspirations — Shorten, Plibersek etc etc. And perhaps Noel Pearson?

Too much has been made of a bit of bolshie barracking from the crowd outside. Boos and cheers went along with the hugs and tears. More intriguing were the tensions in the Town Hall, even more intensely felt at the 'after party' downstairs. Beneath a micron-thin layer of collegiates, many hatreds. PMs don't like each other.

Had Gorton and McMahon been there you could have started with their mutual loathing. But the following survey of the survivors serves. Many have commented on the seating issues — the standoff when Gillard was about to be plonked beside Rudd. (Was this mischief making by the PM's department, in charge of the event and its protocols?)

Gough, of course, had reviled Malcolm who'd certainly grated teeth about Gough. In recent years, of course, they'd kissed and made up. Now it's the Libs rather than the Labs who fulminate against Fraser. Fraser the traitor, the trouser-less turncoat. Malcolm detests John Howard who despises Malcolm in turn. All the Labor PMs who'd hated Malcolm now embrace him like a brother. But they'll forever hate Howard.

It is compulsory for all ex-Labor PMs, Bob, Paul, Kevin, Julia and Kevin to view Abbott as if he were the devil incarnate. The incumbent returns the compliment.

Howard hates Rudd, for ending his era. Ditto and vice-versa. Both hope to attend the other's state funeral, if only to ensure they're dead. Hawke could not possibly be more hostile towards Keating and Keating hates Hawke as only a Keating can hate.

Gillard and Rudd are not close. When Peta Credlin, in a rare flash of humour, tried to put them close there was, as observed a few paras back, a bit of an issue. On the Richter Scale of revulsion their mutual hostility might even exceed Keating's and Hawke's.

Bob likes Julia and doesn't like Kevin. Kevin likes Paul but doesn't, I suspect, like Bob. And the odd thing is that, by and large, they weren't that keen on Gough either. Most Labor leaders of the post-Whitlam years, and there've been a lot of them (both leaders and years) were conflicted. The one Labor PM who was an unequivocal admirer: Kevin.

One of the reasons for privately expressed reservations was the ineptitude of the final months of Gough's government. The other was the fact that his first months were embarrassingly magnificent. Both sides of politics resent that because they can't emulate it.

J. Anus

November 29, 2014

JANUS, WHO GAVE his name to January, was a dinky-di dead-set Roman. Many, even most other gods in Roman mythology were nicked from the neighbours — mainly begged, borrowed or stolen from the Greeks. But not Janus. Not only was he a Roman original but he embodied, or more accurately embodied a quite original notion. The idea of looking in both directions. And not only before you crossed the road lest you be skittled by a chariot.

Imagine playing heads and tails without the tails. Imagine coins with two heads.

With two heads better than one Janus became the god of go-betweening. He looked simultaneously yon and thither. There and here. Forward into the future and back into the past.

So if you wanted to mark a beginning or a transition Janus was your man. Or rather, your god. Hence Janurius, the first month of the Roman year. Janus was also put to work over doorways, gates, passages. He had a mate called Portunus, also popular on portals, and the two shared responsibility for safety in harbours.

There's a few marble Janus heads in my antiquities collection, keeping an eye — or four — on things. But he'd (they'd?) be better employed in diplomacy, stuck over the doorway of the United Nations, as Janus marked the starts and stops of conflict. When a war broke out, the doors of the Temples of Janus were opened wide. When the war ended, they'd be closed. I'm not entirely sure about that symbolism but given that Roman emperors were as warlike as George W. Bush they'd have been open a hell of a lot.

These days, of course, being two-faced is less mythical and more ethical. Specifically, unethical. To be two-faced is no longer a prerogative of a deity but a criticism of a human being; and oft unsuspected and unexpected in an alleged friend, partner, colleague or employer.

Sadly, however, we expect two-facedness in our politicians. Where it can also be known as duplicity or hypocrisy. (Did the Romans also have a god called Hipocratus?) Particularly during election times. The PM, MP or wannabee pronounce on their good intentions, pull more policies out of hats than a magician does rabbits, fully intending to con us. To lie.

Our coat of arms, writ huge on Parliament House, displays two Australian animals that are big of bum and small of head. That should be a warning. The emu is 80% bum, all covered in feathers, with a skull the size of a domestic chook. Whilst the roo is equally ample of buttock with a cranium closely resembling a rabbit. And the pollies sit inside on their backsides backsliding on their policies and promises. Lying their heads off.

I don't believe for a moment that Tony Abbott tells fibs about "no budget cuts to ..." (fill in the blank as you choose). I prefer to accept Malcolm Turnbull's argument, heard when announcing the ABC cuts that were promised not to happen, that Tony's pronouncement could be explained by more of the following: A. The PM's absent mindedness; B.

His early onset dementia; or C. He was taken out of context. D. My hearing aid batteries were flat.

I belong to the Ausflag committee, dedicated to updating our national flappy thing. (Like New Zealanders, we're concerned that you can't tell it from New Zealand's.) Now I'm forming a new committee to update our coat-of-arms, at least the giant metallic one atop Tony's joint. Despite their clear heraldic relevance — to warn us of the bum-versus-brain ratio — down comes the giant chook and the ginormous kanga ... and up goes Janus. Or as I think we should rename him for this particular purpose, J Anus. With the emphasis on the Anus.

Now back to the beginning. When we sing Auld Lang Syne, the Romans trumpeted Janus at the New Year. As I do now. Have a happy one.

2015

Ghosts

January 9, 2015

I DON'T BELIEVE in ghosts. But I've seen a few. The most vivid apparition — nothing spooky, quite matter-of-fact — was of filmmaker Brian Robinson. Though my oldest friend had died days earlier, there he was. In 3D and HD at the ABC. I was seconds from going on air. And there, on the other side of the plate-glass sheet that separates studio from control room, was Brian. Standing quietly between my producer and our techo. As the theme swelled he disappeared. Rational explanation? An image of one of the most important people in my life burned into the retina of memory.

When my wife and young kids insisted they'd repeatedly seen a ghost in our old home in Hawthorn I explained it away by insisting — demonstrating — that the departed soul was simply a flash of reflected light from swinging glass doors that divided the hallway. They were not persuaded.

Many, perhaps most ghosts seem to live (sic?) in England's stately homes or ancient castles where the unquiet dead, like Hamlet's dad at Elsinore (Shakespeare exporting local superstitions to Denmark) walk the battlements, oft with a head tucked underneath an arm. All very posh.

I remember writing a column after my first visit to Auschwitz, almost angrily pointing out the absence of ghosts in that ghastly place. Where millions were murdered the air should be as thick with them as bats in a belfry. Such is the banality of evil that Auschwitz is instead thick with tourists.

I recall a literally haunting program we did on the ghosts of the Vietnam War. The Vietnamese passionately believe that the armies of the dead remain restless, and the population shares their pain. But most ghosts in western culture are loners, and generally upper class.

This column was provoked by 7.30's recent report on death, or lack thereof, in the digital age, where countless dead denizens of Facebook and social media will live on, despite the protests of friends and family who'd like to see them rest in peace. Others disagree and some have made "living will" arrangements to continue emailing, texting or tweeting from the other side. To send prepared messages to their children, for example, that would arrive on significant days in their lives.

Legislation is being proposed in some countries to allow family members to pull the plug on their nearest and dearest, an idea energetically opposed by some of the big players in cyberspace as an invasion of privacy.

I once sat with an ancient Jimmy Stewart to watch *Rear Window*. He told me he hadn't seen it in 20 years. On the screen was the vibrant ghost of Grace Kelly — and, effectively, his own. The old man watching his youthful self. I took many a sidelong glance at Jimmy. He wasn't enjoying it at all.

Thus film, a technology well over 100 years old, brought ghosts to life. What Shakespeare could merely imagine, film delivered, even industrialised. Now as populations live on in features, news footage, home movies. I looked again at Dennis O'Rourke's great doco *Cunnamulla*, that most remarkable portrait of a small town. In the few short years since 2000 so many of the dramatis personae have passed on, to use one of the preferred euphemisms. As has Dennis. But not the dead in his loving record of struggles, loves and conflicts.

The digital era will undoubtedly take an artificial after-life so much further than film, democratising the eternity once reserved for the highest and mightiest via grand tombs and pyramids. Instead of a head living on in a pickle jar there's now talk of downloading the entire mind, with all its ideas and memories, of preserving the psyche in binary code. Some of us, however, would prefer oblivion. Of fading away as the memories of those who knew us fade.

Nigel Grey

January 31, 2015

DR NIGEL GREY AO was the Marlboro Man of anti-smoking. Riding tall in the saddle he was Shane and the Pale Rider as well. As head honcho of the Anti-Cancer Council, rootin' tootin' Nigel organised any number of shootouts at the OK Corral, caught many a 310 to Yuma and pretty much ran the US cigarette industry out of town. And he needed the armour of Ned Kelly to survive the vilification of his powerful enemies.

Lovingly known as Nige, the good doctor had a genius for educating the public and an ability to muster support across the political spectrum. His quick-on-the-draw skills outsmarted the blokes in the black hats, gang-members of one of the world's toughest, deadliest industries. Thanks to Nige, Australia was (and remains) the test-bed for the world's anti-smoking policies and legislation. His death at 85 will not be mourned at Philip Morris.

With colleague Dr David Hill playing Tonto to his Lone Ranger, Nigel used a double-barrel approach to saving lives — a combination of humour to mock cigarette ads and pricing mechanisms to force down usage. Nigel and David were largely responsible for progressive restrictions on advertising culminating in laws passed by Keating in 1992.

Nigel's battles with smoking began when the industry was still bribing 'scientists' to dispute any link between smoking and lung cancer, a pre-echo of the continuing arguments denying linkage between the heavy smoking of coal-fired power and climate change. We're talking of the times when one fag company had the hutzpah and hypocrisy to market a brand under the slogan: 'You've nothing to lose but your smoker's cough.'

Having out-manoeuvred the tobacco industry in Australia, Nigel would go on to be world champion, leading the International Union Against Cancer and working with the WHO. And I had the privilege of working with him for a decade.

We devised educational campaigns on cervical cancer and breast self-examination. Our 'Slip Slop Slap' ads, with Sid the sibilant seagull, took on the major public health problem of skin cancer — and became the longest running ad campaign in the country. We also worked to educate doctors to be more empathetic in their interactions with women fearful of breast cancer — and with cancer patients in general. I learned a great deal from Nigel. So did everybody. And he was still at it in his ninth decade.

Nigel employed science and psychology in his strategies. We deployed any weapon and argument we could scrounge. I remember a discussion after we'd seen ultra-scans showing babies sucking their thumbs in utero. That sucking (aka 'oral gratification') shifted to the mother's breast and would be echoed for the rest of our lives as we chewed pencils, nibbled our nails or chomped on cigars.

I wrote a script that *This Day Tonight* turned into a parody 60-second commercial. It began with a silhouetted figure of man-on-horse-with-Stetson, posed heroically on a distant hill. As the lens slowly zoomed in on our version of Marlboro's hyper-masculine Man, we intercut images of lips nibbling nipples and pencils. Finally our hero filled the frame. Tall in the saddle. But instead of drawing deeply on a manly Marlboro our cowboy was ... sucking his thumb. And the voice-over said, "Smoking is for suckers".

Philip Morris went berserk and our anti-ad got only one airing. But in broad terms it symbolised Nigel's approach — his unrelenting combination of rigour and ridicule. Of horror and humour. Over the protests of the tobacco companies the health warnings on packs became increasingly brutal — and visual. Australian experiments with blank packets (where the marketer's 'brand image' is invisible) have been successful, with Britain's Conservative government introducing the same approach.

Of course the ciggy industry is unrepentant and continues its unconscionable behaviour in the vast markets of Asia and anywhere else it can get away with murder. But an Australian doctor has shown the world the tactics needed to turn the tide.

Vale Nigel

Glass

February 6, 2015

THE GLOSS OF GLASS. We look at it and through it and hold it and use it all the time but rarely think about it. Where history salutes a Stone Age, a Bronze Age, an Iron Age, a Steam Age and perhaps the Age of Silicone, we don't record or celebrate a Glass Age.

Nor a Grass Age, or more accurately, an Age of String. I wrote about that oversight earlier. String's the material that made fabric possible. Instead of fig leaves or furs to hide our nakedness we could make clothing. For warmth as well as modesty. By binding together filaments of grass humans could create baskets, cords, twines, ropes. Fishing lines and nets transformed our diet. Using ropes to tie logs together gave us rafts.

Stone, bronze, iron are big and butch, tough materials that last a long long time. The oldest artefact in my collection is an elegant hand tool, a sort of stone Stanley blade with finger and thumb grips. It was found in the Nile Valley and predates the nearby pyramids by 250,000 years. It's an odd feeling to fit your hand around it, to hold it as a human held it all that time ago, and is little different from the stone tools still being made in Africa and Australia in the 20th century.

Just as ancient baskets are little different from those still being made in Arnhem Land. Except very few of them have survived. String doesn't last. It yields to friction and rot. Thus there's not a lot of ancient stringy things awaiting discovery by archaeologists in ancient tombs or for us to inspect in museums. This means the role of women in human progress is understated, for it was women who gathered the grasses and fibres and wove them into a thousand shapes and products — for carrying everything from food to babies.

Although there's the strong possibility that women made the stone tools too. Like many other stone axes and blades in my collection — and in collections all over the world — my 250,000-year-old example doesn't seem to have been used. The blade is pristine, as are countless others from many cultures and millennia. Just one blow with a lovingly shaped and polished stone axe and it'd be chipped. Recently it occurred to scholars that many might have been made for display purposes, or to win a mate. Look at the beautiful axe I've made! Marry me! And it would be left in mint condition, like our good silver cutlery services.

Glass is a comparatively recent invention, one of the few that cannot be claimed by China. It occurs naturally when lightning or meteorites hit desert sand; with an abundance of examples in Egypt and Libya. So-called Edowie glass can be found in sheets near our Flinders Rangers — while "Darwin glass" occurs near Mt Darwin in Tasmania. Naturally occurring glass was used in the Stone Age and extensively traded. But the first manufactured glass was made in Syria, Egypt and Mesopotamia in the third millennium BCE. I've got some ancient Phoenician beads, jewel-like and brilliantly coloured, and a dozen later examples of opalescent Roman glass vases and bowls, instantly identifiable by an airy, almost eerie lightness.

No material is more obedient — more malleable, mould-able, pourable, blowable, versatile, reflective, refractive, stable, sterile, beautiful, artistically expressive, recyclable or as infinitely useful. We get glassy-eyed looking through glass glasses at glass computer screens that can communicate instantly through fibreglass tubes, while drinking from glasses or directly from bottles. We tap at glass screens on our phones or thump reluctant dollops of tomato sauce from glass bottles. Everything we do comes in glass. This is a Glass Age and we're remarkably ungrateful.

So pop the champers, pour some bubbly, lift your glasses and let's have a toast to glass.

Death penalty

February 7, 2015

WE ARE ALL on death row, moving at the same steady pace towards execution. Some of us have our sentences delayed by medical intervention but none of us have them commuted. Why then are we so appalled by official executions, by the noose, the needle, the gas chamber, the electric chair or whatever pitiless means the state employs?

The world is outraged by ISIS beheadings, whilst choosing to ignore the fact that our good friends, the Saudis, perform so many, many more, often for activities that would not be regarded as misdemeanours, let alone 'crimes' anywhere else — not even in China or Texas.

But even when the victim is an undisputed and unrepentant monster — an Adolph Eichmann or a Saddam Hussein — I find the death sentence monstrous. Even when the execution isn't botched in execution, as has been the case in recent US efforts, even when it's carried out with practised professional skill.

I lost my respect for Bill Clinton during his campaign for the Presidency when he returned to Alabama to authorise the execution of a convict who, because of an infantile mind, surely deserved clemency. I never had respect for George W. Bush because of his record-breaking sequence of executions as Governor of Texas, carried out with apparent pleasure.

Compassionate conservative indeed. Bush was continuing the proud American tradition of the lynch mob — with most of his doomed men being African American.

All of us are on death row, but few know the day, let alone the exact moment when our lives will end. That's one of the reasons that an official execution, wherever it's carried out, is a 'cruel and unnatural punishment'. As appalling a prospect and experience for the family as for the doomed person. And often for an entire community. How many of you share my memory of the execution of Robert Ryan at Pentridge? The collective horror and shame felt on that day, over a hanging insisted upon by the detestable Premier Bolte, was so profound that Australia has never had one since. Until Bali, when two Australian executions were conducted offshore thanks to shameful decisions by the Australian Federal Police.

Leave aside that too many innocent people have been subject to official lynchings, as DNA evidence has proved again and again in recently reopened investigations in the US. Or that the poor devils sent to the gas chamber or electric chair were given abysmal representation.

One by one the nations of the world, and many American states, have abandoned the death sentence. Those that retain it should be seen as pariah states.

We have always known that its only purpose is vengeance. (Of those hanged in Britain in the early 20th century many had witnessed public executions in the 19th.) There is no evidence that capital punishment reduces any crime rate anywhere, most certainly not murder — or drug offences. Its purpose is usually shamefully political, or obscenely religious.

Mourning in America? While it's not something that the notoriously sentimental President ever mentioned, Reagan's great biographer Gary Wills records that Ron's dad moved the young family into a new home in the burbs, because a 'Negro' was lynched from a lamp post a few blocks away. Those public spectacles remained popular until a moment ago in US history — the same insanity lingers on in Texas. In Indonesia. And in Saudi Arabia.

The society that practices capital punishment, whatever the pretext, diminishes itself. It makes its citizens complicit in murder. If done in the name of a god, it is blasphemous.

Time to end executions everywhere. Without exception. The more we feel enraged, the more we feel vengeful, the more the criminal seems to deserve it, the greater the temptation to officially kill, the greater the reason to show mercy.

Foreign wars

February 28, 2015

A CONFESSION. I agreed with Tony on one issue ... that Australians shouldn't head for the Middle East to fight for ISIS. Or even against it. Clearly it's very silly and quite dangerous getting involved in other people's wars.

Many Australians have made that exact point throughout our history. My generation recalls the noisy advice we gave Harold "All the Way With LBJ" Holt in regard to the Great Vietnam Fiasco ... and to John Howard while he was urging George W to shock 'n awe Baghdad. From the Great Iraq Farce to the Great Exercise in Futility in Afghanistan. Three wars that were a) none of our business b) not in our interest and c) doomed to failure.

Nor were all Aussies keen on joining the ANZACs at Gallipoli. A few lily-livered white-feathered commos or Catholic locals were sceptical about signing up for that Greatest of Follies, the Great War, in its awesome entirety. (There was another 'stolen generation'. Per capita Australia paid the highest price of any combatant nation in the loss of young lives.)

Tony never saw a war he didn't like. Like John Winston, like Winston Churchill, he was more than willing to put our troops in harm's way. There were, of course, precedents aplenty. Some Australians volunteered to fight the Crimean

War (1853-1856), somewhat anticipating Tony. *Breaker Morant* reminds us of Australian involvement in the Second Boer War (1899-1902), the Boxer Rebellion (1900-1901), the Russian Civil War (1922), Korea (1950-1953), the Malayan Emergency (1950-1960), the Indonesian confrontation (1963-1966), Vietnam (1962-1973) and the First Gulf War (1990-1991). Not to mention our wars against indigenous Australians and, more recently, our contributions to the US Cold War via Pine Gap et al, and our red carpet welcome to Woomera for British nuclear tests. Currently the War on Terror still has us involved in Iraq and Afghanistan — and in an expanding war on the ISIS death cult. We've been eager participants in the US War on Drugs, arguably the most self-destructive and counterproductive nonsense in the history of public policy. And let's not talk about our War on Refugees.

This country all but sinks beneath the weight of war museums and marble memorials. Our most solemn day, April 25, simultaneously honours and mourns a shattering military defeat. Our politicians fight for photo-ops with ancient and current warriors. They shroud our military mistakes in the Australian flag (as Tony so sensitively expressed it, "shit happens") while fighting to claim it as their own.

Some of us predicted that our enthusiastic involvement in Middle Eastern conflicts would detonate the problems we now see in that wrecked region within our borders. And indeed our cities. Far from making us more secure we've continued to make ourselves the target — as did our willingness to aid and abet the US Cold War with Pine Gap and other satellite tracking and signalling installations we accommodate. (Soviet missiles were certainly aimed at us in retaliation.) No sane Australian could deny the importance of our involvement in the Second World War — but the rest of the wars? Past, present and potential? The treaties with the US that lock us in to future conflict with China? At a time when the looney Right are planning their take-over of the White House? I've long argued that the most intelligent policy for this country would be one of armed neutrality. Of being prepared but increasingly unaligned. Of being the last, not the first, to sign up for other nations' wars. Let's not march to the tune of others' drums. With the exception of the Second World War, when what we call civilisation narrowly won — with the immense help of the Soviet who would almost overnight become the enemy — name a war that anyone won!

Let's be recruits for a war on war.

Dearth cult

March 6, 2015

DEATH CULT? Abbott's favourite term for ISIS. Technically, Tony, no. A cult requires a single charismatic and/or deranged leader, a Charlie Manson. A Jim Jones or Alan Jones. Whereas ISIS, with a one-hundred year history, remains hydra-headed. Cut off one head (appropriate! given its preferred mode of execution) and others grow.

It's the same with the Dearth Cult, my name for what passes for Australian democracy. Hardly matters who's heading the government or opposition — we see a dearth of ideas, ideals, imagination, intellect. Mind you, if we did see one or more of them we'd probably run a mile. It's much the same everywhere. Dearth cults are not limited to democracies. Many a dictator is even more deathly dearthly. (Take that egregious brat in North Korea or the brute in Moscow.) No matter how power is attained, whether through ballots or via the barrels of guns, you finish up in dearth valley. Even our least moribund governments are near dearth experiences. And what little policy is proffered the media response is parlous. It falls on dearth ears.

However, we must keep trying to formulate a new improved approach with added vitamins. The business models for state or federal governments are broken. All votes are donkey votes, with elections involving reluctant voters filling front and backbenches with fools, frauds and bitter disappointments.

Apart from being inordinately expensive elections stack branches, stuff envelopes with developers' dollars; further corrupting already corrupt parties leading to 'law 'n order' auctions that increasingly overcrowd prisons. Even worse, even the prospect of an election provokes faux patriotic war mongering and costly, fatal involvements in other people's wars.

A few random thoughts and desperate experiments.

Let us choose our leaders in a raffle, or via Scratchies. Losers become MPs. The pay is good so people would still shell out at the newsagents.

Or let us swap one ballot for another. Remember conscription? All those marbles tumbling around? Happy birthday! You've won an overseas cruise! The chance to kill or be killed in a Vietnamese jungle! I'm sure the Lotto people would lend us their barrel. Hope they haven't lost their marbles.

Or we could borrow from the jury system. You'd get a letter in the mail from the Sherriff and, unless you had a damned good excuse, a letter from the doctor indicating mental illness can pull strings; you find yourself one of twelve angry men and women reluctantly running the nation. Twelve would be plenty — Gough did a good job with two.

Given the politicians' enchantment with law 'n order and the need for ever harsher sentences on any misdemeanour over double parking, perhaps we could make government itself a punishment. By sentencing recalcitrants to parliamentary penal servitude. Four years hard Labor, one year hard Liberal. With no hope of parole. We're half way there with ICAC, that splendid organisation practised in revealing the inherent criminality in the profession.

Law 'n order or alphabetical order, conscripting MPs by going from Z to A? Note the reversal — the current system grossly disadvantages the Zieglers and Zabriskies. (OK, this would be to Adams' personal advantage as he'd rather go to his grave than federal parliament.)

Inspiration has just struck. Ouch! The answer to this problem, as to any and every problem, is an algorithm. These little buggers do all the cutting edge things, proving their unerring capacities by making David MONA Walsh disgustingly rich, leading the lemming-like rush over the precipice of the GFC and helping Obama kill innocents galore in drone attacks. Algorithms run our iPhones and lower our IQs by replacing thought with Googling, and memory with Wikipedia. Let's hand governments over to them. Couldn't be worse than the dearth cult.

Wagstaff

March 13, 2015

WHEN I HEARD a few weeks back that Stuart Wagstaff had died at 90, I remembered a chance encounter long ago and far away. When he was in his 50s.

I'd arrived at JFK very early and checked into the Algonquin on a day when a team of huskies would've been a help on the streets on New York. Snow, sleet, wind chill. Having left an Australian summer I was sartorially ill-prepared and slipped and slid on the sidewalk as I sought somewhere to buy a raincoat and a brolly. The scene was now Fifth Avenue and, as I hadn't eaten, passing Tiffany's brought thoughts of breakfast. At that exact moment I felt a tap on the shoulder and heard a familiar voice. "Hello, old chap!" It was Stuart.

So we breakfasted and thawed together in the pre-Trump vulgarity of the Helmsley Palace. "It's good to see you, Stuart, because I wanted to apologise."

"What for, old chap?"

"I got you wrong."

Older readers will recall that Waggers came to Australia to play Henry Higgins in *My Fair Lady*, staying on to become even more famous as the insouciant star of Benson and Hedges ads. So his public persona was of the poshest of Poms, very Eton and Knightsbridge. But just as Noel

Coward had upgraded himself to posh pommydom, it turned out that Stuart was wearing thick make-up and full camouflage.

As I had, Stuart appeared on an ABC radio show lifted from the BBC's *Desert Island Discs*, where the guest talks about some favourite records and discusses his or her life. A very gentle but skilled interrogator, Mary Adams (no relation) would turn her studio into a confessional. But Stuart was determined to keep things light, camping it up with recordings of Broadway musicals. Mary, however, wanted more ... and the mask slipped. Out came the story of Stuart's appalling childhood. Born in 1924 he was raised on a dirt poor farm in Wiltshire — by a father who'd brutalised him. Given some parallels with my own childhood, I was riveted. It seemed the only real happiness in Stuart's life had been when his emotionally remote mother took him to the odd play or panto. And the rest, as they say, was history.

That's why I wanted to say sorry to Stuart. And I reminded him how the programme had ended. Mary had asked her final question very quietly.

"Does that make it hard for you to love?"

A moment's silence. "No, but it makes it almost impossible to be loved."

Anyone who has had a childhood like his will understand that answer very well. Irrespective of social class it's a common reaction to abuse — even if the abuse was emotional rather than physical or sexual. It would be a familiar outcome to the countless damaged childhoods being revealed in the Royal Commission.

I once told Stuart's story — and repeated his words — to Kerry Packer. Their economic circumstances could not have been more different. But both Packer and Wagstaff had been severely damaged by thug fathers. So Kerry understood those words all too well.

(I've written before about my first long and most revelatory conversation with Kerry — hours long, lasting from dinner to dawn — when all of a sudden he asked me, "What's a black hole?" And I made an inadequate attempt to explain what that young Stephen Hawking was arguing. Packer brushed the science aside. "That's what I've got inside me," he murmured. "A black hole.")

So stage and screen gave Stuart a means of escape from the gravitational pull of an unhappy past. The term 'Doctor Theatre' is used to describe the way the demands of tonight's performance can, for the time being, mask the pains of an actor's sudden illness. But in another sense it can provide therapy forever.

Doctor Theatre seemed to work very well for Stuart Wagstaff AM. Dead at 90.

Fun on the farm ...

March 13, 2015

JUST DRAGGED TWO dead cows into a gully. Poor dears were standing side-by-side in the sudden storm that swept through the place a few hours ago. During a fusillade of flash photography accompanied by the theatrical thunder, seems lightning struck the fence beside them.

(Already the good news will have reached the cleanup crew — everything from ants to eagles, flies to feral pigs. Helped along by dingoes, dogs and dinosaur-sized goannas, the huge corpses will quickly be picked clean, leaving a leathery blanket draped over the bones.)

We were getting desperate for rain and God punishes atheists' prayers by hurling hurricanes at us. Thirsting for a transfusion our emaciated river's little more than a series of stagnant pools in which the feral fish were crowded fin-to-fin. It's one thing to enjoy the claustrophobia of European carp but you fear for the traditional residents, from the catfish to the platupussies. Even the yabbies and the tortoises have been doing it tough in their desiccated dams, most already sunbaked into glazed bowls.

Then God says let there be light-ning! Let there be a great deafening! And let mighty winds tear the branches from the trees! Let my wrath topple mighty trunks! All of which, thanks to the big bully who nuked Sodom and Gomorrah (and ethnic-cleansed the entire planet during Noah's Flood) just happened here.

The biggest tree in our tiny town that loomed large near the Linga-Longa Pub and our beloved Gundy Store was skittled in seconds. After a century on duty it's now a vast cadaver awaiting the chain saw's roar. And to add insult to injury and dead cows, all this meteorological mayhem delivered bugger all rain. Yes, some car-denting hail. But only enough of the wet stuff to settle the dust.

And what about Pat's olives? Drought hasn't been kind to the groves in the region — for years we've produced pack-able crops. Just enough olives for a few martinis. This year was looking good — now we dread to think what the hail's done to the fruit.

Yep, it's a laugh a minute in the rural sector. And scouts' honour, that previous sentence was provoked by a kooka-burra mocking me from the proximity of a shredded tree. For city-dwellers 'the weather' is something they tack on the end of the News. Apart from the need to carry an umbrella the citizens of cities are conned — air-conned — into a delusion of security. They are lulled and cosseted in car and office building. Whereas those humans who share the land-scape with roo and wombat dread it. Weather is the other Big W, and farmers are caught between both of them. The power of the supermarket and the whims of Huey.

OK, this was only a quasi-catastrophe. The last time a really histrionic hairy-chested hurricane hit us — about 5 years back — it uprooted literally thousands of trees, crushed farm vehicles, ripped off roofs, toppled fuel tanks and tossed buildings about the place — in the ten most ter-rifying minutes I've experienced since hearing that Howard had won a federal election.

To be in a storm that tore your farm and your life apart is to find yourself in a dream-sequence, a digital disaster movie, experiencing something you can neither comprehend nor compute. You cannot believe your eyes or ears.

The scars of our own personal hurricane (and we took it very personally as it seemed focused on Elmswood, leaving many of our neighbours untouched) are still to be seen all around us, and can be felt within us. Thus we utterly empathise with those who've experienced Big W at its worst, via flood, wind or fire.

Wither the weather? It's destined to get even bigger and ever wilder as climate change gets more climactic. Big W is getting bigger.

Winging it

March 28, 2015

WE KNOW WE'RE a thousand times more likely to die in the bath and a million times more likely to die in bed than in a Boeing or Airbus. Recent fatalities and mysteries involving aviation persuade me that human flight is a flight from sanity and the Wright Brothers were wrong. I'm with the flightless birds — that've come to the same decision about winging it. The very sensible penguin, kiwi and moa. I like to see the emu sitting safely on our coat of arms, opposite the kangaroo, which has, as we know from Qantas, yearnings to fly.

My first flight, age 12, scattered sheep in a paddock. It was in a Tiger Moth, an apt name for a vehicle of such frailty. Wood, wires, fabric. A few years later I'd be taking every opportunity to catch a Concorde — until that wondrous machine's final flight smack-bang into a hotel in Gonesse. 65 years of flying in every imaginable aircraft, from hot air balloons to Dick Smith's helicopters.

(At one point Dick was insistent I buy one to commute betwixt Sydney and the bush and arranged for me to have lessons from his instructor. It proved quite easy to buzz around Bankstown like a Mortein'd blowie — but getting the throbbing velocipede to go vertical proved counter-intuitive. Dick's instructor whispered that Dick had been on the verge of giving up — then suddenly got it! I never did.)

I was once climbing into a plane at the Vienna airport when my travelling companion, a certain Barry Jones, who shall remain nameless, had a vivid premonition that it was going to crash. I pushed him into his seat and while BOJ palpitated, I'd never felt safer. Yet to be honest, every second person on any flight anywhere has the same premonition. And often they're right.

On a flight in the backblocks of China, when my travelling companion was Jack Thompson, we barely survived a botched take-off and forced landing. I once managed to miss an airliner that crashed and I walked wobbily away from a crash landing in a small Piaggo; the same eccentric aircraft with propellers facing backwards that had recently killed a beloved son of Onassis. I even flew repeatedly in Soviet Ilyushins when Aeroflot was the world's worst airline.

Yet like 99.9999% of the flying public I survived. I've outlived many of the airlines I've booked on. From Ansett and TAA to PanAm, which Kubrick had taking passengers to the moon in 2001, but didn't. It ceased flying in 1991.

My most memorable flight? A tense Qantas flight from Greece to Italy during the hijack season. The grisly evidence of a terrorist attack on Athens airport (3 dead, 55 wounded) was still to be seen. So tension was high as we climbed onboard. And as we approached Rome there was a thunderous explosion and all was blackness. A bomb! Much screaming! Then the lights flickered on and we heard the voice of the Captain struggling to be calm. "It's alright! We've just been struck by lightning." He tried to cheer us up by repeating the soothing adage that it never struck twice in the same place. When it did! Another explosion! More darkness. More screams.

A few days earlier, anticipating Dawkins and Hitchins by decades, I'd published my atheistic diatribe *Adams Versus God*, and as the latter is my witness, a journo was interviewing me about the book mid-flight at exactly the moment the lightning struck.

Later the Captain told me we'd been directly over the Vatican at the time. And both strikes had hit the plane within inches of my seat ...

Kirk Douglas

April 18, 2015

MY CAREER IN newspapers began with a billy cart; which I'd drag around the streets at dawn, delivering *The Sun, The Argus, The Age*. At night I'd reload the cart with *Herald*s and head for my pozzie. Paperboys fought it out for the best pozzies. I finished up with a crappy one: a tram stop opposite Jolimont Railway Station where, decades later, Hilton would open their first Melbourne Hotel. I'd stand there in all weathers, yodelling, "Getcha paper!!! The Hair-Oiled!!! Read all about it!!!!"

With my rain-sodden Hair-Oilds substituting for the red cape, I was a twelve-year-old toreador dodging the charging cars. Leaping on and off moving trams. It was dead dangerous. Risking your life for a penny per paper. A deener a dozen.

And there I was, in my early thirties, standing on the very same corner, looking up at the Hilton where I was to have a meeting with a movie star. I half-owned a busy production company called Adams Packer — and Kerry had made an urgent phone call. "Kirk Douglas wants us to make a film."

I held Kirk Douglas in high regard. I admired the courage of his films and the bravery of his politics. More than anyone else Kirk broke the back of the Hollywood Black List. He gave the young Kubrick the chance to direct him in both *Paths of Glory* and *Spartacus* — and son Michael the chance to make *One Flew Over the Cuckoo's Nest*. His list of credits was remarkable. And here was a paperboy hearing him pitch a picture. Later we'd form a friendship, but on that night, things did not go well.

His wife opened the door — they'd been married for 60 years — and introduced me to the world's most famous dimple. Kirk was almost reverent as handed me "a really great script, really really great!" and asked me to read it there and then. But I insisted he tell me about it instead. "You're a great actor, I'm a good listener."

Within seconds I wished I hadn't.

It was set in the 1860s with Kirk as a US cowboy brought to Western Australia by "a sheep rancher to shoot roos, dingoes and Abos ... but I get a change of heart."

"About the roos, Kirk?"

"No, about the Abos." And things got rapidly worse. The cowboy leads "a revolution of Abos." (!!!) Kirk became more and more excited as the story unfolded, all but incandescent as he described the final scene.

"I come over a big bare hill, riding tall in the saddle — and behind me are 10,000 Abos!"

After a shocked silence I quietly suggested, "Kirk, you've got Aborigines confused with Zulus. We are talking of a nomadic people who lived in small groups — and while, yes, there was an heroic struggle against invading cattlemen the indigenous warriors fought as guerillas and were NOT led by an American cowboy. This story would outrage my Aboriginal friends and ..."

He silenced me with an imperious gesture. His dimple took on a somewhat menacing quality.

"Don't tell me about movies, Phil."

"Don't tell me about Aborigines, Kirk."

So the film wasn't made. At least not by us. Kerry wasn't happy. In 1990 a modified version was produced under the title *Quigley Down Under* co-starring Tom Selleck and Alan Rickman. I couldn't bring myself to see it.

I talked to Rickman a few weeks back — on his first trip to Oz since *Quigley*. Alan seemed reluctant to discuss it, only willing to recall the scenery. In 1982 Kirk had returned to play another redundant cowboy in *The Man from Snowy River*. Kerry had wanted to make that, too. Once again I didn't. Bad decision on my part. It made a fortune.

Street University

May 18, 2015

OVER THE DECADES readers of this column donated millions to Melbourne's Families in Distress Foundation, co-founded by John Embling and Heather Pilcher. As John put it, "With this help we saved countless street kids from homicide or suicide."

The on-going era of greed-is-good saw an economic juggernaut crushing lives and hope throughout the world. It rolled through the western suburbs of Melbourne and countless young were road-kill. Victims of parental violence and societal neglect they'd have been lost to the black economy of drug addition, prostitution, and criminality. Worn out from their heroic efforts John and Heather finally retired hurt. John survives with a serious illness, Heather is dead.

Now I'm working with Matt and Naomi Noffs. In 2004, 24-year-old Matt, grandson of the sainted Ted, told me of his inspirational idea — the 'Street University'. He wanted to transform a few derelict buildings into somewhere to transform kids' lives — an unofficial Uni in Liverpool, a drop-in place to create some optimism, teach skills, give hope and create a sense of community. I wrote the first column on the project in 2008 and you gave enough money to get things running by 2009.

Matt and wife Naomi opened a second Uni at Mt. Druitt, in 2013. While business at both is booming, funding is an endless struggle. Struggle Street University?

Progress report. Day one at Liverpool, a few sceptical kids drifted in. A week later, hundreds. Soon thousands were regulars, coming to play sport and music, read books and choose courses in sound engineering, dance, drama, gardening, cooking — even how to be an entrepreneur.

(The Uni has started a few small businesses, including the design, manufacture and successful marketing of Australia's first homegrown sneaker!)

Now Matt and Naomi get 14,000 visits per annum, with academics from 'real universities' — UNSW, Sydney Uni and UWS — joining their volunteers to lecture on everything from sociology to Latin. The Street Uni has helped with housing issues and achieved success in reducing drugs usage and consequent crime. Suicidal ideation has dropped from 40 to 11%. Kids have graduated to become 'proper' university students.

Here's a few case studies. Brother and sister refugees, their father killed by the Taliban. Mum spoke no English. The kids spent arvos after school at the Uni where Naomi helped with their homework. Now both are realising ambitions — one in engineering, the other in dentistry. Living as a petty thief, a young graffiti artist arrives at the Uni, gets trained in less controversial forms of graphic art, goes on to a BA at UWS, starts his own ad agency and shows his work around the world. An indigenous boy whose stomach was blown out during a drug deal was rehabilitated at the Uni and now studies HR in Queensland.

Homeless at 15 (he'd been kicked out by his parents for being gay) arrived at the Uni and formed a dance crew of 25 kids. They recently won a national championship. Now 19, he's a dance instructor.

Warning to the ANU. This year we launch Street University Canberra. Yes, even the city of gilded halls has intractable social problems. (Perhaps MPs could benefit from the Uni's courses or its counselling and mentoring.) Family breakdowns, mental health and drug problems are all on the curriculum. As usual the focus is on 11- to 25-year-olds at risk because of difficulties with the mainstream education system. The Fed government has provided a small amount of core funding for the next two years but your help is needed for staff, equipment and materials.

Donations to the Uni can be made by web at www.noffs.org.au.

Maddening Max

May 26, 2015

IN 1971, EIGHT years before *Mad Max*, George Miller and Byron Kennedy gave the world fair warning of what they were planning. Their first film, 20 minutes of mounting mayhem called *Violence in the Cinema Part 1*, won oodles of festival awards. It was a cultural manifesto, a declaration of war.

It depicted a rather boring man pontificating on media violence at a conference. As he speaks he is stabbed, sliced, diced and finally eviscerated. (As I recall the entrails were donated by a dead pig.) Until all that's left is a bloodied mouth that keeps droning on. Arthur Dingam played the part. He was playing me.

For years I'd been attacking porn — not the sexual variety that seemed to me comparatively harmless but 'the pornography of violence' — the escalation of sadistic images that had turned "channels into charnel houses, cinemas into abattoirs". Sexual pornography had the sex-hating churches, censors and customs officers enfrenzied. Yet such sexual gymnastics seemed far less a threat than mass entertainments based on people butchering each other. Behold Hollywood's version of the Roman arena.

And it would only be a matter of time until audiences became active participants in the slaughter via ever more vicious video games. And you'll never convince me that the pornographies of violence don't normalise and encourage real violence — whilst dulling our sensibilities.

I thought Mad Max some sort of masterpiece, far and away the best directed film of our new wave. Which made me loath it all the more. Working on a tiny budget, long before the era of digital delusions, George showed a genius for what the droogs in Kubrick's *A Clockwork Orange* would describe as a 'bit of ultra violence'.

Never had I seen executions so beautifully executed, savagery so exquisitely choreographed. And what happened when my protests appeared in print? George and Byron proudly quoted them in their ads.

I walked out on the latest incarnation of Max after twenty deafening minutes. (George hasn't needed to get better but he's certainly got louder.) And I hereby declare my total and abject surrender. Violence has won.

Whilst Kubrick suffered some agonies of doubt about the social impact of *A Clockwork Orange* (too many real-life thugs mimicking his) and withdrew it from UK screens, George remains impervious to wowsers like me and keeps upping the ante. The cruelty in the original plot, which puts the most vulnerable characters in harm's way is replaced by sheer momentum, with only a vestigial hint of morality. It's a non-stop joust of juggernauts and sub-human flotsam wherein the newly-minted Max mutters menacingly while his female counterpart, a Ms Furiosa, mows 'em down in the millions. And everyone loves it.

Ninety per cent of contemporary cinema is recycled imaginings from Marvel comics, not so such movies as Iraq-style shock 'n awe. Made by the brain-dead for the brain-dead. Half close your eyes and cough and they're the same movie, merging, blending, blurring — gore galore to add flavour to your choc-top and popcorn. Add Madder Max to the mix and you get the Miller bonus — a far greater sensory onslaught. In 4D. Deafening, Destructive, Diabolical, Demented. And once more, your enfeebled critic feels he's been stabbed, sliced, diced and eviscerated. Mouth still emitting futile sounds. Even close friends have told me how much they loved George's genial genocide. It's as if they saw it as a Keystone comedy. Or a ride at a Gold Coast theme park — which it will no doubt become.

Our most profound and defining fear is death. Which is why we fight it with science, medicine and cosmetic surgery — and desperately deny it with religion. Is that mortal dread why we've made death our most popular form of entertainment?

A little knowledge

June 30, 2015

IF A LITTLE knowledge is a dangerous thing, I'm in trouble. You're meant to acquire knowledge with the passing of years, even attain a modicum of wisdom, yet the longer I live the less I know. I try to keep up, read a lot, talk to clever people. But I've fallen further and further behind. There's so much more to know every day as human genius, at least in science, adds to the quantum. Thus I know less and less of more and more. I feel like a chimpanzee surrounded by Nobel laureates.

And it's not just up-market knowledge that eludes me; not only the counter-intuitive world of quantum (that word again) mechanics or big bangs. As I turn the pages, yes I still read paper newspapers, there's hardly anything or anyone I know. I don't know the people in the social columns. I neither know nor care about the Kardashians. Or the pompous portraits shown on the business pages. I don't begin to understand the stock market listings. The racing guide might as well be printed in Aramaic. I am blissfully ignorant of sport up the back.

I became confused by pop music shortly after Johnny Ray wept over a cloud and Bill Haley rocked around his clock, though I sort of 'got' the Beatles. But all the rest of them, those gorillas with guitars growing from their groins?

I can no more tell them apart than distinguish between wines or whiskeys. Wine? Apart from detecting the subtle difference between red and white and observing a dramatic difference in prices, wine's something of which I know naught.

I've been looking at TV weather forecasts since 1956 and as a farmer I need to know about matters meteorological, yet I don't begin to understand the maps and the squiggles. The only bit I do comprehend is when the bloke or the blonde says whether the weather will be wet tomorrow. I don't understand Alan Kohler's squiggles either.

And it's not just weather maps that bewilder me. It's maps per se. I can barely follow the dominatrix giving instructions on my GPS.

Here are a few more things I don't know about, starting with what I didn't learn at school prior to my escape at age 15. Algebra, Geometry, Maths, Grammar, Chemistry, Biology, Latin and French. I also failed woodwork. Since then I've achieved high levels of ignorance in (and the list is by no means complete) algorithms, computers, the Federal budget, nuclear fission, fusion and basic electricity, the internal combustion engine and, after 30 years in radio, the Boeing-like array of knobs and dials in my studio. Nor do I get podcasting, streaming or Netflix.

I did a dozen telly shows and two books with Paul Davies — *The Big Questions* — yet still find the astronomic and sub-atomic realms as incomprehensible as theological explanations of the Holy Trinity and transubstantiation. I couldn't fathom Facebook and am only a basic Tweeter, without the foggiest about hash tags. I don't know the Periodic Table and get confused by where places are, from the Middle East to the Caucasus. (I've long suspected that given a globe, few TV newsreaders could locate the countries they talk about if their lives depended on it. Another confession: despite umpteen surgical procedures, I'd have some difficulty in locating my major body organs.

I don't know what really happened in the GFC or have a glimmering of how a GPS functions. And I have no idea why anyone believes in God or votes Liberal. (Mind you, in recent times it's hard to see why people vote Labor, or at all.)

Thus Alzheimer's does not represent an urgent threat. I'm there already.

Hair

July 14, 2015

"MR HAWKE, could I ask you whether you feel a little embarrassed tonight at the blood that's on your hands?" The late Richard Carleton's immortal first question to Bob Hawke in his very first interview as opposition leader. And if that infuriated the Silver Bodgie, how did he feel about the observation of Robert Haupt's comparison of his hair to a scoop of meringue? Like Richard, Robert was a fine journo who died young, but you can bet Hawke's anger lingers on. As I can attest he's a good hater. And ask Blanche — he's very proud of his hair.

I've written before of the importance of follicles in political leadership, of the way Robert Menzies' sacred eyebrows were handed down to succeeding, if not necessarily successful Lib leaders. The hapless Bill Sneddon was one inheritor, as was the equally inept Andrew Peacock. More recently they've been worn by John Howard — and I can imagine Malcolm Turnbull, whose current models aren't particularly notable, praying for those caterpillar-like brows to crawl onto and distinguish the Turnbull forehead. Having shunned Tony's, they'd be worth fifty votes in caucus.

But today it's hair on the head, or the lack of it, that is our follicular focus. The politically pappous. The hirsute pursuing high office. Consider the case of Donald M.

Trump, the silliest of the many silly candidates contesting the Republican nomination, a silliness he emphasises by having the silliest hair. (And you thought Neville Wran had a ludicrous comb-over!) With all the money he claims to have, why doesn't he invest in a good rug? A Trump-towering toupee? Is it too late to call in Advance Hair Studios?

In the interests of Australian-US relations I wrote to Mr Trump about this, pointing out that the kings of England, and France, like the Pharaohs of Egypt wore elaborate wigs to magnify their majesty. And I included photos of Bronwyn Bishop.

It's widely known amongst members of the press gallery that Ms Bishop's as bald as a badger. Or Peter Garret. That the towering edifice on her noggin is confected, if not an actual confection like Hawkie's meringue. There are times when you'd swear Bronwyn Bishop went to the same stylist as Dame Edna, but most of the time she's a dead ringer for Marge Simpson. Bronnie and Marge like to pile it up like ...? Given that meringue is taken ... like a three-layer wedding cake? A teetering cone of gelati? And both women love the same colour. Blue.

As far as I can see all creatures great and small have a choice of just four coverings. Skin, hide, feathers or scales. Add up all the fish and reptiles and scales would be the most popular, with hide — or if you prefer fur — coming in second. Or would second be feathers? There are lots of birds. Either way humans, with just bare skin and a few tufty pieces for groin, armpits and scalp, are by no means as numerous. Perhaps it's time for cosmetic surgery to offer alternatives — Hawke and Peacock would have been much happier with feathers. And Tony Abbott would look great in scales or armadilloish armour. (Ask Kevin and Julia

— Prime Ministers need the hide of a rhino!) Apart from protecting him from Turnbull it would proclaim our PM's toughness and imperviousness to unpopularity.

Greens? With their love of trees they might prefer a fifth covering. Bark.

Haven't heard back from Trump yet. Given his loathing of foreigners he mightn't be impressed with English, French or Egyptian examples. That's why my letter pointed out that from some angles his comb-over resembles a sombrero. And we know how much he hates Mexicans.

Ellis

July 20, 2015

BLESSINGS UPON Bob Ellis. His talents and eccentricities coil around and confuse each other like a drunken version of the DNA's double helix. Of many memories of Bob accumulated over our half-century friendship, my favourite involves a tumultuous event on an awards night in Perth.

But first, an operatic story from London, the relevance of which will become obvious at the end of this fond recollection.

It stars British conductor, Sir Thomas Beecham, who ruled his roost with an iron baton for much of the 20th century. Beecham was taking his cast, including two elephants, through a dress rehearsal of Aida and was having trouble with his diva and her aria. Again and again he insisted she and an increasingly aggrieved tenor try again. Whereupon one of the elephants turned its bum to the stalls and pooped all over the stage.

Sir Thomas stopped conducting, lay down his baton and said, "Terrible stage manners, but what a critic!"

The scene shifts to a jet, jam-packed with Australian filmmakers — producers, directors and stars flying to Perth and the biggest-budget AFI Awards in the history of what I'd dubbed the Ozcars. Sir Charles Court's government was using the occasion to launch a super-duper new convention centre and no expense had been spared. To add some Hollywood glam to the event they'd even imported Esome internationals, the dilapidated duo of Fred McMurray and June Haver, while I'd have the dubious pleasure of partnering Peter Sellers' merry widow, Britt Ekland.

(They'd also flown in dotty thespian Brenda Vacarro who took the opportunity to protest the current vogue of vaginal deodorants by promoting her 'Society for the Promotion of Natural Body Odours'.)

Bob, or Ellis, as he was invariably named, was a nominee for Best Screenplay. As Chairman of the Australian Film Commission, I was dreading his threatened acceptance speech. All the way to Perth he rehearsed and refined an attack on Malcolm Fraser, that all the way I implored him not to make. Ellis was, of course, still 'maintaining the rage' after the Dismissal — which I shared — but negotiations on government support for film were at a delicate point, with Malcolm no more as sympathetic as patron saint Gorton. Finally, as the plane landed, Ellis surrendered.

That year the AFI unveiled a new physical embodiment for the Ozcar. A fragile, filmy fantasy of perspex swirls it revealed an appalling tendency to disintegrate in the grateful grip of recipients. Soon the stage was littered with glistening shards. No wonder the design was promptly retired, replaced for the next twenty years by a solid, no-nonsense plastic brick.

The moment when Ellis might be announced a winner came ever closer. And Bob was dangerously pissed. Which tended to distract me from the companionship of the glamorous Ms Ekland who, being a connoisseur of male bottoms, repeatedly murmured "great tush" whenever she sighted an appropriately endowed actor.

Then the worst happened. Bloody Ellis bloody won. And waddled unsteadily across the stage crunching the detritus of perspex from previous awards to claim his own. And rather than thanking his colleagues, his family and God, as per tradition, Ellis's mumbling baritone fulminated against Fraser. And with every word amplified from coast to coast I could hear any residual hint of governmental enthusiasm for Australian film evaporating. Who was the hapless presenter? I can't remember. Perhaps it was Britt. Whoever would have been in shock. I was in shock. The audience was in shock. But Ellis was in his element.

And then came Ellis's greatest moment. He grabbed at the statuette, did a drunken pirouette and vomited all over the stage.

Terrible stage manners. But what a critic.

Things

October 23, 2015

MUMBAI, LATE AT NIGHT. Behind 5-star hotels full of the fortunate, I find hundreds of sleeping figures crowding a footpath. Men, women, kids, as rats scurry around and over them I step carefully. Many have laid out flattened cardboard cartons over the filth. I look down at upturned faces while trying to avoid their akimbo legs, outflung arms, bare feet, and vulnerable fingers.

One sleeper lingers in my memory. He has two possessions, just two, apart from his cardboard mattress. A toothbrush down to its last bristles and a bent aluminium spoon.

Phnom Penh, blazing noon. Buddhist monks, heads shaven, saffron-robed, glide by, their begging bowls in one hand, smart phones in the other. And here, on the footpath I come across perhaps the world's smallest small business. Rather than beg outright a wizened man begs to weigh passers-by. As he squats beside his rusted set of bathroom scales a customer climbs aboard. The old bloke murmurs the figure and receives a coin.

Just as it's mostly Mercedes that purr past the sleepers at midnight in Mumbai, it's the luxurious Lexus that are bumper-to-bumper here, in the capital of Cambodia. The obscenely rich are oblivious to the obscenity of poverty.

Poor is a poor word for people beyond and beneath destitution. Poor suggests less, not nothing.

A brushless toothbrush, a bent spoon, a set of rusty scales. Things. It's like that parody of hard times in Monty Python, with the old codgers out-bidding each other on who had the toughest childhood.

In contrast to my fraternity on the footpath we have many more things in a pocket, a purse or a glove box, whilst just one kitchen drawer is a cornucopia. Even our dustbins are full of riches — ask the scavengers who survive on the municipal tips from Cambodia to the Philippines.

As bad as the most deranged hoarder we see confronting a local council, I collect everything. A bit like Andy Warhol who threw everything into a box every day, leaving it for others to sort; I've kept every letter from every reader I've ever received, even the anonymous and abusive ones. And just about every book I've ever read or even half-read. The National Library has the letters — hundreds of boxes filled in Warholian style over half-a-century, and the books, in their tens of thousands, from Williams and Biggles to the latest effort by the learned scholar I interviewed last night, fill room after room.

No one seems to want books any more. Redundant technology. Can't bear to toss them out. Can't give them away. They'll finish up as landfill. Meanwhile fellow humans pile up collections of anything and everything, from Bronze Age artefacts to Barbie Dolls. Think of all the eccentric objects and collections thereof that are celebrated — and highly valued — on *Antiques Roadshow*. (Memo to the ABC: bring back *Collectors*!) While some of our domestic detritus makes it to the Tip, more and more is detoured to Vinnies, the toffier junk-shops and antique dealers. Antique? It used to take 100 years for something to be considered antique, at least 1000 to be an antiquity. Now, no matter how god-awful or kitsch, if it lasts a decade it becomes a curio, a collectable. It won't be too long before Tupperware is taken as seriously as Greek vases.

Things used to be handmade, took a bit of time and trouble. Whereas we dwell within the era of mass and messy production. Now we drown in things — the good, the bad and the ugly. Think of how many things you own. Versus how many things you need.

Phillip Adams on
Ho Chi Minh

September 13, 2015

GOOD MORNING Viet Nam! It's 6 am in Hanoi, the city's in lockdown and the loudspeakers are blaring patriotic messages. Big day. One of the biggest. Today the city will host a parade worthy of North Korea, Tiananmen or Moscow's May Day.

Seventy years ago Ho Chi Minh declared Vietnam an independent nation. More prediction than proclamation it would take decades and millions of deaths in wars with the French, South Vietnamese, Filipinos, Khmer, the Americans, the South Koreans, the Thais, Laotians, Taiwanese and, yes, Australians and New Zealanders until it finally came true. No wonder the citizenry is flocking to Ba Dinh Square to watch 20,000 men and women march past Ho's tomb. Not just regiments of soldiers but also members of the fire brigade. Pretty much anyone with a dress uniform. The program also promises a march-past of Vietnamese intellectuals but I didn't spot them. Although a couple of blokes walked by looking intensely thoughtful. Thinking, thinking.

When Ho gave the heave-ho to the Americans — the Lilliputians defeating Gulliver — Hanoi, with understandable triumphalism renamed Saigon Ho Chi Minh City.

But it isn't. Hanoi — Ho-noi? — deserves that designation. Few in Saigon use the official name, pretty much reserved for official buildings and airline boarding passes. Whereas the Northern capital was the scene of his triumphs and the place of his entombment. And below his mausoleum, pretty much exactly on the site of Ho's Declaration of Independence, the latest President gives the one-and-only speech, dutifully applauded by regional dignitaries and a 21-gun salute.

In recognition of our notorious political bias I call LNL LeninL, and we've a great pozzie opposite the Tomb and the official party. Unlike Red Square where Soviet heavies were perched over Lenin's pickled cadaver to watch the strutting soldiers and menacing missiles, their Vietnamese counterparts stand beneath the looming monolith — the last resting place Ho never wanted. Just as he'd refused to move into the vainglorious Presidential Palace left by the French. But like Lenin and Mao the mortal remains of this immortal hero were too valuable to waste in the simple village burial he'd thought appropriate.

As the thousands march past us, in a modified goosestep, followed by the massed ranks of 'ethnic minorities' waving flowers, I wonder why communist nations do this to their defunct dictators. And I recall a column I wrote decades ago called "The Twin Religions", comparing Communism with Catholicism — the Vatican endorsing a huge trade in the corpses and spare parts of their saints. So many parallels — from an Index of approved writings to their respective Inquisitions, from confession to excommunication. With the writings of Marx and Lenin representing the Old and New Testaments.

Next day I head back to say 'Hi' to Ho, just as one likes to call in on Lenin and Mao. But just as Christ vanished from his tomb, Ho had disappeared from his. Knock, knock, no answer. It seems that within hours of the march he'd been packed off and sent on his annual hols to Russia. Two months in Moscow with the post-morticians who keep Vladimir Ilyich in non-working order. Ho travels with the entire conservation team in his refrigerated plant to Red Square — where after trial and error Lenin's team has learned a few tricks. In the Soviet in the early 70s I was told — in a whisper — that Lenin's nose had fallen off and that little by little he's become more Tussaud's than the genuine article.

I commend this approach to the National Portrait Gallery — pickled Prime Ministers — I'm sure that an embalmed Abbott would be a real crowd pleaser.

Radicalised youth

November 12, 2015

IT'S NOT NEW for Australian security agencies to keep an eye on radicalised teenagers. I know, because ASIO first opened my file 61 years ago. When I was 15. I wasn't radicalised by mad mullahs in a mosque but by reading John Steinbeck's *Grapes of Wrath*, borrowed from the Kew Municipal Library when I'd exhausted the possibilities of William and Biggles.

You can't blame ASIO for their interest in young Adams' subversive views. No sooner had I left the Boy Scouts than I joined the Communist Party.

(This didn't make my ASIO file but I was actually expelled from the broomstick warriors for setting fire to the Scoutmaster's desk. We were sharing a packet of Turf when we heard him coming. So I shoved our smouldering butts into the drawer where they kindled some memos from Baden-Powell. Ignition! Blast-off! I was drummed from the regiment.)

Having replaced scouting's woggle and knots with Stalin's hammer and sickle I clearly represented an urgent threat to national security.

Serious point here. The young have always been susceptible to a clarion call. Australian boys understated their age to fight in WWI. Volunteers like the Hemmingway, young lefties from all over joined the International Brigade to fight fascism in the Spanish Civil War. More recently many young Australian Jews have headed to Israel and joined the IDF to fight Palestinians. Our watchful spooks have no probs with this.

The process of 'radicalisation', of signing up for distant conflicts, may involve religious and /or ideological fervour for Zionists and ISIS recruits. Some of the current crop of would-be jihadists may be mentally unstable or feel alienated in their families or communities. But there's also the issue of teenage boredom versus the pangs of pubescent sexuality. Plus the simple seduction of guns and explosives, fantasies encouraged by violent media and video games. The same phenomena also play a deadly role in the secular slaughters in US schools, aided and abetted by the nation's most powerful terrorist organisation, the NRA.

Boys will be boys. And they love dangerous toys. Hence the glossy and sanitised images that seek to recruit kids for our armed services are not entirely different from ISIS' propaganda on anti-social media. Long before ISIS protestations of patriotism by our opportunistic politicians grew ever louder and more manipulative. It's been going on for centuries, millennia. So many opposing forces seeking child soldiers, kids as cannon fodder.

What I christened 'the pornography of violence' has turned slaughter into laughter. You see it in the trajectory and tactics of Australia's *Mad Max* movies. Miller's first effort took its killing and cruelty very seriously. His last effort played more lurid violence as slapstick. And critics who should have known better (and thought deeper) laughed along.

Abbott was right to describe ISIS as a death cult. It is. My wireless programme has spent much time explaining the significance — and the lure — of its apocalyptic theology. But it flourishes within a greater death cult. Over 100,000,000 died in wars and genocides in the last century — yet we seem to want more. Thus killing people remains the most popular form of mass entertainment. The video games are today's Roman arena, TV channels are charnel houses. We huffed 'n puffed about sexual porn, rather than the pornography of violence. The links between those school massacres in US (the perps largely devoid of ideology or theology) and the ISIS atrocities should not be denied.

Kids are easy targets for killers — from the jihadists to the cigarette companies.

Identity

November 9, 2015

AT LAST COUNT, sixty three years writing for newspapers and magazines, with millions more words for books, scripts, speeches, broadcasts. Mostly ephemeral, forgettable — forgotten even by the author who, when devoting some days to bon-firing decades of press clippings, discovered he was destroying the writings and memories of a stranger. Along with the arguments and accounts of so many long-dead controversies. They'd seemed all-consuming at the time. Now they were being consumed by flames.

Of all the words I've written only a few changed anything: a one-page report to Prime Minister John Gorton. It began with "We hold these truths to be self-evident" — a borrowing close to satire given the issue: the need to give Australia some chance of fighting the growing dominance of US culture, particularly film and television. The 'we' included my friend — and Gorton's — Barry Jones. Our report mapped out a plan for a revived film industry.

But first, the rhetoric. "We hold these truths to be self-evident. It is time to see our own landscapes, hear our own voices and dream our dreams." Gorton accepted the three-part plan without bothering to discuss it with his cabinet, McMahon would try to scrap it but Whitlam would carry it through. And the plan worked wonderfully. Within a few years Australian films were a global phenomenon.

Our landscapes, voices, dreams. Our painters, poets, historians and novelists had been doing their best. But our cinemas showed only the vistas and cities of the US, told us their history, sold us their heroes. Our industry had made 500 films during the silent era alone, but soon after sound we'd fallen silent. Destroyed by Hollywood.

Generations of our actors lived and died without ever playing an Australian. They could mimic English and American accents to perfection — still can, but did not know their own. And we mimicked America in many other ways — from food to foreign policy. When I wrote that report for Gorton, 96% of the Australian box office takings went to US films, leaving 4% for the rest of the filmmaking countries. Including us.

Having devoted much of my life to the cause of Australian film I saw my dream of a cinema of national identity come true — only to be wrecked by a return to American landscapes, voices, dreams. With honourable exceptions, including the new wave of Aboriginal filmmakers, our industry is once more held hostage by Hollywood. Our box office share is much the same as it was 40 years ago — while grovelling governments bribe US studios to shoot in Sydney. Behold the Hollywood hybrids: *The Great Gatsby*, *Star Wars*, an assembly line of epics starring Depp, DiCaprio, Jolie. And our best and brightest are Hollywood stars with Hollywood accents.

So be it? A process involving osmosis and bullying that began in the 1860s has made us as American as apple pie, as Apple. We are overwhelmed by every aspect of US culture. Even our vernacular is disappearing. What movies, music and television started, the internet has finished.

We are connected to the American bloodstream. It flows into our political style and policies. If they are cut, do we not bleed? We become blood donors; the first to share American delusions and fight America's wars. Vietnam wars, Iraq wars, drug wars, terror wars.

Our painters still paint Australian landscapes and faces. Our poets and novelists still find inspiration at home. And some of our filmmakers dream our dreams ... Distinctive cultures blur and blend, are buried in a placeless brand-name world. I'm not sure what we've gained. But I know what we've lost.

2016

Dumbocracy

January 6, 2016

A PARADOX. Around our politically polluted planet voters express their deepening contempt for democracy by voting for the politicians most determined to debauch it.

Foremost amongst the current examples — the Republicans jostling for their Party's poisoned chalice, the right to run for the presidency. Resplendent in their ignorance, beatific in their bigotry, glorious in their stupidity and cupidity they are not content to wrestle in mere mud but seek to wallow in excrement.

And who has emerged triumphant from this ordeal of ordure? Trump. The sleaziest, greediest and silliest of the election's selection. Trump, the only leading candidate of any party in the US's modern era who makes George W look like Plato. Trump. Beyond the skills of a political cartoon because he is one. The inevitable outcome of celebrity culture.

Anyone with a brain larger than a Surprise Pea laughs at the thought of President Trump — except for the millions who seek to vote for him. But let us remember that the world laughed nervously at the prospect of B-feature Reagan in the White House. And laughed louder at the idea of George W. Admittedly Dubyah's successes (sic) were dubious. While Gore out-polled Bush he lost in a photo-shopped finish thanks to electoral shenanigans organised by brother Jeb in Florida that were endorsed by family friends in the Supreme Court. But the voters bear the blame for George Jr's second term — which gave us World War III in instalments.

Not that skulduggery is the exclusive domain of the Republicans. I was amused when one of the heavies sent by the Democrat leadership to Florida to vet the vote-counting fraud was Richard M. Daley — son of the notorious Major Richard J. Daley of Chicago who is widely believed to have stuffed enough ballot boxes to rob Nixon of the White House and give JFK the Presidency. What goes around ...

Not that Australian dumbocracy is devoid of gullibility. Queenslanders showed theirs by electing and re-electing that most scandalous and scabrous of scoundrels Joh Bjelke Peterson, whom such idiotic savants as Alan Jones would seriously propose as PM.

It's not only the cream that rises. Bolte, Askin, McMahon, Hanson and Abbott are amongst the multitude of mediocrities who've bobbed, albeit briefly, on the surface of power. (Remember that swimming pool scene in *Caddyshack*?) Indeed given the choice between brains and bullshit Australian voters have long shown an eagerness to elevate the unworthy.

To hell with the virtuous. Villains are not only the most entertaining characters in drama but we seem to prefer them in politics, giving brownie points to the more cunning and devious.

Trump is not the first rich celebrity to do an overnight switch to rough-as-guts politics. Lest we forget: the rise of Malcolm Turnbull in the Liberal Party when a wealthy merchant banker brutally disposed of sitting member Peter King by branch-stacking the Wentworth branch with such newly recruited members as James Packer. In the fall-out it was the decent King who was expelled from the Liberal Party while the Turnbully was propelled into parliament, hence into the leadership and finally to the Prime Ministership.

It is a poor workman who blames his tools. If politics in the western world disappoint and disgust it's the foolishness and wilful ignorance of the electorate that must bear both the responsibility and the burden. All too often what we say we detest in democracy is what we've done to it. The qualities or lack of them in the politicians we elect is finally our responsibility. As the Trump campaign deafeningly demonstrates at a thousand decibels, we reward machinations over merit, fail to distinguish sincerity from cynicism, and then have the audacity to complain.

Dimocracy, damnocracy, dumbocracy.

Houses

February 3, 2016

HOW MANY HOMES IN an average lifetime? The
Australian Bureau of Statistics' statistics were unfathomable
to this innumerate. The US stats were simpler. Between go
and whoa the average American moves 11.4 times.

(That .4 seems ominous. Perhaps it represents being
made homeless, tossed into the streets after the Sub Prime
Mortgage disaster.)

So let us both try to remember our domestic perambu-
lations. My first — the decidedly humble Congregational
manse in Maryborough, Victoria. Between the church and
the tennis courts, home to the Rev Charles Adams and his
bride, Sylvia nee Smith. We all left in 1941 — Dad off to provide spiritual guidance to soldiers in New Guinea, Mum to
work in 'the Rationing' and to have a wild time in her husband's absence. Can someone tell me if the manse survives?

Surplus to her requirements Mum billeted me with my
grandparents on their little farm on the then outskirts of
Melbourne. Now only the address remains.

Here's how I recorded it on the front of every schoolbook:
Phillip Andrew Adams/798 High St/ East Kew/
Melbourne/Victoria/Australia/the Southern Hemisphere/
the British Empire /the World / the Universe. The Empire
and the house are gone.

In fact I didn't actually live in the house. My real address was a sleep-out beside it, shrouded in soughing pine trees. Farmer grandpa Bill Smith was a twin, as was his little weatherboard — side-by-side and identical to brother Ed's. Ed, whose house as well as his person, would be carted up High Street to the Kew's Bundoora Cemetery. Caretakers lived in it for decades.

When finally Bill joined Ed up the road Mum reluctantly reclaimed her surplus son, moving me into a flat in East Melbourne with her second husband, a fully-fledged psychopath. I was 11 and it was hell. As was our next move to the open spaces of Briar Hill. Another weatherboard, more horrors.

To escape I left Eltham High at 15 to return to 798 to nurse my beloved grandma. All the land had been subdivided. Only the house was left, soon to be bulldozed. Nan was shunted into an 'old ladies' home' and I shared an old house in Brighton with would-be bohemians. Soon thereafter, a too-young marriage led to a decaying two-storey place in Oakleigh, a dead ringer for the Addams Family dwelling, though some insisted it was closer to the even spookier house in *Psycho* ...

As economics improved the removalists were kept busy. Off to a tiny rented place in South Yarra, to a tenement in a shabby part of Toorak (it had them) and hence to a large, likeable old pile in Hawthorn.

An affair of the heart sent a romantic refugee up the Hume Highway to rented digs in Rose Bay, to a flat in King's Cross, and to a sandstone pile (1820, Nat Trust listed) in what was still dangerous, decadent Darlinghurst. Driven out by a full-scale attack by neo-Nazis (true story) I moved to my first-ever 20th century home in Paddington. And finally to Elmswood, a farm at Gundy, 9,996 acres larger than the little plot Grandpa had farmed in the 30s and 40s. If only he'd lived to see it.

And this, I trust, is stumps. Last resting place.

How many homes, houses, bolt-holes is that? Might have missed a couple. For a few years, for example, I all but lived in the legendary Sebel Town House, the hotel in Elizabeth Bay frequented by show biz lowlifes. Plus a few longish-term stays in foreign parts.

Just as homes aren't always houses, houses aren't always homes. Too many homes aren't homes but places as intimidating, dangerous and claustrophobic as any prison. Whereas life in a caravan park can be content.

Cars

February 8, 2016

IN THE EARLY '70S, when shooting a fillum in London, I was introduced to the dreaded weed by Richard Neville. Puffed furiously, coughed hackingly, no measurable, let alone pleasurable after-effects. Rated it overrated.

Decades later, in San Francisco, I was persuaded to try again by a hugely famous film director. Didn't stop laughing for days. Far too much fun. As Methodists warn couples having stand-up sex in doorways "beware, this could lead to dancing". Ceased and desisted.

Tried cocaine at a Hollywood party. Only noticeable reaction? Dental, not mental. Numb teeth. Reminded me of having a filling.

Once spent a few days carting Timothy Leary around Sydney. He recommended

LSD. Very tempted, too timid.

That's about it. Apart from enjoying a rare rollie my drug of choice is English Breakfast.

Yet I admit to sharing a lifelong addiction with Mr Toad. Automobiles. I've long since lost count of them and the money I've wasted. Can't even remember how many work-horse 4WDs we've bought for the farm.

My first transport of joy was a very second-hand Austin A30, bought from a car yard in Essendon. To this point I'd ridden pushbikes and motor scooters. I'd never driven a car and had no licence. The dealer said no probs, indicated brake versus accelerator and gave me the name of an understanding police officer in the city. "He'll sort it in return for a counter lunch."

I bunny-hopped my little green car to the Exhibition Buildings, located the cop, took him across the road to the pub. I can still remember what he ordered sixty years later. Pork chops with apple sauce. No bother with a test, I bunny-hopped off with my automotive passport.

Unsurprisingly I climbed out of the beyond-repair wreckage of the A30 a few months later — and bought the cheapest new car in Australia. Even tinier than the Austin, a fibre-glass Goggomobile sedan sold by a motorbike dealer. I felt elated as it put-putted down Elizabeth Street. But at the first traffic lights I heard a five-year-old boy say, "Look Mummy, Noddy's car!" All pride of ownership vanished.

Twenty years and many cars later I stopped at the very same lights in my latest and ultimate mistake. No Noddy's car this, but an elderly Rolls Royce, a ginormous drop-head Corniche. A bloke awaiting a tram snarled, "Die rich man!" So I sold it to Kerry Packer who, driving at warp-speed from Sydney to Canberra, blew the engine. Bugger the NRMA, he got the TCN helicopter to fly down and pick him up.

As an addict I've had fixes with every imaginable make and model — but very little luck. My fixes forever needed fixing. On the day of delivery a famous grille fell off one as if it were spitting out a set of dentures. I've jousted with Jaguar and the Japanese, raged at Range Rover, tiffed with Italians and had an atrocious Audi. Only the last couple of cars, both Citroen CXs (including the very last one off the assembly line) have been pleasurable, although they've eaten tyres as if they were liquorice. Perhaps they are liquorice. The French are eccentric.

Next, the era when people don't drive cars but cars drive people. When the song of the cylinders is replaced by the whirr of electricity in cars closely related to Hoovers.

I've probably bought my last car. Nothing flash. Korean, devoid of karisma. Main attraction? The 5-year warranty, clearly exceeding my own. What Mr Toad and I exulted in will be forgotten, as Gens X, Y or Z (?) lose interest in the other form of autoerotica ... in this age of Uber and the iCar. Somehow Google lacks the frisson of Ferrari!

Fillums

February 21, 2016

ON SATURDAY ARVOS, having begged a couple of bob from Grandpa, I'd leave our little farm and catch the tram up High Street to Kew's Rialto, where, as I recall, it cost a deener to get in. The Hoyt's Matinee, jammed with raucous prepubescents, stuffing their gobs with the lollies they didn't roll down the aisles or hurl at an already blotched screen. The manager/usher in his ill-fitting red jacket tried and failed to keep order — until a brief hush as the first shafts of light flexed from the M bio-box ... only to become a triumphant chorus of the Matinee's official anthem. Follow the bouncing ball:

Here we are again
Happy as can be
All good pals
And members of the CCC.

CCC? The Children's Cinema Club. Three rowdy choruses led to a couple of cartoons: Heckle and Jeckle, Tom and Jerry, Sylvester and Tweetie Pie, Bugs Bunny and Elmer Fudd. "That's all folks!" from Porky Pig, followed by one or another of our serials. Batman and Robin versus evil Japs, Superman, starring the plump George Reeves in wrinkled undies, or woeful Western — Hopalong Cassidy, Tom

Mix, the Scarlet Horseman — all filmed between the same familiar Hollywood boulders. Despite the fact they were crap — and we knew it — we loved them. The way the hero was left dangling at an ep's end, often literally dangling from a cliff or the wing of a crashing plane, in a situation from which escape was impossible; only to miraculously survive via manifestly fraudulent editing.

(Deafening boos from a couple of hundred critics, then out to get more lollies.)

My favourite Matinee movies were anything starring Johnny Weissmuller, preferably being Tarzan, though a jungle Jim was acceptable. (When Johnny became too heavy to swing from a vine, producer Sam Katzman squeezed him into a safari suit.) While writing these words I'm holding a photo of Tarz doing his yodel — signed by Big W — and recall his sad end in a Hollywood retirement home for actors on hard times. Seems he'd frightened the old ladies by lumbering up the corridors beating his withered pectorals and yodelling for his elephant.

The trick at the end was to run for the EXIT — a thunder of feet and flipping seats — before THE END became the National Anthem. God Save The King? Bugger that! We were Republicans ...

Apart from the Movietone and Cinesound Newsreels, the first with its kookaburra, the latter with a kanga jumping from the screen, there was no Australian fillum, and few of my contemporaries — like Fred Schepisi and Peter Carey — conceived them possible.

By the time my first fillum was complete Hoyt's Rialto was long gone, despite a brief second life as a Revival Centre for what were known as Jesus Jumpers. I reckon the Rialto was more a religious venue for us.

Apart from going to the pictures with parents — perhaps once a week as well as the Matinee — that was that. Television? A decade away. All we had were Batman and Superman comics, scratched 78s on a hand-cranked record-player, and the wireless. My favourite program, a radio serial called *David and Dawn and the Search for the Golden Boomerang*, an Australian precursor to movies about searching for golden rings.

So we weren't overloaded, drowning in images. What we saw on the Rialto's blotched screen was precious and magical.

And wireless was wonderful — because it wasn't done for you. You just listened ... and conjured the pictures, faces, sets, costumes.

Imagine that. Imagine kids having to use their imaginations.

Branch stacking

February 29, 2016

FORGET THE TEA PARTY. Welcome to another secret meeting of the Tree Party here in the Bot Gardens, held after hours when we're not exhausted by our work photo synthesising and sequestering carbon.

It's good to see so many indigenous and foreign trees here tonight. As you know we large woody perennials believe in multi-horticulturalism. Abhorring arboreal bigotry we welcome the participation of eucalypts, oaks, elms, palms — the evergreen and the deciduous. Though we do draw the line at cacti.

As usual we'll open with a reading of "I Think that I Shall Never See a Poem Lovely as a Tree", followed by a chorus of "I'm a Lumberjack" which lists so many of our species in its lyrics while, at the same time, mourning fallen comrades.

Thus begins a new stage in our campaign to get the vote — to have trees given their democratic rights in federal, state and local elections—and to have our role recognised in the constitution. We also demand trees be honoured in the Order of Australia and the introduction of Living National Treesures, particularly those magnificent organisms who've lived for centuries or millennia.

Apart from being ignored in the constitution (itself, like all our legislation and regulations, printed on trees) we don't get a mention in the National Anthem. Though 'young and free' rhymes with tree, not a word about us. 'Girt by sea' (rhymes with tree) 'golden soil', 'boundless plains' — yet not one of us cracks it. Talk about the Nullarbor! Tree Nullius!

Even Dorothea Mackeller only mentions us in passing — and in the unsung third verse. 'The stark white ring-barked forests / all tragic to the moon'. Only *Waltzing Matilda* puts us centre stage, with its swaggie in the shade of a Coolabah tree. All praise to our dear friends, the landscape painters.

Our original plan was to infiltrate the major parties, Labor and Liberal. (We've already succeeded with the Greens, declaring Bob Brown an Honorary Tree.) Sadly we gave up on the Nats because of their genocidal attacks on trees everywhere.

With this infiltration going well (who better than trees to organise branch stacking?) solid legislative gains had been few and far between, with more and more of us being bulldozed and wood-chipped. Even the National Treesures in Old Growth forests chain-sawed! This, when every tree is desperately needed to capture carbon and provide oxygen.

Enter splinter groups, pun intended. Humiliated, radicalised young trees wanted war against our human tormentors. They imagined wood everywhere (in their furniture, cars, buildings — even newsprint) in a mass uprising! We'd have had them on their knees. Where even the timber floors would rise up against them.

Militant pencils stabbing at hands! Chopsticks lunging from the bowl! Angry doors slamming in faces! But wiser counsel from distinguished older trees containing many rings of experience, argued against it. Let's give humans one last chance.

Hence our final attempt to gain political power through the ballot box, itself originating in the tree. Votes for Trees! Trees in the Reps! Trees in the Senate! Trees running Tasmania! Trees on the High Court! Trees on the UN Security Council!

I'll be treeific, treemendous! With Treed Unions! The Forests United Can Never Be Divided! And we're backed by arborists, dendrologists, the birds and climate change scientists.

We're barking mad and aren't going to take it anymore! Enough of being nailed to the cross! From the bonsai to the giant Redwoods—from the olive groves to the conifers — and not forgetting Australia's 739 eucalypts — we're on the march, albeit a motionless march given we're rooted. We demand that humans turn over a new leaf.

Vatican't

March 6, 2016

PROVOKED BY PELL I'm reminded of an (im)pertinent archaeological discovery I made in Rome.

The painful fact that the Vatican's vast collection of Greek and Roman sculptures depicting nuddy blokes had been attacked by a team of Goths or Toths with hammers. The entire marble army denuded of their masculine marbles. Denuded of their dicks. Snipped of their trouser snakes. Pruned of their penises.

(Let the record show that one cock escaped the carnage. I found a Roman cherub still in possession of his, the size of a jellybean.)

Toths? Laszlo Toth, the deranged Australian who attacked Michelangelo's Pieta in St Peter's with a sledgehammer. But further researches cleared Lazlo. So was it an early effort of ISIS? No. The vandalism was an inside job, carried out by the Vatican itself.

A hit squad of nuns had been charged with the choppings off. After taking circumcision a bit too far they were then required to hide the genital mutilations beneath crudely plastered plaster fig leaves.

Doesn't this (dis)embody all the inanities of Catholic teachings on sex? I prayed for a future with a Holy Father who hadn't entirely lost his marbles (a Pope Francis?) ending the emasculation of his marble menfolk by returning theirs. By getting modern nuns (hopefully Josephites) to 'pin the tail on the donkey' — to sort through the chest of amputated appendages to find the right fits. Then out with the Araldite.

Yes, a dumpster full of dongers does exist in the dungeons. I wrote to Rome offering to buy the shattered shlongs as a job lot, either to swell my personal collection of antiquities or to flog at a huge profit as executive paperweights. Or as pets — to compete with the 'pet rock' craze. No reply.

Then an Emeritus Professor from Milan wrote to confirm the Papal pile of Percies. He'd seen it.

Searching St Peter's ruins in 1000 years, a Martian archaeologist will discover not only the dumpster but further evidence of a religion obsessed with sex. With an Immaculate Conception. With a Virgin Mary and a Virgin Birth. With a horror of sexual intercourse unless its purpose is procreative. With an abhorrence of adultery or bonking outside or before marriage. With women renouncing their sexuality to be Brides of Christ. With an unmarried priesthood expected to share the Church's lust for celibacy. A church that regards the humble, useful condom as the devil's tool.

I feel some pity for young men in the church copping the Vatican's brutal and unnatural bans on sexual expression. Inevitably some, hetero or homo, cross the line. I commend to readers writings of my favourite US Catholic, Emeritus Professor Gary Wills — his books galore or essays in the *New York Review*. Wills writes of the emasculation of young priests with a mixture of enragement and compassion. We share the view that it's as wounding as the hammering of classic statues.

The Catholic Church is not alone in its fear and hatred of the sexuality that drives all life, not just human life, for any creature more complex than the amoeba. Apart from a few permissive moments in Hindu history, and the free-and-easy culture on the Trobriand Islands, most religions (and even Lenin's Soviet) proscribed sexual pleasure, dogma and taboos creating destructive guilt and what hierarchies damn-to-hell as perversions. When it is their own teach-ings, their own inventions of sins, their own taboos that are perverse. Paedophilia is not the only problem created by archaic theology.

Wills is right. Generations of young priests have been abused by the dogmas of their own church, denied any chance of sexual maturation. Some are destined to abuse others.

Sorry Day

March 9, 2016

HERE IS THE NEWS.

Donald Trump has surprised the US and the wider world by apologising for his conduct "both as a candidate and a human being".

"I've been rude, rotten and repulsive throughout my personal and business life. I sincerely regret this, and the way my unpalatable proclivities have spilled into an increasingly thuggish political campaign. Unlike my trade-mark hair my racism has not been thinly veiled but central to my dubious success. My nudge-nudge dislike of blacks and my ten-decibel detestation of Mexicans and Muslims won support from many of the nastiest elements in this nation — from the Ku Klux Klan to rabid anti-Semites. And my plans to build the Great Wall of Trump across our southern borders have alienated global opinion. I have been seen as a nasty hybrid of Berlusconi and Putin. But a long private audience with Pope Francis has changed everything. I am withdrawing from the contest, shaved off my silly comb-over and joined a silent order of Benedictine monks."

(Apart from noting his change of heart and hair, political commentators have observed a marked improvement in Trump's vocabulary.)

Ignoring the health risks palpitating beneath his pectoral cross, Cardinal Pell has had a change of heart and returned to Australia. As an act of penance he flew economy with Virgin (the plane re-branded Virgin Mary for the purpose) and having kissed the tarmac at Mascot he proceeded to wash the feet of abuse victims. "It will take me weeks to confess my many sins, but for now, let this be my Sorry Day. I am totally and utterly ashamed of acts of commission and omission during my years in Australia and hope that the victims of predatory priests and those who obfuscated the evidence, mainly myself, can forgive me. I am handing in my Cardinal's cap, shaving my head and joining a silent order of Benedictine monks."

(Founded by Benedict of Nursia in 529AD, and known as the Black Monks, the order has produced almost a dozen popes — and leading apostles include Wolfgang of Regensburg and, my special favourite, Gerard of Csanaid.)

Tony Abbott has apologised for running what he now admits was a ghastly, grotesque government. He insists it was his fault and responsibility, adding with characteristic chivalry, "Stop picking on Peta".

Last week Abbott confessed to confessing his sins, personal and political, via video link to Cardinal Pell in the Vatican, and was absolved of guilt. Abbott has said sorry to Malcolm Turnbull for saying awful things about him and has announced his intention of resigning from parliament to join a silent order of Benedictine monks.

Bill Shorten has broken his silence and resigned as a Benedictine monk to resume duties as the Leader of the Opposition. "With a July election it's probably time people heard from me."

Others have apologised for expressing bigoted or overly aggressive points of view. These include scores amongst the conservative commentariat of shock jocks and print pundits. Topping the list, Alan Jones, Ray Hadley, and Andrew Bolt.

"We don't know what came over us," they said in a joint statement. All are quitting their media pulpits to join a silent order of Benedictine monks.

Few of the above were Catholics, which makes their conversions all the more notable. However, one apologetic pundit was already within the faith. Australia's latter-day Gerard of Csanaid, our own Gerard of Henderson. He admits it was difficult to admit to error, "and it will be even harder observing an oath of silence." Yet the leading Pell apologist will also enter the Benedictine order.

One's pacemaker'd heart goes out to Donald, George, Tony, Alan, Ray, Andrew and Gerard. And even more to the Benedictines.

Is this a hospital?

March 17, 2016

I'M WORKING AT 2UE with John Laws, Alan Jones, Stan Zenamek and other shock jocks and although station management regards my jocking as insufficiently shocking it's me being stalked ... by a punch-drunk ex-boxer with a gun.

The police aren't being particularly helpful. ("Don't hesitate to call if he kills you.") So I'm forced to hire some 'muscle'. However, as my bodyguard's not available 24/ 7, long periods remain tense; exiting home at 9pm — and leaving the studios around midnight.

My Kings Cross home seems secure. Built of solid sandstone in the 1830s, it is surrounded by high walls with even higher metal gates. My study and bedroom are on the third floor.

Having arrived home unscathed, I'm reading my hate mail when I sense someone's in the room. Close behind me. I await the bullet. And then I slowly, slowly turn, to face my fate. However, it's not the punch-drunk ex-boxer but a frail old bloke who looks more afraid than me. And he asks me a very sad question:

"Is this a hospital?"

This is the year the Mental Asylums (aka 'the Loonie Bins') are being closed down in pretence of progressive social policy. But it's really to save money. The official line is that the patients (inmates? prisoners?) are to be 'returned to the community'.

Trouble is, bugger all preparation has been made. The asylums are emptying but many have nowhere to go. No family that cares. No halfway houses. Yes, Australia's Bedlams are god-awful places, but many shown the door will be homeless, helpless. And they're heading for Kings Cross, where tourists can watch the drunks, the drug-addicted, the prostituted street kids in that neon-lit theme park of human misery.

I still don't know how he got in. Perhaps he saw the high walls as comforting and managed to climb the tall iron gates. And the steep and darkened flights of stairs, until he found someone, anyone who might help him.

Explaining that no, this isn't a hospital, I calm us both down with cups of tea. And ring the Kings Cross Police Station. No, I haven't been murdered by my ex-boxer. But can you come around anyway?

Cops in Kings Cross have one of the toughest beats in Australia. Many retire early, suffering from what will be known in the future as PTSD. In my years here they visit me and, while I make cups of tea, they tell me their horror stories.

(Two cops are in the kitchen, one veteran, one rookie. The older bloke is telling the young cop [and me] how to take down the corpse of someone who's hanged himself. How the body has invariably defecated. How it can burst. And how hard it is to get help when the police force has only two staff psychiatrists.)

The cops who come this night are gentle with the old bloke. Off he goes into the night. God knows where.

And where are they all today? Some are still homeless, still living rough at the Cross; bag ladies and blokes. You see them in the nooks and crannies, or queuing for cups of tea from the samovars of various good Samaritans, or the Wayside Chapel.

We finally got my punch-drunk, ex-boxer sorted. And Mr Plod has been far more helpful with subsequent death threats. One of the more serious — proclaiming himself a suicide bomber intent on vengeance was under surveillance for months. My crime? Refusing to share his 9/11 conspiracy theories. The bomber also had John Howard on his hit list. So the PM and I had another reason to avoid each other's company.

Unpopulation

April 30, 2016

THERE'S LITTLE CONSENSUS on our census. As 2016 approaches, many question the questions and are suspicious of what might be done with the info. Both libertarians and lefties advocate non-cooperation. Governments know too much already—why add to the massive amount of mega-data? Isn't it enough to know the gross population tops 24,000,000?

Had God conducted a census since the death of the dinosaurs we'd know for certain what the experts suspect — that the number of humans who've ever lived nudges 107 billion. So for every one alive, 100 are dead.

But business is booming. Despite international conflicts, terrorism, epidemics, famines, China's One Child policy and advances in contraception, our population continues to soar. In the 20th century it's estimated that 140 million died in wars and genocides. Yet we've continued to breed like rabbits and cane toads. Out of control and birth control we're like other feral species: a growing threat to the environment. Our genius for desertification, salination, deforestation and other epic forms of vandalism, is killing off habitat and the hapless creatures within — both on the land and in the oceans. Any census shows that whether furred, feathered or scaled, special species galore have been driven into extinction or the growing queue of the endangered.

A queue we've chosen to join ourselves. For the very same reason — habitat destruction. Firstly in blissful ignorance, now in wilful ignorance or, even worse, murderous intent we're destroying our habitat.

Because we refuse to give up smoking. For years the cigarette industry used tame scientists to dispute and deny the clear evidence linking tobacco with cancer. More recently scientists — including some of the same scoundrels — have been trotted out to deny any link between the smoking of industry and climate change. The heavy smoking of a billion exhaust pipes, of countless factory chimneys and power stations, is turning the planet into an ashtray. With corporate greed's burning ambitions even those of us who've given up the fags are forced to be passive smokers.

In his early 80s James "Gaia" Lovelock told me two things, one optimistic, one fatalistic. Firstly, his cheerful statistic that no matter your age it was 90% certain you'd still be alive in two years. (In his case that proved accurate — he's now 96.) Secondly, what climate change would do for humanity in the 21st century — that we'd be 'lucky if there were a few breeding pairs surviving in a temperate Arctic'.

(Incidentally, DNA records suggest that there was a time, a bad time for humans, when our total population got down to a few thousand. So there's no need to worry. Let's keep puffing away.)

Will the Australian census count those criminals; child drowners and terrorists who pretend to be refugees, in offshore detention? If so, prepare to see our population soar as ocean levels make refugees out of countless millions. Pacific neighbours will be amongst the first; rising levels are already leaking into the fresh water tables. Next, on a far larger scale, those driven to desperation by increasing droughts or inundation.

We live in the lotus land of the deniers, Pell, Abbott, Jones; where the new head of the CSIRO sacks climate scientists. Where we approve ever-larger coalmines. Where a Prime Minister who knows and accepts the truth of climate change changes his tune.

But don't worry. There's a 90% likelihood we'll still be alive in two years.

Health warnings

May 10, 2016

PLEASE TURN YOUR Bibles to Matthew 5:5. In his account of the Sermon on the Mount — also in what's known as the Beatitudes — Matt quotes the Lord: "The Meek Shall Inherit the Earth". This is a fib that dwarfs Everest. They haven't, they aren't and they won't.

Not only do the meek NOT inherit, they're very rarely mentioned in the Will. Name me one place on Earth when the meek inherited it. One time in history. Oh, there've been moments when they seemed to have cracked it — as when those Bolshie atheists claimed to have launched a dictatorship of the proletariat — but it never happened. Soon the proles were being dictated to by another mob of Kremlin dictators. The Czars replaced by the Commissars. The Commie czars.

In *The Life of Brian* those too far from the Mount misheard the Saviour — thought He'd said the "Greeks Shall Inherit the Earth". Had they had better seats I'm sure it would've been clear that a prescient Jesus really said, "The Geek will inherit the Earth". This is manifestly correct — geeks like Gates, Musk and the disciples of Jobs (what a wonderfully Old Testament name) increasingly dominate the 1%.

The Bible is full of well-intentioned fibs. "They shalt beat the swords into ploughshares" (Isaiah 2:4) has not, is not and will not occur while there's more money in weapons than in agriculture. Indeed much of the Good Book gives bad advice. Scroll through God's most famous download, the Ten Commandments.

"Thou shalt not kill." Yes thou shalt — in the 20th century alone around 150,000,000 were killed in wars and genocides. Sadly God himself ignored that commandment with his A-bombing of Sodom and Gomorrah and His genocidal Flood.

Thou shalt not covet thy neighbour's ass? Well, perhaps not his donkey — but you certainly lust after his BMW or Tesla. As for coveting his wife ...

Before TV shows they screen an audio-visual health warning: "Contains violence, bad language and sex scenes". Does this warn off the viewers or welcome them? Admit it, it's an inducement. Programs lacking such naughty ingredients rate like Question Time. Though, on second thoughts that piece of local drama contains material unsuitable for viewers under 15 — or over it.

The world is full of ambit claims. Remember them? The pay rates unions demanded? When they knew they'd have to settle for half? The 'United Nation's Declaration of Human Rights' is a classic case. Nations sign up without any intention of providing them. Just as Australia is a signatory to the international convention on refugees.

Remember the way Phil Ruddock defiantly wore his amnesty badge (depicting a candle shining through barbed wire) while opening up concentration camps for asylum seekers? Amnesty repeatedly demanded Ruddock take his badge off. Phil had, after all, put up the barbed wire and blown out the candle.

(He was still wearing it when he left parliament, heading

for a ludicrous Job for the Boy, "Australia's Special Envoy for Human Rights".)

The Seven Deadly Sins? Pride? Envy? Wrath? Gluttony? Lust? Sloth? Greed? Like Moses' Big 10 that's not so much a don't-do-this-don't-do-that list as an agenda. A shopping list. And the creatures used to symbolise them: toad for avarice, snake for envy, lion for wrath, snail for sloth, pig for gluttony, goat for lust and peacock for pride must be the popular pets in the metaphoric menagerie.

So don't buy shares in plough shares. Have your super-fund invest in munitions. Bombs and bullets are safer than real estate. As for the meek — follow Ruddock's example on refugees and shun compassion. As successor Dutton recently warned: warm fuzzies about the meek only gives them false hope.

The mighty pencil

May 27, 2016

THE MOST POWERFUL bloke in Australian politics isn't Billion Dollar Bill or Mr Harbourside Mansion. It's Mr Squiggle ...

We're all familiar with the whereabouts of Auntie's pen. "La plume de ma tante est sur le bureau de mon oncle." I'm not sure whether this is the same pen that's mightier than the sword — "le plume est plus forte que l'epee" — but there's also a French connection. Not via Baron Bic, who went from pen to sword (i.e., from ballpoint to disposable razor) but with Cardinal Richelieu in Edward Bulwer-Lytton's 1839 play.

Whatever the language it's a load of horse merde, as non-sensical as 'the meek shall inherit the Earth'. In any fight I'll take the sword, even the littlest one, against the biggest pen — one of those duty-free Mont Blancs. History proves the sharpest nib is powerless against a well-honed blade. Writers may be messianic and courageous, but the odds have always favoured the bloke with the bayonet.

(Had I been doing the dialogue for Richelieu I'd have written "the word is mightier than the sword". Not that it's any truer, but word /sword seems more stylish.)

On the other hand, there is clear proof of the might of the pencil. We'll witness it once more in the imminent if not eminent election. That Commonwealth of Australia pencil, dangling from its piece of string, in every polling booth across this wide brown land.

America's voting machines have voters yanking levers like old-style Australian pokies. And this is an appropriate simile, given US election scandals. Thus Jack Kennedy won the 1960 Presidential election when Mayor Daley — that corrupt mate of his criminally connected father — rigged the machines in Chicago. Yet they had the cheek to call Nixon "Tricky Dicky".

(In every election the US 'pokie' system's a gamble that the bank — or the bankers — always wins. Or the Supreme Court will dud the Democrats and give the job to a lemon like George W. or Donald Trump.)

Discussing election matters with Antony Green confirmed my worst fears: it's only a matter of time until we'll be waving our iPhones in the booth, having been handed 'How to Vote' cards by a hovering drone. Or we'll vote online from home, ordering our MPs from Amazon. One can anticipate entire elections being manipulated by foreign powers (not just by the US as is currently the case) or being hacked by acned teenagers in jumbled bedrooms.

So let us enjoy the power of the pencil while it lasts. Neither Antony nor I could recall if the official government pencils are HB or 2B, but legislation puts lead in the pencil of our democracy. The law insists you have one, though you may choose not to use it. Some heretics use ballpoints.

Think of the mighty forests felled for the wooden casing. The open-cuts of graphite gouged for the innards. The epic amount of string produced for the tethering. This is a vast undertaking — one of Snowy Mountains scale. And I presume the Greens, other than Antony, make sure the pencil timber doesn't come from old-growth forests or the wood-chip industry.

And what happens to them after Election Day? Are they dumped as landfill? Or recycled like election promises? Did the very same pencil you'll use on July 2 say NO to Menzies' plan to ban the Commos? YES to giving Aboriginal people access to the pencil? Did it elect Whitlam? Eject Abbott? If so, my point is made. The pencil is mightier than the pen.

Recently a plethora of PMs and Premiers have lost their jobs without the pencil, without giving us the pleasure. But our ailing body politic is about to get another jab of pencilillin.

Supermarket

June 6, 2016

BORROWING ITS TITLE from Hamlet, *To the Manor Born* was set in a hamlet of great tranquillity. No mountain of corpses as in murderous 'Midsummer', not so much as a skull of Yorick. More Dibley than Elsinore, the 1979 series told the story of the posh Audrey fforbes-Hamilton (Penelope Keith) losing her mansion to *nouveau riche* supermarket owner, Richard DeVere (Peter Bowles) and their slow-motion romance. Every episode concerned the British obsession with class.

My favourite moment involved fforbes-Hamilton's first visit to a supermarket. As shopping had been left to servants, she's mystified. Stands alone and confused amidst the shelves. At last she speaks sternly, desperately to anyone in earshot: "If someone doesn't serve me I shall serve myself!"

Almost 40 years later I share poor Audrey's confusion. Whether it's Woolies, Coles or Aldi, I feel like a rat in a maze, the victim of scientific sadists who are looking down measuring and pleasuring in my discomfort. Trundling a trolley with a wonky wheel I can't find anything. And if I do I'm confused by choice. (How can there be so many milks, such a blur of detergents?) Then, no matter how hard I try to nut things out, I choose the slowest checkout.

Oh, for the days of the local grocer. When bread was white and cheese was Kraft — one of the few items that came in a pack. Everything else was bulk. Grandma would send the six-year-old me off with a list and the grocer would do the rest. Running up and down his ladder, slicing butter from the block. Biscuits (Milk Arrowroot mainly) were measured into paper-bags — with 'broken bickies' given in a cone of brown paper as a treat, an early version of the loyalty program. The bread was invariably High Tin, a loaf shaped like a bum. "Don't pick at the bread," Nanny would warn me, but I always did on the way home, having parted the buttocks.

The grocers was dim and fragrant, and when you pushed open the wire door it rang a bell. A real bell, not electric. And Mr W would emerge from the gloom, take the list, and load your bag. The string bag of loving memory.

Now it's all fluoro lights, crap music, victims with vacant eyes. You'd swear the entire system was being run by Peter Dutton using the techniques of oppression developed for offshore detention. And just when you've spent weeks mapping out more-or-less where things are, they shuffle their shelves and, yet again, you need GPS to find the yoghurt.

I miss our grocer. Mr W had a gammy leg, but it didn't slow him on the ladder. And he gave me broken bickies. True the store had about 5% of the stock of a supermarket, but it seemed more than enough — except for what you got from the Haycraft brothers who ran the East Kew butcher shop, and the Italian bloke who sold fruit and veg. (Only one sort of lettuce.) In that pre-freezer era shopping was more frequent and more friendly, gave a sense of community.

Fforbes-Hamilton was right to protest. What next? Self service petrol? Where they don't check your oil, water and tyres? Money-vending machines outside banks? Robot voices that so 'value our call' that we're put on endless hold to a sardonic soundtrack of mechanical music?

As a symbol of cruelty the supermarket trolley has replaced the tumbrel. One led to the guillotine, the other to the checkout.

Donations

July 18, 2016

THOUGH HE COULD easily afford to give it — and perhaps couldn't afford not to — Malcolm Turnbull's generous donation to himself has raised as many issues, hackles and eyebrows as his footnote in the Panama papers.

I do not see any ethical issues here. If Turnbull was for sale, and we can be sure he neither was nor is, as he doesn't need the money, he's surely entitled to get a good price. After all, more than anyone else, Malcolm knows what he's worth. At worst we're looking at a case of insider trading.

It's not like the Hockey donation drama — leading to a court case betwixt Joe and nudge-nudging-wink-winking Fairfax — where the implication of a SMH headline seemed to be that big donors would be guaranteed access to the Living National Treasurer. Malcolm doesn't need to bribe Malcolm because he already has access to himself. Only Mrs Malcolm is more intimate.

It's not as if Malcolm did something iffy. Like declaring himself a charity so his donation to himself would be tax-deductible. The Turnbull transaction was entirely transparent, or would have been had we known about it and, subsequently, been able to see right through it.

Thanks to this newspaper's front-page story Malcolm's donation has become transparent — transparently obvious that it would have confused the voters had they learned about it during rather than after the election. And it's clear as mud that the self-donation would have deflected our attention away from important policy issues. Like political donations.

There's continuing scuttlebutt about the need for federal ICAC. Who wants one of those? Neither the Libs nor the Labor Party. It's no more necessary than a Royal Commission into the banks. Waste of money. Ask the banks. They don't want one. And if you can't trust the banks, who can you trust? Enough of this class-war carping from the impecunious and envious.

True story. Above my desk are two framed financial documents, one irrelevant, one on the money. The former is a cheque signed with a flourish, in blue ink, by Charles Dickens. Dated the Third of January 1859, it seeks to draw the princely amount of Six Pounds from his bankers, Coutts & Company of No 59 the Strand. As far as we know this was not a political donation.

The latter document, however, certainly was. It says so. On a page torn from the sort of cheap receipt book you got from a newsagent and stationer. The date — 90 years later. November 16, 1949. It thanks a J B Foster for donating 'to the Australian Federal Labor Party Campaign Fund'. The amount? The unprincely sum of '4 shillings'.

And it's signed, in pencil, by Ben Chifley, just a few days before his election defeat.

A Prime Minister signing a receipt for a miserable four bob. Forgive the rhetorical question — but why do I find this scrap of paper so unutterably poignant?

But back to our two million-dollar donating PM. Sixty six years later, everything is more expensive. Cars, real estate, food, politicians. We live at a time when raffling a duck in a country pub doesn't measure up. When elections are so costly that only the rich can afford them. Around the world it costs more and more to own a politician. (Look at billionaire Trump versus the cashed-up Clintons.) So the question arises, do we really need to out-and-out buy them?

Couldn't we just rent them? For the occasion? Over and above their official and clearly inadequate salaries? Couldn't we lease them for a year or so? Get them on layby? Rather than raffling ducks, why don't we simply raffle our politicians?

Why the Queen is a Republican

August 7, 2016

WE ARE NOW the longest running, longest reigning monarch in English history. And we're heartily sick of it.

We yearn to abdicate. But the thought of handing over the family business to Charles fills us with despair. Like most of the Windsors, his choice of women has been calamitous. First his affair with that excessively bouncy Australian. No wonder they called her Kanga. Then Diana, enough said. And now that wretched Camilla for God's sake!

Uncle Edward set a very bad example, of course, with that American person. Had to go, of course, and we should be grateful that she provided an excuse. The real problem was his infatuation with Hitler. Would have been back in the throne in five minutes flat had the Nazis invaded.

(Thank God the nice chap who looked after my paintings got the incriminating letters back. So he was another of those Soviet spies like Burgess and McLain. So what? Nobody's perfect. And Uncle Ed's letters to Berlin were almost as embarrassing as the Palace's correspondence with that farting Falstaff from Canberra, Sir John Kerr. Note to self: We must remember to burn them at Balmoral next time Philip fires up the barbie.)

Margaret was hopeless with men. That air-force bloke she fell in love with! Couldn't have let her marry him in a fit. Not that that photographer Jones was much better. Let alone that Roddie bloke. Thank God we got the naughty photographs. Would have made the Profumo affair look tame. Philip burnt them at Balmoral during that sausage sizzle for that Australian PM who groped me. Paul ... Paul? Tip of the tongue.

Talking of sausages, Ann married that young chap whose family made a fortune out of sausages. And Andrew! What's a Queen to say? When all her kids, heirs to the throne in the event of another plague sweeping London, married embarrassments.

At least we did alright. With Philip. He might be as thick as a brick and a bit inclined to stray, but he knows his place. Coming up the rear.

The real problem as Queen is having to have weekly meetings with the endless succession of dopes from Number 10. Quite liked Harold Wilson, but that Thatcher woman! And that two-faced twerp Tony Blair!

The Royal Tours were appalling chores, particularly after they evicted we from the Royal Yacht. And the endless investitures. And the effing garden parties. And having to dress up in full regalia, heavy as a horse's harness, to read those absurd Parliamentary prologues.

But the worst is the curse of the Anthem. The Royal advertising jingle. 'Jingle Bells' has a better tune, and that other dirge 'Happy Birthday' has better lyrics. Can you imagine how many times we've had to endure God Save Me? How many times we've been sent Victorious, Happy and Glorious? How we hate it.

Let's do the math. We've been HM for about a century. We cop God Save, on average, four times a day. That 100 times 365 times 4, equals ...? Where's HM's iPhone ... it's got a calculator. And it's not as though we get paid royalties. If we did we'd out-earn Lennon, McCartney and that other Queen. And we'd have a slush fund for my retirement.

Our only consolations are our corgis and our horsies. Nobody knows, but we call the corgis after the kids and their wives. Give 'em kicks in the arse when nobody's looking.

So roll on the republic. We'll flog the pictures at Sotheby's, turn Buckingham Palace into top-end condos. Get the Royal Yacht back from the scrap yard and sail off into the sunset. Victorious, happy and glorious at last.

Curtains

September 18, 2016

IT IS NOW OFFICIAL. This is our last day on Earth. The sad fact has been confirmed by Pope Gladys in Rome, by King Charles in London and by other heads of state, a plethora of presidents including our own President Wu. We failed to deflect the asteroid with IGBMs.

At first there was that familiar response to a looming planetary catastrophe: denialism. Those who saw climate change as a left-wing plot echoed familiar arguments. A: it wasn't happening. B: the dangers were wildly exaggerated by scientists seeking grant money or C: it was as joke, a latter-day version of Orson Welles' *War of the Worlds*.

Now that we can see the approaching monster and know it will impact with the force of seven billion nuclear bombs; equivalent to one bomb for each of us, the responses are even more varied. Millions have already crowded into churches, mosques, synagogues and temples for collective prayer. Some true believers, however, seem angry with their priests and are demanding their money back.

Others, in a desperate attempt to reach religious destinations, for whatever reason, are gridlocked in their final traffic jams.

Almost as many are gathered in street parties, intent on mass inebriation. Sad that the end of everything has led to such a decline in moral standards. Dieters have stopped bothering with gluten-free bread, teetotallers have taken up drink and many, having sworn off smoking, have resumed the filthy habit. And speaking of filthy habits there are many reports of public fornication, in parks and on footpaths. Even worse, few participants are practising safe sex.

Nor are people putting coins in the parking metres.

No longer fearful of legal consequences others have taken up arms and are shooting unpopular neighbours or assassinating leading politicians. President Trump, mid-way through his third term, was finally moved to appeal for tougher gun laws when shot by his own bodyguards.

You are probably feeling the earthquakes or being drowned in the tsunamis. These were predicted in last night's weather forecasts as the gravitational pull of the approaching asteroid tugs at the oceans and tectonic plates. In the apocalyptic drama *On the Beach* the world ended in Melbourne. Now, in reality, it will end in Australia. As a point of pride the point of impact will be close to Maralinga where Mr Menzies persuaded the Brits to hold their nuclear tests in the 1950s (something the late John Howard forgot to mention in his TV series).

For my own part I am observing a personal Sorry Day, seeking to express regret to all those I've in any way hurt or disappointed. This will, as you can appreciate, keep me fully occupied.

(This includes you, Arthur. I should have returned your leaf-blower.)

And while realising that no one will read this final column — I may not have time to finish it — I'd like to wish you all a fond farewell.

PS: Not everyone is blaming God. Some blame the Muslims, the CFMEU or the Carbon Tax.

Happy days

November 3, 2016

IN 1926 IRVING BERLIN tried to banish America's blues with Blue Skies ('all of them gone!') that had them brimming with bluebirds. As performed by Jolson in *The Jazz Singer* it would become one of the first songs to be heard in a 'talkie'. Three years later, in another attempt to provide an anti-depressant for the Great Depression, Hollywood released *Chasing Rainbows*. The theme 'Happy Days Are Here Again' had lyricist Jack Yellen again rejoicing in blue skies and urging the audience to 'sing a song of cheer again'.

Given that we live in equally parlous and perilous times, with every day delivering bad, badder, baddest news, it seems time to direct our feet, at least for a moment, to the sunny side of the street, the sidestep suggested by Dorothy Fields in her song of 1930. Let us forget the turbulence of Trump, the continuing shambles of our own Trumpbull government. Though our quota of bluebirds have been driven away by circling vultures, though our economy is on life support, though we are living in the environmental End Times, let us pretend we're happy.

Surely the most optimistic of all lyricists was Oscar Hammerstein Jr. (I know nothing of Oscar Hammerstein Sr.) For example, whenever you feel little, Oscar suggests you whistle a happy tune. And should malevolent meteorology force us to walk through a storm he urges us to hold our heads up high. And most famously of all, Oscar advises us to prepare an inventory of favourite things. Like whiskers on kittens and snowflakes on eye-lashes.

I'm not mad on cats, so will replace kittens (which Oscar wistfully rhymes with 'warm woollen mittens') and go for puppies, particularly in their early wriggling stage before they start chewing your shoes. And looking around the farm today I also observe any number of newborn lambs, very bo-peepish and cute, particularly two sets of black twins. Calves too, and foals. And little tweetie-pie birdies sticking their bald heads out of nests. Farms are very fecund this time of year and, let's face it, baby anythings, particularly human ones, appeal to the hardest heart, which in my case is pacemaker'd. Not fond of ferals, but our wild pigs are having lots of piglets. Soon they'll be wrecking everything but, at the moment, they're cute.

Seeing the dogs, Squire and CJ, dancing on their chains as I approach to untie them. Taking them and going for the morning walk. Letting the sheep out of the yards by the shearing shed. Saying hello to the donkeys. Getting warm eggs from the chooks. Loading ecstatic Squire and CJ into the ute and driving to the Gundy Store for the newspapers. Reading them with the first coffee of the day. Wishing the Oz would bring back Doonesbury. Feeling pity for poor Malcolm. Considering a furtive roll-your-own. Favourite things.

After years of drought the river's full. The grass is lush. The sheep are now moving through the olive grove and mowing the grass. Cattle prices? Good. The garlic crop? Great. The trees are alive with blossom, bees, maggies, finches, parrots. Kookaburras are pissing themselves. I'm alcoholic with the bucolic.

So come on. Let's pretend the world isn't totally utterly stuffed. Let's pretend that there are no wars, woes, refugees, Trumps, One Nations, environmental crises, human rights abuses, and domestic violence. No trubs.

2017

Adelaide Festival of Ideas

February 1, 2017

In 2016 The Adelaide Festival of Ideas was dedicated to Phillip Adams. The dedication was delivered by Barry Jones. The following was Adams' response.

THANK YOU FESTIVAL for an undeserved honour. And thank you, Barry. It's not often that you live long enough to hear your own obituary.

Let us now leave Adelaide and head for Hollywood. Known for over a century as 'the dream factory' — manufacturing filmic fantasies for both its domestic audience and much of the world. And for generations a cauldron for madness — as attested by, for example, the Manson family, the OJ Simpson case and Scientology. Hollywood is a prime source of supernatural phenomena and, during the '70s, the likes of Shirley MacLaine, Sylvester Stallone and Ronald Reagan all famously confused past roles with past lives, encouraging a rapture around reincarnation.

With La-La Land creating as many newly-minted religions as musicals and westerns, and with enough close encounters to clog the freeways, a committee of fine minds — the likes of Carl Sagan, Isaac Asimov and various categories of Nobel Laureate — coalesced around CSICOP — the Committee for the Scientific Investigation of Claims of the Paranormal.

Dick Smith and I agreed that we needed an Antipodean branch of CSICOP. A particular concern was cancer quackery, with people being deflected from life-saving procedures by manipulation of their credulity. The current fad was 'psychic surgery', a procedure wherein the surgeon (sic) seems to make an incision in the belly of a cancer patient without a scalpel — just using bare fingers to open a gushing wound. Almost the entire hand would disappear into the crater and, lo and behold, would emerge with what was claimed to be a piece of malignant tissue. I was taught to replicate this fraud and should someone in the audience be willing to disrobe and lie here on stage, I will demonstrate. Perhaps later in the evening.

We talk of a time when innocent scientists were being tricked by conmen, even within their sacrosanct laboratories. Uri Geller, a conjurer from Tel Aviv, was the most skilful, demonstrating a marvellous ability to melt metal with his mind and, as well, to 'remote view' — an ability to see inside an envelope in another room. The room could be next door or on the other side of the planet.

Seeking a second opinion, some called him Geller's nemesis, a gentleman with the somewhat unfortunate name of Randy. James Randy. Stage name? The Amazing Randy. Perhaps more appropriate to a porn star.

So Dick brought James to Australia where he and I and Richard Carleton offered $50,000 to anyone who, under reasonable scrutiny, under Randy's scrutiny, could demonstrate any form of psychic power. (That offer would subsequently be increased to a million dollars US with countless tests undertaken in many countries over almost 50 years — and not one person, not one, has been able to prove even the most commonplace psychic power, like telepathy.) Dick, Richard and I took the view that we'd be happy to hand over the $50,000 if someone could, for example, demonstrate the popular Australian agricultural skill of water divining. But it was not to be then — and has never been since. Though, let it be said, water diviners are not frauds like Geller. But true believers are absolutely convinced of their gifts. And it comes as a great surprise to them, sometimes verging on the tragic, when it is demonstrated to them that they are deluded.

What does this have to do with politics? The story begins in Dick's office where we were to hold a press conference — and every television network had sent a reporter and a cameraman. ABC, SBS, 9, 7 and 10. Their crews crowded into Smith's office.

First up Randy explained how he'd unmasked Uri and effortlessly survived any number of subsequent libel actions brought by the Israeli conjurer. As a professional magician James could see what scientists failed to see — because he knew the tricks of the trade.

Mid-conference Randy saw that I was about to light a cigarette and grabbed the offending tube from my lips. 'Dirty habit,' he said and placed the cigarette on Dick's desk. He then told us that he would demonstrate psycho-kinesis — the ability of the human brain to move solid objects, by paranormal power. And he wandered around the room rubbing his fingers on people's clothing. The leather jacket of a cameraman, the lapel of a reporter's suit. Finally he found a textile he deemed appropriate and asked us to cluster around. Remember we had two categories of trained observers — the journalists and the cameramen. People paid to see things with clarity. Randy once more rubbed his fingers on the fabric of his choice and extended them towards the cigarette; his fingers atremble with pent-up energy. The zoom lenses clustered to view the goings on from every possible angle. Dozens of eyes focusing intently on the fingers and the fag. And as Randy continued his spiel, lo and behold, the cigarette began first to tremble, then to move. Up the desk. Down the desk. Rolling left, rolling right. Gasps of wonderment and disbelief!

Then James asked the assembly to explain how he'd done it. Everyone had a theory, most involving static electricity, the sort of charge generated by walking on a synthetic carpet. You know, you approach a doorknob and get a mild shock.

No, he said. It was much simpler than that: 'I was blowing.' And he demonstrated how, though talking non-stop, he'd managed to emit little puffs that had propelled the cigarette. And yet none of us had noticed.

As Randy pointed out it was a classic demonstration of what's basic to all magic. Mis-direction. 'All of you were focused on my fingertips and the cigarette — not one of you looked at my mouth.' And for me it was a Eureka moment, an epiphany. For at that moment I realised that mis-direction, the basis of all conjuring, was perhaps the greatest tool in politics. Politics at every level, from the gubernatorial to the global.

Later I'd watch an associate of Randy's, stage name David Copperfield, 'vanish' the entire Statue of Liberty in front of a sizeable crowd gathered on its tiny island. Once again, dead simple if you understood the principle of mis-direction.

Managing the audience's attention is of course the aim of all theatre. And it's the aim of almost all politics. Mis-direction takes advantage of the limits of the human mind in order to give the wrong picture and a false memory. Research suggests that the mind of a magician's audience — or a politician's — can barely concentrate on one thing at a time. Which makes it easy for the magician (or the politician) to manipulate ideas or perceptions and lead the audience towards a wrong conclusion.

It doesn't matter whether you're performing table magic with a blown cigarette or Three Card Monty or one of Copperfield's large-scale illusions. Mis-direction is the tool, the trick.

Before I give some primary examples of its application in the illusionism of politics let us recognise that it's also a basic device in the animal kingdom with mis-direction taking the form of camouflage. And we see it in the bullfight. It's an interesting fact that bulls don't see red. It's the one colour they're blind to — whether it's their own gore or that of a gored toreador. The colour has nothing to do with it. It's the mis-direction of that flapping cape. Having been goaded and quilled by the picadors the poor brute lunges hopelessly at the cape, completely failing to observe its tormentor. And we, the public, are a bit like that. Goaded by the picadors of shock jockery, by the strident commentariat we become as blundering and as blind to the truth as that bull.

'If the Jews did not exist it would be necessary to invent them.' A quotation attributed to Hitler though Jean-Paul Sartre made the same point in regard to anti-Semitism — and he was paraphrasing Voltaire. 'If God did not exist it would be necessary to invent him.' So we did. For an atheist like myself I'd have to suggest there might even have been mis-direction at the Resurrection.

For centuries, for millennia, Jews were the most popular racial or religious scapegoat. We currently see variations of the theme in relation to Muslims and Mexicans in the Trump campaign. We've seen it applied for decades in regard to our rabid response to refugees. We saw it a few weeks ago in a new poll suggesting that Australians accept the Trump/Hanson policy of restricting Muslim immigration — nothing short of a fully-fledged reintroduction of the White Australia policy, Australia's pre-emptive version of ethnic cleansing. And we saw it in 'kids overboard'. Politics don't get more magical. Like David Copperfield, Donald Trump wants the Statue of Liberty, and all it symbolises, disappeared. And here, politicians in all parties, major or minor, have managed to 'disappear' ethics, decency and compassion. Now you see it. Now you don't.

'Kids overboard'. Mis-direction is built into language. Asylum seekers become 'queue jumpers', or 'illegals'.

The elderly amongst us will remember a mis-directed Neville Chamberlain waving a piece of paper in the air and proclaiming 'peace in our time'. Some will remember Joseph McCarthy waving another piece of paper in the air — a list he insisted contained the names of 200 Communists working in the state department. It was the reddest of red herrings and there is an argument that what McCarthy held in his hand was a laundry list.

Lyndon Johnson famously — infamously — used the TonKin incident of August 2, 1964 to justify his massive escalation in Vietnam. An alleged attack on the USS Maddox that we've long known didn't actually occur. It was, if you like, a porky. Or, to use a more Australian piece of vernacular, a furphy.

But like the Reichstag fire, another classic piece of mis-direction, it was more than enough to energise an ideological and military onslaught — a massive escalation in one of the most appalling and unnecessary conflicts of the modern era. We call it the Vietnam War, they call it the American War.

So many appalling, unnecessary and ill-advised conflicts. George W. Bush's Middle East adventurism was arguably the most catastrophic. You will recall that that invasion was enthusiastically endorsed by the Coalition of the Willing, the Coalition of the Killing, in which John Howard played an underrated role. (Bernstein, of Woodward and Bernstein fame, became a rather conservative commentator in his latter years and was the ultimate Washington insider. He wrote a series of books on the history of George W.'s invasion — and I will never forget him telling me, on *Late Night Live*, that Howard was not simply a supporter but one of the most enthusiastic and influential advocates. 'The man of steel' had Bush's ear and endlessly, insistently whispered what the President wanted to hear.)

Hans Blix was on the program quietly arguing the case for the non-existence of Weapons of Mass Destruction. Most of us in this room knew what the President of the United States and the Prime Ministers of Australia and Great Britain claimed not to know — chose not to know — that Saddam's nuclear program had been abandoned and his swords, if not turned into ploughshares, had at least become scrap metal.

But what a magnificent piece of mis-direction that was — a war opposed by a majority of the human population, protested in unprecedented mass marches in scores of major cities, went ahead justified by a total fiction. Weapons of mis-direction. A fiction which, to this day, is endlessly recycled by Bush's bullies, by Blair and Howard. The Three Tenors supported by the deafening chorus of Australia's right-wing commentariat.

9/11 was, in and of itself, a monstrous act of mis-direction. Not by those who perpetrated it but by those who used it to justify an immense and ongoing calamity. George W. Bush insisted that 9/11 had been a personal project of Saddam Hussein's. Tis said that war exists to teach Americans geography — but to this day I doubt that Bush could point to Iraq on a map. But it was known within minutes of the event that most of the plotting and planning came not from Iraqis but from Saudis — from a country with which George H. Bush had uncomfortably close business affiliations. Yet Bin Laden's ethnicity would be ignored — and the Iraqis would be beaten into submission by Shock and Awe. Mission accomplished! Washington had updated the domino theory, used the towers as the biggest dominos in history. Dominos that continue to topple in the Middle East and beyond — to this day, to this minute.

Mis-direction takes so many forms. I took the programme to Tiananmen Square on one of its most significant anniversaries and our puny efforts at broadcasting were immediately closed down and *Late Night Live* was hustled away under threat of arrest. But the strange thing was that there were hardly any Chinese in the square that day — and not simply because of the police presence. But because of mis-direction on a grand scale. The children of Beijing knew little and cared less of Tiananmen. They'd formed huge crowds elsewhere in the city. In the shopping malls. We left a vacant Tiananmen to watch the young, the rising middle-class of China, crowding into the big-name stores just a few blocks away.

And it has to be said that around the world shopping has become one of the great mis-directions. The young are as likely to hyperventilate with excitement at the news of a new iPhone than they are to protest a political outrage. And this links to the other great form of mis-direction — the insatiable interest in celebrity. If shopping is the new religion, celebrities are its priesthood. As media cashes in on such human brand names as the Kardashians — and other human variants on the meretricious and the meaningless — political responses are dulled and distracted. Now we are witnessing its apotheosis. A world wherein brand names and celebrity overlap to produce a Trump candidacy, where someone of soaring, stratospheric stupidity is so dangerously close to becoming the most powerful person on earth.

Endlessly, easily distracted. We now have the attention span of insects. And the biggest issues have the shelf life of yoghurt. Executions in Bali are forgotten almost as soon as they occur. And we forget the context of everything. Which is why we recently chose to misunderstand the responses of locals to an Australian military ceremony in Vietnam.

Mis-direction is everywhere. Alfred Hitchcock invented his own version — the Maguffin. To Alfred a Maguffin was a little something he introduced to his thrillers to distract from the momentum of the plot. A false clue.

Another version is the straw man. The gay marriage plebiscite is a classic case — the most cynical of manoeuvres, a sort of legal filibuster. Which takes us away from Trump to Turnbull. One could suggest that Malcolm's beliefs, so passionately expressed over the years, have all been mis-directions in that none of them manifest themselves as policy.

His passionate belief in the Republic? His concern for climate change? Evaporated.

Such policies, such alleged enthusiasms are to be dismissed as though they were nothing more than puffery. The sort of puffery that moves cigarettes.

Around the world political confidence is not merely eroding but collapsing. You see it in Trump, we saw it in Brexit. We lose faith in our democratic structures, in our great institutions, in our churches. Healthy scepticism morphs into cynicism and into self-destructive, almost suicidal voting behaviour.

It occurs to me that the very term 'newspaper' is mis-direction as, God knows, they contain less and less news and more and more views of intensifying toxicity.

We are so easily distracted. And our ignorance is wilful. We collaborate in our own decline. We seek not to know. We have deaf ears, blind eyes. And that is why this festival, this little festival, that generated so many others around the country, plays an honourable role. You will not be mis-directed here. And your mere presence demonstrates a desire, a demand for the truth. And let the record show that thinking can be fun. That kicking ideas around can be far more entertaining than kicking a football. Think of it as the sport of thought.

For me the largest current use of mis-direction involves climate change. It is now over 30 years since Barry and I, through our Commission for the Future, introduced the issue of the Greenhouse Effect to this country. It's thirty years since we organised Australia's first national and international conferences on what would become 'global warming' and, in due course 'climate change', that latter term being in and of itself a mis-direction.

At the time I thought that here, at last, was an issue that would unite us all, that would soar above politics. But that was not to be. The cigarette companies hired corrupt scientists to dissemble and deny. The same tactics and some of the same charlatans are now employed by the fossil fuel industry. Then they denied any links between smoking and lung cancer. Now, as we try to stop the world smoking itself to death, they refute any human role in the crisis.

Finally, to another form of mis-direction deployed in the debate on refugees. This is the binary concept which postulates either total border protection or total disaster. And we fall for it. The false dichotomy, the either/or fallacy. The trick of false choice. The false dichotomy that there is no choice between razor wire and the red carpet.

'Read my lips: no new taxes' was a phrase spoken by the then American presidential candidate George H. Bush during the 1988 contest. The words we read on politicians' lips are unlikely to be the truth, the whole truth. Instead they're anything but the truth.

What I learnt from the Amazing Randy, and what I ask you to consider on this occasion, is to watch your politicians' lips anyway. To watch them very, very closely.

If only to see that they're ... blowing.

Thank you.

Fibs

February 10, 2017

IN THIS ERA of technological triumphalism and digital dazzlements you'd think that someone would have come up with a BSD. A bullshit detector. With circuitry installed in your TV, computer or cell phone ready to buzz or blink when someone tries to lay it on with a trowel.

In the case of a TV set, you'd have to turn the BSD off during the ads, pulling the plug whilst actors, hucksters and bribed celebrities feign multi-orgasmic ecstasy in the service of Mammon, lest all that twaddle about cosmetics turning the tide on time caused a Chernobyl-style melt-down. But a BSD during News or public affairs programs, particularly when PMs or presidents are bee-essing, would be far more useful than electric insect zappers or missile defence systems.

Perhaps it could be an electronic blurt, with little rasp-berries for minor fibs and echoing "oinks!" for major porkies. Or perhaps the BSD could employ the sub-titling abilities of SBS or the Caption Centre, simply supering "MORE BULLSHIT!" on the screen.

Though not much employed in Australia, the venerable Lie Detector has been a tool in US criminal investigations for years. And, more recently, we were told of a technology that can detect lies in the voices on the phone. ("Darling, I can't get home for dinner. I have to work late at the office.") Then there are the new gizmos scanning the faces of passengers at airports, trying to separate terrorists from tourists. 'Tis said that the system can see through beards and disguises — so don't tell me that between Microsoft and the CIA there isn't an appropriate variation that can see through whoppers. A counterpart of fingerprinting. Fibprinting.

And we need a variation on the technology for newspapers, a sort of litmus test that turns columns, news stories and editorials bright blue when their authors are being duplicitous.

The old joke that asks, "How can you tell when a politician's lying?" is answered by, "When his lips move." Yet too many people remain oblivious to political lying. In many cases such credulity is wilful, a deliberate choice. How else could this ongoing BS about WMDs remain an issue? Those fortunate enough to have a natural aptitude for BS detection were trying to warn the world of what was going on throughout the preamble to the war in Iraq. When the only people on earth who believed, or pretended to believe that Bush, Blair and Howard were telling the truth were to be found among the gullible and the culpable in the US, the UK and Australia.

The great fraud that went on for month after month, wherein our PM echoed the nonsense being pumped out in Washington and London, failed to convince a majority of Australians whilst being rejected and ridiculed by nations and populations around the world. The thuggery that went on at the UN, the revelations of Steve Ritter, the blundering attacks on Hans Blix were clear evidence of Bush's and Blair's determination to bulldoze their countries into an unnecessary conflict. The BS was laid on so thick that you didn't need a detector. It was clear that Howard didn't believe what he was saying — and hardly cared if we didn't believe him either.

Remember Howard's twaddle about "No final decision" having been made about our involvement? Australia's media was all but buried in Uluru-sized dollops of BS in an ongoing piece of political and media theatrics that was even less convincing, less plausible, than the silliest cosmetic ads.

Whilst Baghdad's Baathists would be stunned by the scale of Washington's war, many of us were more shocked and awed by the scale of its BS. It wasn't the WMDs we were worrying about but the WBS. The powerful weapons of bullshit.

It's not an issue of the reliability of US Intelligence. When has it ever been reliable? Intelligence (sic) failed to notice that North Korea was about to invade the South. It was responsible for such glorious stuff-ups as the Bay of Pigs and, subsequently, failed to protect President Kennedy from those who wanted him dead. Having grotesquely exaggerated the military might of the Soviet Union throughout the Cold War, "Intelligence" failed to predict Communism's collapse. Then there was the small problem of its failure to protect the US from September 11.

But all this low IQ Intelligence is nothing beside the unintelligence, the idiocy of what passes for political leadership. It was the scale of the exaggerations, the out-and-out fabrications, the bare-faced fraudulence of the whole preamble to the war in Iraq, that critics found profoundly offensive. One might have forgiven Bush and Co if, for a moment, they'd believed what they were saying. If they'd simply been misinformed. Or mistaken. But it was all chicanery and charades, sexing up any Intelligence that could be conjured by Washington whilst utterly ignoring any contradictory information or advice. Critics were vilified, having their patriotism questioned. It became treasonable to protest.

We've witnessed an ugly war waged by ugly people against, yes, an ugly despot. And the WMDs were just one of the lies used to justify it. Never forget the vacuous allegation (more unintelligent Intelligence) that the invasion was an essential part of the war against terror because Iraq was in league with Al Qaida. Of course it was. Just as Harold Holt was plucked off Cheviot Beach by a Chinese submarine.

Intelligence? Washington would have been better off relying on the revelations in owls' entrails or the horoscopes in women's mags.

Resistance is futile

February 21, 2017

A DEFINITION DERIVING from the Greek for 'all people'
pandemics have long plagued humanity, and many of our
fellow creatures. Some of the worst have been transgenic
— beginning in the jungles or farmyards and migrating
to human populations. Amongst our worst pandemics —
the Black Death, cholera, smallpox, tuberculosis, polio,
malaria, dengue fever, yellow fever, HIV, SARS, Ebola, and
avian flu.

And, of course, influenza. I like the origin of its name —
Italian for 'influence' because the outbreaks were believed to
coincide with the visits of comets.

The list of pandemics — or very near things — is long
and seems to be getting longer. Think Zika. And in many
cases our chances of containing them is problematic as anti-
biotics decline in effectiveness.

I raise the issue because of a new threat to world health
— to outbreaks of diseases the likes of which we haven't
seen since the 1930s: Pandemics of political insanity. One
of the worst cases was Pox Americana caused by George W.
Bush. Backed by the Coalition of the Killing (Blair, Howard
etc) it destroyed the lives of millions in the Middle East
— and continues to afflict a dozen nations in the region.
Current outbreaks include deadly ISIS. Tony Blair has

belatedly apologised for his role in spreading this latter-day Black Death, but not a hint of regret from Howard.

Australia's had domestic outbreaks of political insanity. The vector was One Nation. Hansonitis is now rapidly infecting a body politic that seems to have lost any natural resistance. Previously quarantined Hansonitis is spreading ever faster, thanks to PM Turnbull's decision to be doubly dissolute. And many of the worst symptoms are now clearly visible in the LNP, in sick and sickening MPs like Christensen and Bernardi.

Overheated rhetoric. Escalating racism. Religious bigotry. Ideological dementia blinding the afflicted to issues like climate change — or leading to hatred of refugees. If the symptoms are serious here they're probably worse in Europe. Take Brexit and the rise of the lunatic right in France, Poland, just about everywhere.

But the pandemic of political madness is at its deadliest and most dangerous in the (Dis)united States of America, with previously mild Trumpculosis leading to the tragic Trumporrhagic Fever. Scenes of utter madness occur on a daily basis in various Trumporrhagic centres like the White House and the Donald's glitzy venues — and the mental health system cannot cope.

The hope that the pandemic could be contained by: a) venerable institutions like the courts or b) that the President's ravings might subside following his inauguration have proved wildly optimistic. POTUS' dementia worsens by the hour with the small problem he could launch a nuclear war in one of his escalating attacks of anger or hubris. Labs are working overtime to find a cure (what is the source, the 'influenza' of what ails him?) and to produce a vaccine. There's an irony here — that Trump is so hostile to science.

(This is an all-too familiar symptom in Australia. One Nation's Malcolm Roberts is the most afflicted, but apparently sane LNP MPs have brought lumps of coal into the Reps claiming it to be 'clean' and needed to be tranquilised by parliamentary security.)

It's a race to find a pill, a jab, or to get world leaders to undergo electro-convulsive therapy, using their preferred source of power. Clearly most would refuse renewables. Clean coal?

The 1930s outbreak of political insanity lead to the madness of WW3. The well-named policy of MAD (Mutually Assured Destruction) dominated the decades that followed, taking us to the brink of nuclear Armageddon. We're back there again.

Phillip Adams
AO FAHA

DESPITE LEAVING SCHOOL at 15 Phillip is now Dr Dr Dr Dr Dr Dr Adams – having received a record-breaking six honorary doctorates from major universities. Elected as one of Australia's official National Living Treasures in a poll conducted by the National Trust he has received two Orders of Australia and the International Astronomical Union named 'a minor planet orbiting the sun between Mars and Jupiter' in his honour. He has won Australia's highest awards in film, journalism, broadcasting and human rights – and was elected to the Media Hall of Fame.

Billed as the 'Godfather' of the Australian film industry he has made over 20 films – including *The Adventures of Barry McKenzie, Don's Party, The Getting of Wisdom* and *We of the Never Never*. His scores of books include works on politics and Australian humour.

Described in the influential journal *The Monthly* as 'perhaps the most remarkable broadcaster in the history of this country' he has presented ABC's *Late Night Live* for almost 30 years. Broadcast twice daily around the world his tens of thousands of interviewees have included national leaders from Gorbachev to Kissinger and countless prime ministers and presidents. As Australia's longest running newspaper columnist he has contributed to most of Australia's major newspapers and journals over the last 60 years and to the London *Times*, the *Financial Times* and the *New York Times*.

He has been Republican of the Year and Humanist of the Year. Adams has chaired the Australian Film Commission, the Australian Film Institute, Film Australia, the film board of The Australia Council, the Commission for the Future, the National Australia Day Council, the Centre for the Mind, the Australian Centre for Social Innovation and many other state and federal government bodies. Board memberships include Wikileaks, Greenpeace, Clean-Up Australia, the National Museum, Manning Clark House, and the Don Dunstan Foundation.

Adams had a major impact on Australian advertising through his business Monahan Dayman Adams, his most famous campaigns including 'Life Be In It', 'Slip Slap Slop' and Qantas' 'Spirit of Australia'.

He lives on a large cattle property in the upper Hunter of New South Wales.